# THE PERFECT HUMAN REBIRTH

FPMT Lineage is a series of books of Lama Zopa Rinpoche's teachings on the graduated path to enlightenment drawn from his four decades of discourses on the topic based on his own textbook, *The Wish-fulfilling Golden Sun,* and several traditional *lam-rim* texts, and in general arranged according to the outline of *Liberation in the Palm of Your Hand.* This series is the most extensive contemporary lam-rim commentary available and comprises the essence of the FPMT's education program.

The FPMT Lineage Series is dedicated to the long life and perfect health of Lama Zopa Rinpoche, to his continuous teaching activity and to the fulfillment of all his holy wishes.

*May whoever sees, touches, reads, remembers, or talks or thinks about these books never be reborn in unfortunate circumstances, receive only rebirths in situations conducive to the perfect practice of Dharma, meet only perfectly qualified spiritual guides, quickly develop bodhicitta and immediately attain enlightenment for the sake of all sentient beings.*

FPMT LINEAGE SERIES

Lama Zopa Rinpoche

# The Perfect Human Rebirth
*Freedom and Richness on the Path to Enlightenment*

Edited by Gordon McDougall
Series editor Nicholas Ribush

LAMA YESHE WISDOM ARCHIVE • BOSTON
www.LamaYeshe.com

A non-profit charitable organization for the benefit of all
sentient beings and an affiliate of the Foundation for
the Preservation of the Mahayana Tradition
www.fpmt.org

Colleen

First published 2013

Lama Yeshe Wisdom Archive
PO Box 636
Lincoln
MA 01773, USA

*Library of Congress Cataloging-in-Publication Data* To come

Thubten Zopa, Rinpoche, 1945-
The perfect human rebirth : freedom and richness on the path
to enlightenment / Thubten Zopa, Rinpoche ; edited by
Gordon McDougall ; series editor, Nicholas Ribush.
pages cm. — (FPMT lineage series)
Includes bibliographical references and index.
Summary: "This book is drawn from Lama Zopa Rinpoche's graduated path
to enlightenment teachings given over a four decade period, starting from the
early 1970s, and deals with how rare and precious it is to receive not just
a human rebirth but a perfect human rebirth, with eight freedoms and
ten richnesses, the best possible conditions for practicing Dharma"
—Provided by publisher.
ISBN 978-1-891868-50-4
1. Lam-rim. 2. Meditation—Buddhism. I. McDougall,
Gordon, 1948– editor of compilation. II. Title.
BQ7645.L35T52 2013
294.3'444—dc23
2013035486

ISBN 978-1-891868-50-4

10 9 8 7 6 5 4 3 2 1

Cover and interior photographs by Carol Royce-Wilder:
Lama Zopa Rinpoche at Lake Arrowhead, 1975
Line drawing by Lama Zopa Rinpoche
Designed by Gopa&Ted2 Inc.

♻ Printed in the USA with environmental mindfulness on 30% PCW recycled paper.
The following resources have been saved: 21 trees, 618 lbs. of solid waste, 9.742 gallons of
water, 2,160 lbs. of greenhouse gases and 9 million BTUs of energy. (papercalculator.org)

# Contents

❧❦

# Publisher's Acknowledgments

—————————— ❧ ——————————

I N OUR PREVIOUS title, Lama Zopa Rinpoche's *How to Practice Dharma*, I explained in detail how the FPMT Lineage Series, of which this book is the third, came about. So I won't repeat all that here.

In brief, the aim of the series is to publish all of Rinpoche's *lam-rim* teachings as a sequence of commentaries on the key points of the path for both a general audience and a more specialized readership—serious lam-rim meditators trying to attain realizations and lam-rim teachers in need of the ultimate resource to enhance their knowledge. Our editor, Gordon McDougall, to whom we're most grateful, talks more about the process in his preface.

In 1996, Rinpoche asked me to establish the LYWA as a stand-alone FPMT entity. In 2007, thanks to an inexpressibly kind benefactor who offered us a $500,000 matching grant that allowed us to hire the staff we needed to go ahead, we came up with a plan to make this series of commentaries a reality, Publishing the FPMT Lineage (PFL). Gordon has taken the lead in combing through nearly four decades of Rinpoche's teachings to create the series, building on the previous "basketing" work done by Ven. Trisha Donnelly and Tenzin Namdrol (Miranda Adams). You can see more details of the PFL program on the LYWA website under "Current Projects."

In our previous books and on our website we have also mentioned in detail all the people who have made the ARCHIVE possible and continue to do so, so there's no need to repeat that here either. I would, however, like to thank those who directly supported the editing and printing of *The Perfect Human Rebirth*—the Hao Ran Foundation, Losang Dragpa Centre, Malaysia, our kind benefactor again, and all the people who have made matching grants to this program. We still have a ways to go to match the entire grant, so if you would like to support the preparation of more of Lama Zopa Rinpoche's peerless lam-rim commentaries, please do so at LamaYeshe.com. Thank you so much.

*Dr. Nicholas Ribush*

# Editor's Preface

As I started collecting material for this book, the World Cup was drawing to a close. For somebody living in England (or many of the other countries participating), for over a month it seemed as if nothing in the world existed except football. Red-and-white English flags were everywhere and national pride was vociferous and, as it turned out, unjustified.

A year earlier, I was among four hundred people who took part in the hundred-million mani retreat in France with Lama Zopa Rinpoche. It was quite an experience. If you have ever done an extended retreat with Rinpoche, you'll know that there is a lot of Dharma and not much sleep, and we all knew from the beginning that Rinpoche wanted us to complete the seemingly impossible recitation of a hundred million OM MANI PADME HUM mantras. Some of us started the retreat with a degree of trepidation. And so it is significant that Rinpoche's very opening words were those that start the first chapter of this book, explaining that the real reason for joy is having this precious human body, not kicking a ball into a net.

But Dharma isn't just retreats; everything we do can be Dharma. (I can't quite see how supporting a particular football team would qualify, but I'm sure it can.) And it all stems from understanding our true potential. That is the essence of the teachings on the perfect human rebirth.

Generally, when the graduated path to enlightenment (Tib: *lam-rim*) is presented to Western students, the subjects are listed as a step-by-step instruction manual on how to be completely happy and attain enlightenment, with each subject being given equal weight. While this may be true, it is instructive to see how the traditional Tibetan texts divide the lam-rim. In Lama Tsongkhapa's seminal *Great Treatise on the Stages of the Path to Enlightenment* (Tib: *Lam-rim Chen-mo*) and the works by other authors that follow his structure, after establishing the lineage and talking of the importance of the teacher and the meditation session, the main body of the work is divided into two: appreciating the human life of freedom and richness and how to take advantage of such a life. From this we can see that understanding and appreciating the perfect human rebirth is pivotal to the entire spiritual journey. As Lama Zopa Rinpoche says, it is the key that opens the door to understanding.

I think this is especially true for the Western student, because one of our greatest demons is lack of self-worth, or low self-esteem. Amid a lifestyle that is so comfortable and supportive but at the same time so competitive and goal-oriented, we can feel inadequate, even worthless. We are so busy that we miss the essential point of why we are busy. The teachings on the perfect human rebirth are a wake-up call. Through them we can see just how unique our situation is and how remarkable our potential is. When we can truly see this we will have the momentum to really develop our mind, which is the purpose of the rest of the subjects of the lam-rim.

Quite early in the piece, students at the initial month-long meditation courses led by Lama Zopa Rinpoche at Kopan Monastery recognized the importance of recording Lama Yeshe's and Rinpoche's teachings in full, and over the decades we have collected almost 2,000 teachings—ranging from a single evening's discourse to a full three-month retreat. This collection was formalized in 1996, when Lama Zopa Rinpoche established the LAMA YESHE WISDOM ARCHIVE. In 2007, *Publishing the FPMT Lineage* commenced, a project to make Rinpoche's lam-rim teachings available. The aim is to extract individual lam-rim topics from all the teachings recorded and assemble, edit and publish them in a series of detailed commentaries. Until now, the ARCHIVE has generally published edited teachings of one particular course or teaching, but with the books of *FPMT Lineage series* we will offer a comprehensive presentation of everything Rinpoche has said on each lam-rim topic.

*The Perfect Human Rebirth* was created in this fashion. Having collected as much of Rinpoche's teachings on perfect human rebirth as possible, I assembled them into topics. Then, using the outline from Pabongka Rinpoche's *Liberation in the Palm of Your Hand*, the structure that Lama Zopa Rinpoche followed in his early courses, I built a template from the various teachings given by Rinpoche at Kopan Monastery, Kathmandu, in the one-month lam-rim courses he gave every year. I then trawled the entire ARCHIVE to find whatever else Rinpoche had said on the perfect human rebirth and added it to the template.

The whole text was then edited. I have tried to keep the informal, experiential style that Rinpoche uses and have included many of the anecdotal and almost parable-like stories that often pepper his discourses.

The edited text comes from verbatim transcripts that have been checked for accuracy, so we can be confident that what is here is exactly what Rinpoche has taught. Mistakes and confusions belong one hundred per cent to the editor. Taking it from so many sources, with Rinpoche teaching to different audiences at different times, it is inevitable that no matter how much I have tried to avoid repetition, there will be some sections that reflect others. Hopefully these will serve to reinforce the message rather than create any sense of tedium. Textual quotations should be regarded more as paraphrase than word-for-word translation. When Rinpoche cites a text I have listed it in English only, the one exception being the *Lam-rim Chenmo*, which is better known to many people by its Tibetan title than the much longer English one. For the Sanskrit or Tibetan titles of other works, please see the bibliography.

In all, more than 140 of Rinpoche's courses around the world constitute the source material for this book.[1] How many hours of labor does that represent for all those many people involved? And how many people have actually been involved in the creation of this book? I can't start to name names; there are just too many. All I can do is offer each and every one of you who have given so much a huge thank you.

But most of all, I wish to thank from the bottom of my heart Lama Zopa Rinpoche, the inspiration for all this, the source of all this incredible knowledge. To me he is the living example of how one person can make a huge difference and how everything is possible when one's mind is imbued with

---

[1] From the 1972 third Kopan course to the 2009 Mani retreat at Institut Vajra Yogini, the ARCHIVE numbers of the courses used for the final edit are: 005, 014, 017, 018, 022, 027, 028, 029, 081, 089, 091, 092, 095, 096, 102, 107, 111, 119, 122, 139, 149, 163, 169, 170, 181, 182, 203, 278, 328, 350, 359, 368, 395, 399, 425, 436, 469, 475, 476, 488, 511, 514, 566, 627, 634, 737, 788, 823, 831, 836, 851, 852, 984, 944, 996, 1005, 1045, 1055, 1061, 1090, 1095, 1111, 1124, 1152, 1169, 1172, 1184, 1186, 1203, 1238, 1247, 1331, 1372, 1381, 1388, 1399, 1402, 1410, 1413, 1441, 1443, 1470, 1478, 1588, 1604.

compassion and wisdom. May whatever small merit gained from the creation of this book be dedicated to his continued long life, good health and the attainment of all his holy wishes.

Bath, England
March 2013

# 1. What is Dharma?

### THE PATH WE MUST FOLLOW

PEOPLE GET EXCITED about strange things. I recently saw a group of men kicking a ball into a big net between two sticks and hundreds of thousands of people were cheering and throwing their hands up in the air, while millions watched on television. Everybody was totally out of control with excitement. In fact, their faces were so distorted I couldn't tell whether they were very happy or in great pain. This World Cup seems extremely important to many people, but it also brings misery and jealousy, as well as anger and hatred when *your* country beats *my* country.

On the other hand, a real cause for excitement and happiness is simply having this human body. If we could truly understand even a tiny part of its value, we would have a million times more reason for jumping in the air and shouting for joy the way those soccer fans do. Every day—every second— we should have a huge feeling of joy in our hearts that we have this precious possession that gives us the opportunity to do whatever we want. With it, we can achieve anything we want, to benefit ourselves and to benefit others.

In sports and in worldly activities, people are always chasing the best and trying to be first in whatever they do. But winning at the Olympics, climbing Mount Everest, whatever people consider to be a great achievement, is really nothing. We have all done this kind of thing innumerable times, in past lives if not in this one, and it certainly hasn't made us any happier.

In fact, in our countless previous lives we have enjoyed every kind of pleasure innumerable times. We have achieved states we can't even imagine. There is no new pleasure or experience that we have never had. We have been born in god realms where there is no overt suffering at all. We have achieved great powers of concentration, a concentration so profound

2 THE PERFECT HUMAN REBIRTH

that, as the great master Pabongka Dechen Nyingpo explains in his commentary on *The Three Principal Aspects of the Path to Enlightenment*,[2] even a big drum beating right next to our ear could not disturb us. And we have even attained high psychic powers such as clairvoyance and the ability to fly. None of this is new. Such things seem special only because we don't understand reincarnation and therefore don't realize that in our beginningless previous lives we have done it all over and over again.

The first students at the early meditation courses at Kopan Monastery in Nepal,[3] came for many different reasons. Many of them were hippies and had read in books like *The Tibetan Book of the Dead* or *The Third Eye*[4] how meditation can bring about magic powers, like flying. There is nothing special about flying. Billions of birds can fly but does that mean they have the secret to happiness? Some students were interested in astral travel or developing the aura around their bodies. Fireflies emit light but do we really want to be like them?

In fact, although the greatest magic powers may sound wonderful, they are really just mundane achievements that mean very little in the long run. They cannot assure real happiness for us and they cannot free us from *samsara*, this cycle of dissatisfaction in which we are trapped. They have no power to eliminate or even diminish our delusions, which is the only real way of destroying our suffering and becoming happy.

None of these samsaric things can even last. That is their very nature. To achieve them we undergo much hardship, have them for a short while and then they're gone, leaving us discontented again. Furthermore, everything of this nature is achieved through a motivation that longs for the mundane

---

[2] Pabongka Dechen Nyingpo Rinpoche (1871–1941) was a highly regarded lama, root guru of His Holiness the Dalai Lama's senior and junior tutors and author of *Liberation in the Palm of Your Hand*, which served as the structure for most of Lama Zopa's early meditation courses (and hence this series of books). *The Three Principal Aspects of the Path*, a letter written by Lama Tsongkhapa to a disciple, is a key text in the Gelug tradition.

[3] Kopan, the FPMT's main monastery, has hosted annual one-month meditation courses since 1971.

[4] The Evans-Wentz translation of the *Tibetan Book of the Dead* was one of the few books on Tibetan Buddhism available in English in the early 1970s. It recounts the stages a person travels through in the intermediate state between this life and the next. Many of its passages would have seemed quite fantastical to a reader unfamiliar with any Buddhist concepts. *The Third Eye*, by "Lama" Lobsang Rampa, was very popular then, all about Tibetan monks attaining great powers through concentration, including the attaining of a physical third eye in the center of the forehead. Rampa was later exposed as a fraud.

pleasures of this life, which, as we will see, is a nonvirtuous motivation and the cause of future suffering.[5]

Many of the other Kopan students, of course, came because they could see that the happiness being offered them in the West was somehow illusory. Even those from great cities like New York could see through the material progress that had been made there and realized that it was not enough. Every year there was more progress but somehow there was never any more happiness. A new invention solved one problem but immediately there were more problems to be solved. As their societies became more and more complex, the problems became more and more complicated. These students could see that there was something missing in the methods being used to overcome problems. Those who made it to those early Kopan courses shared a dissatisfaction with their societies' reliance on external methods to fix external problems, and somehow intuitively knew that there must be a deeper, more meaningful way of attaining happiness. Just taking this step was a very wise action; it opened the door to inner peace. Outside in the street was the crazy, confusing world, but they had found the gate to a beautiful park.

Right now, with this precious human body, we have the perfect conditions to see beyond this external confusion—we can understand what suffering is and how to overcome it and what true happiness is and how to attain it. We have the Dharma.

The Dharma is whatever leads us toward happiness and away from suffering; it is whatever destroys the root of suffering—delusion and karma. It is the path we all must take, whether we consider ourselves Buddhist or not. Only by renouncing the causes of suffering, such as attachment, and developing compassion and a correct understanding of the nature of reality can we truly liberate ourselves. *This* is the new experience we should strive for, not clairvoyance or flying; this what we have never achieved in the past.

The Dharma is anything that can do that, but it is often specifically used to mean the teachings of the Buddha. It is said that the historical Buddha, Shakyamuni, gave 84,000 teachings in the forty years between his enlightenment in India 2,600 years ago and his death. In Tibetan Buddhism these incredible teachings have been classified into a system that makes them easy to study and actualize—the graduated path to enlightenment, the lam-rim.

Here, the three main areas we need to develop—*renunciation* of samsara;

---

[5] Rinpoche's *How to Practice Dharma* covers this point in great detail.

*bodhicitta*, the altruistic intention to become enlightened in order to benefit all sentient beings; and *right view*, the understanding of emptiness—
are set out in a progressive series of teachings, from the need for a spiritual
guide at the very beginning to the most subtle minds needed for enlightenment at the very end. The lam-rim contains everything we need to take us
all the way to the ultimate state of enlightenment.

In fact, I can definitely say that the lam-rim is the very essence of the
Dharma. When the great Indian teacher Atisha went to Tibet from the
Buddhist university of Vikramashila in India in the tenth century, he condensed everything the Buddha taught into this graduated path, with nothing missing. After that, Tibetan teachers such as Lama Tsongkhapa[6] wrote
commentaries on the lam-rim, and to study these commentaries is to see just
how the lam-rim presents the whole picture.

The comparison is made to butter. Milk is very nutritious but the very
essence of milk is butter. We can use milk to make other things but still,
butter is its ultimate essence. The great philosophers and yogis like Lama
Tsongkhapa gave incredible teachings based on their own experience. They
had a knowledge and an understanding so deep that we can't even begin
to fathom it. From that profound understanding they were able to distill
the essence—the butter—and clearly show us the path we must take from
where we are now all the way to enlightenment.

Just now we have incredible freedom. We have enough intelligence and
leisure and we have the interest to learn. I think if you investigate a little
you will see that this is true. Traditional teachings on the perfect human
rebirth explain the eight freedoms and the ten richnesses. These teachings
show us very clearly just how fortunate we are and how rare it is to be in the
position in which we now find ourselves. At this moment we have in our
hand the means to attain anything we want; we have the means to create
the causes for perfect happiness. It is crucial that we don't waste this precious opportunity.

Without studying the lam-rim it is very difficult to appreciate how rare
this chance is and how to make best use of it. Perhaps we try to meditate,
perhaps we pray or read sutras; perhaps we even call ourselves a Buddhist,
but without a good background in the lam-rim it is very difficult to see how

---

[6] Lama Je Tsongkhapa (1357–1417) was the founder of the Gelug tradition, one of the four
main Tibetan traditions, and revitalized many sutra and tantra lineages and the monastic
tradition in Tibet.

crucial it is not only to practice Dharma but to do nothing else. Dharma practice is the most important thing in life.

First we should know that without the Dharma there is no happiness at all. No happiness *at all*. The very definition of Dharma is that which brings happiness. Any tiny happiness that we experience today comes directly from having acted virtuously in the past, and that act was Dharma, whether it was generosity or kindness, patience or right understanding. And all the happiness we will experience in the future is entirely dependent on our creating only virtuous actions from now on, and that is Dharma as well.

To make our life meaningful, we have to do meaningful actions. That means recognizing how fortunate we are to have this precious opportunity and determining never to squander it. This is the main thing that allows us to generate the energy we need to undertake the long path ahead of us. This is going to be a long, hard journey and we will need to develop many skills— like a major expedition requires many porters. It will be hard because we have never made it before and because it is a solely mental trip with many obscurations and hindrances blocking the way. To attain complete freedom from suffering, liberation and enlightenment, we have to destroy all our self-created mental hindrances. Destroying the earth would be easier.

But, this is a great journey we must undertake and the lam-rim is the road map that will take us all the way on the shortest route without getting lost, and it starts from understanding the perfect human rebirth. Therefore, it is very good, at this initial stage of our journey, to have a very clear understanding of what the perfect human rebirth is, its incredible rarity, its fragility and the wonderful benefits it can bring.

Traditionally, in texts such as Lama Tsongkhapa's *Great Treatise* and Pabongka Dechen Nyingpo's *Liberation in the Palm of Your Hand*, after an explanation of the lineage of the great teachers that have expounded the lam-rim and their direct link to Shakyamuni Buddha and the importance of the spiritual teacher, the guru, the main body of the lam-rim teachings is divided into two:

- ▶ persuading your mind to take the essence from your perfect human rebirth
- ▶ how to extract the essence from your perfect human rebirth—the actual method

The actual method is the rest of the entire path to enlightenment, so you can see that in this great store of teachings, the perfect human rebirth is at its very core; it is the foundation.

In this book I will try to show something of this first point, understanding what the perfect human rebirth is and why it is so important. In Lama Tsongkhapa's and Pabongka Rinpoche's texts, the teaching on the perfect human rebirth has three main sections:

- identifying the perfect human rebirth with its the eight freedoms and ten richnesses
- the great benefits of the perfect human rebirth
- the difficulty of acquiring the perfect human rebirth

Furthermore, teachers such as Lama Tsongkhapa and Pabongka Dechen Nyingpo start their extensive lam-rim texts with a section encouraging the student to take advantage of the perfect human rebirth. That is basically the structure we will be following here.

### What is Dharma?

The meaning of the Sanskrit word *Dharma* is "that which saves." Dharma is whatever saves sentient beings from all forms of suffering and the causes of suffering. This is completely inclusive. A sentient being is any unenlightened being that has sentience—a mind that can function and therefore naturally wants to have happiness and avoid suffering—and suffering is anything undesirable, from the worst suffering of the hot hells to the most subtle pervasive suffering a god experiences.

Say we are slipping down a steep cliff face, with the rocks way down below waiting to smash us to pieces. The only thing that can save us is a rope at the edge of the cliff. Holding onto that rope is the most important thing we can do; that is what can save our life. That is what the Dharma is. It is that which saves us from falling into suffering. Thus we can say that Dharma is whatever leads us to happiness and allows us to eliminate suffering. The analogy of the rope is a good one because it also shows that we are the ones who need to make the effort. The rope is there to help us but we ourselves must hold on to it and pull ourselves out of danger.

Once, Lama Atisha's disciple Dromtönpa[7] asked him to explain the results of actions done with what Buddhism calls the three poisons—igno-

---

[7] Lama Atisha (982–1054) was the renowned Indian master who went to Tibet in 1042 to help in the revival of Buddhism and established the Kadam tradition. His text *A Lamp for the Path to Enlightenment* was the first lam-rim text. Dromtönpa (1005–64) was his interpreter and heart disciple and propagator of the Kadam tradition.

rance, anger and attachment—and of actions done without these attitudes. Lama Atisha answered,

> Actions done with ignorance, anger and attachment bring rebirth in the lower realms as a suffering transmigratory[8] being. Greed causes rebirth in the hungry ghost realm, hatred causes rebirth in the hell realm, ignorance causes rebirth in the animal realm and so forth. Actions done with an attitude not possessed by the three poisonous minds bring the result of rebirth as a happy transmigratory being [in one of the three upper realms].

Here, Lama Atisha clearly delineates between what is Dharma and what is not Dharma, what is a worldly action. Just as actions that arise from delusions result in suffering, actions that arise from a virtuous mind, Dharma actions, are the source of all happiness.

If we want to be happy, the very first thing we need to know is what actions will make us happy and cultivate those, and what actions will bring us suffering and avoid those. This is the very essence of Dharma practice. When we investigate, we will see that any action stained with the deluded minds of ignorance, anger and attachment and the many, many other delusions that derive from these three will create suffering, and any action done with a virtuous motivation, one of love, kindness, generosity and so forth, will bring a happy result. This is definite. In fact, this is the fundamental fact about karma.[9]

We can easily see that hatred, jealousy and so forth are negative and bring all sorts of problems, but so too does attachment. Simple actions like eating, reading and walking, when stained by attachment, are nonvirtuous and the cause of future suffering. Any action motivated by self-interest and attachment is nonvirtuous. We can say prayers for hours every day, we can meditate or make offerings, we can read countless Dharma books—but if those actions are motivated by attachment, such as the wish for a good reputation, then those seemingly good actions are in fact nonvirtuous. They may look

---

[8] A being who "transmigrates" from one life to the next and so is trapped in cyclic existence or samsara.
[9] That karma is definite is one of the four aspects of karma. See Rinpoche's forthcoming book on karma.

like Dharma but they are not Dharma; we may look like a Dharma practitioner but we are not a Dharma practitioner.

We need to be very clear about this. It is not the action but the mind behind the action, the motivation that creates it, that determines whether it is positive or negative, whether it is Dharma or non-Dharma. Eating, sleeping or working can just as easily be unstained by the mind clinging to the happiness of this life, and hence be virtuous Dharma actions, as reciting mantras can be nonvirtuous when done with greed or anger. The action might seem similar, but the difference in the result of happiness or suffering it brings is like that between earth and sky.

Whether the motivation is virtuous or nonvirtuous determines whether the action that results is virtuous or nonvirtuous.

## Happiness and suffering come from the mind

There are two kinds of happiness: worldly, mundane happiness and Dharma happiness. Beings in the lower realms are essentially unable to experience either kind and apart from humans, those in the upper realms are mostly unable to experience Dharma happiness. When we can start to understand that worldly happiness, chasing sense pleasure, is in fact another form of suffering, then we can start to appreciate how it is only in this human form—and only when we have all the unique conditions that we currently have—that we can go beyond mundane concerns and become truly happy by practicing Dharma. That is why this time is so precious.

We will be looking at the beings of the other realms later, those in the lower suffering realms and those in the god realms, but let us now briefly consider the state of most human beings on this planet. If we look beyond the surface differences to try to understand what every single person is doing every single day, we will see that all of us are only looking to have happiness and avoid suffering. No matter what form it takes—success at our career, a good relationship, lots of possessions—that is what we are all doing.

But how many people are successful at attaining that simple goal, happiness? How many are truly satisfied and content? How many can say that they have no suffering in their lives? I think, if you look deeply enough, you will find that there are very few people who can truthfully answer yes to all those questions.

Why is there no real peace for the people of this planet? It is because the vast majority are still ruled by ignorance. With minds that are agitated and unsubdued, they don't understand how to find real happiness.

For most people, happiness is something that is grabbed from the things around them, from relationships, money, travel, possessions and so forth, and obtaining these things requires great effort and often harms others in some way. They cannot appreciate that happiness is in fact a state of mind and that it comes from virtue. They try to get happiness by creating non-virtue and wonder why they are never really happy. They equate happiness with obtaining external objects of desire without understanding that peace is real happiness, the peace of Dharma.

Without relying on the practice of Dharma, people go around the world looking for happiness, not realizing that it is inside them all the time. From childhood until death they visit different countries, climb different mountains, go around and around, yet still they are not free, still there is something missing. Acquiring possessions, experiences, knowledge, no matter what form the quest for happiness takes, when people rely on external methods there is always something missing.

This is where an understanding of karma is so important. Until we can see clearly that both happiness and suffering are created by the mind and that happiness is the result of a virtuous mind and that suffering is the result of a nonvirtuous mind, we will continue to make the mistake of chasing happiness by doing negative actions. There is no happiness at all in external things. Just as a sunflower grows from a sunflower seed, happiness grows from past virtue. If we are unhappy now it is because we have done negative actions in the past. If we want to be happy in the future, we must do only positive actions from now on. The choice is that simple. But we cannot start to work skillfully toward happiness until we have a firm conviction that all happiness and suffering come from the mind, not external factors, and a good understanding of what positive and negative actions are.

We need to see the fault in thinking that material things equate to happiness. Are we, the people of the twenty-first century, any happier than the people of two centuries or two millennia ago? We certainly have more. I'm not contesting that we have more comfort, more knowledge, more possessions, but do we have more happiness? If material possessions were the cause of happiness then there should be far more peace and happiness now than there has ever been, but that is clearly not the case. In fact, the original human beings, without the comforts we have, without houses filled with material possessions, without the electronic things we have, were far happier than we are. There was much greater peace then, even though there was not one machine on the entire planet. We can see this even without looking that far back. If we look at today's very advanced countries and compare them with poorer "backward" countries, we will see that those with more possessions are not necessarily happier than those without.

Can we find any very rich person who is freer and more peaceful than somebody who is not rich? If you investigate you will see that wealth does not equate to happiness. For most people, more wealth and power means more responsibility and worry, more stress and misery. There are many miserable millionaires and the suicide rate in rich countries is much higher than in poor ones.

If material possessions and wealth were the cause of perfect peace and happiness we would have already obtained it, because in past lives we have had great wealth and numberless possessions. But our mind is still ignorant. To change our mind's orientation from a negative, grasping, "me, me, me" mind to a positive, open, selfless one is the way to perfect peace. All the jewels in existence cannot destroy even one of the thousands of negative minds, cannot diminish in the slightest one of the delusions that cause us to act harmfully. We may forget our unhappiness for a while and pretend it is not there, but we are really just habituating ourselves to needing material comfort. Momentary cessation of some mental pain is not the end of all suffering. True cessation from a Dharma point of view is ending the continuity of suffering by eradicating its cause.

Unless we can recognize the nature of suffering we cannot recognize its cause. Nor can we recognize perfect happiness and the way to attain it. Using temporary means to stop suffering momentarily only creates the cause for more suffering; doing this, we are creating more suffering while mistakenly thinking we are stopping it. Locked into always chasing worldly happiness and mundane pleasure, we not only destroy our chances of gaining real happiness but we also ensure that we will never be completely successful at getting the small, temporary happiness we seek. We can never be free from problems, and seeking mundane happiness requires great and repeated effort. We become slaves to our greed, to the mind that wants worldly happiness, the mind that forces us to work ourselves to exhaustion trying to fulfill its needs.

What is so unique about the position we are in is that we have a choice. Animals don't have a choice; people locked into complete poverty don't have a choice; but what places the perfect human rebirth between the two is that we have neither too much suffering nor too much pleasure. We have enough suffering to wish to renounce it but not so much that we are helpless and overwhelmed by it; we can easily see how others are suffering and thus can develop compassion for them.

We can choose to study about the cause of happiness; we can choose to learn to use our mind as a tool to create that happiness by learning how to meditate. We can listen to great teachers and we have the intelligence to understand their message; we have the literacy to read Dharma books, the wisdom to see the truth in them and the intelligence to start to live our life according to the Dharma.

We have the capacity to create the causes for perfect happiness and completely eliminate all the seeds of suffering. Isn't that amazing? Within a minute we can hear an explanation of karma and the cause of happiness and understand it. Furthermore, our mind is not obscured by gross negativities, so when we hear about karma and suffering it makes sense and we have the wisdom to make the right choice. Then everything we do every moment of each twenty-four hours can become Dharma.

## THE INNER SCIENCE OF HAPPINESS

There is still so much that is beyond our understanding—the subtle explanations of emptiness and so forth—and because other realms are not part of our daily experience, when we hear about them we might find it hard to believe that they actually exist. But these explanations have come from the Buddha and been verified by the great sages and yogis down through the ages, in India, Tibet and other Buddhist countries. Just because they are hard to fathom does not mean we should dismiss them. We can see the animal realm and accept that animals have miserable existences, but there are other realms as well. There are the realms of the gods, the hungry ghosts, which are dominated by incredible hunger and thirst, and the hell beings, where the suffering is beyond description. Many great yogis, whose minds are highly developed, have actually seen these realms and told us about them. Our not seeing them is insufficient reason for us to deny that they exist; our karmic obscurations, the delusions that fog our mind, prevent us from seeing reality.

Our obscurations also stop us from realizing that the mind is beginningless. Possibly we have never thought of it, or maybe we have but rejected it, or else not really considered its consequences, but when we see that the mind we currently have has been with us since beginningless time and will continue after our death into our next life, and the next and the next—

when we start to understand all this—it can come as a big shock. But without the fundamental understanding of mental continuity, the rest of the meditations on the lam-rim will make little sense—they'll feel like a heavy rock or an unclimbable mountain. And so we might prefer to just believe in the fairy tales we've grown up with rather than explore exactly what these meditations mean.

It is extremely important to clearly see how the mind is beginningless, because then reincarnation becomes a reality to us, and with that comes the understanding of how the imprints of actions we did in previous lives are ripening on our mindstream right now, causing happiness or misery, and how what we are doing now will have consequences not just in the future in this life, but in countless future lives. Seeing this, suddenly our world becomes huge. Everything becomes much more significant.

Buddhism is really the science of the mind. We need to know the mind—what it is, how it works and how to use it to gain real happiness and ultimately enlightenment. And this is why there is so much emphasis in Buddhism on meditation. It is only through observing our own mind in meditation that we can really start to understand it. Reading about it in books but not meditating on it is like reading about India but never actually going there.

This is inner science, not the external materialistic science they teach in schools. Here we are studying what is vitally important in order to see the reality of this world. True understanding is not a field of empirical knowledge but an inner wisdom that comes from understanding the mind. A medical researcher might be able to tell us why a particular person died of a certain disease but he[10] can never tell us why human beings have to die in the first place. By relying on external experimentation and not investigating inner causes, modern science will always be flawed. It can never penetrate deeply enough to give ultimate answers. Without relying on the inner science of Buddhadharma, the principal cause for why animate beings have to die and be reborn can never be found in outer objects, no matter how many eons are spent in research.

For instance, human beings used to live for thousands of years and now the lifespan is decreasing. Why is that so? A scientist might even deny this

[10] Or she. There is no really satisfactory way in English of referring to the third person unspecified—the use of "they" for a singular subject is clumsy—so we will simply alternate genders.

fact but he would be ignoring the findings of the great yogis who had clear knowledge of this. As meditators reach higher and higher stages of development, subtle understandings such as this become clearer. This is not just one person's experience but the experience of countless buddhas.

Only we, with this perfect human rebirth, can become inner scientists and discover the true cause of happiness. Our pets can't. Even if we play recordings of Dharma teachings to them all day long, they have no power to understand, no freedom to listen and no way to communicate anything meaningful.

There are people who live in countries where religion is suppressed and therefore have no access to wisdom. They have never even seen an image of the Buddha, let alone read his words. There are people with impaired faculties who have no way of understanding the Dharma. There are people who are blind and thus unable to benefit from the psychological effect the image of a buddha has on the mind. There are people with huge karmic obscurations who might be standing right in front of a buddha image yet not see it. There is a story in *Liberation in the Palm of Your Hand* about a person who looked at a buddha statue but, because of his karmic obscurations, saw instead a great pile of meat.

We have none of these problems, so we're unbelievably fortunate. We have the opportunity to study, meditate and understand everything that the Buddha taught, from the simplest lam-rim topic to the most advanced. We have the opportunity to develop the altruistic heart, the attitude that wishes to be fully awakened to benefit others, and to understand the reality of things and events—emptiness. There is nothing we cannot understand with this perfect human rebirth.

Only through the blessings of the Buddha can we do this. And we have received these precious teachings from a fully-qualified teacher. Without this direct link to the Buddha there is no assurance that the teaching is pure and able to lead us all the way. That is why the very first topic in the lam-rim concerns the qualities of the teacher. That is the start. Without a fully-qualified teacher we have no way of knowing if what we are studying is really of benefit to us. From that vital beginning the whole path is laid out, and that is the lam-rim, the graduated path to enlightenment, each topic fitting into the three levels of practice. It is all there: the path of the lower capable being that leads to a better future rebirth, the path of the middle capable being that leads to individual liberation, and the path of the higher capable being that leads to full enlightenment. The two higher scopes rely on the complete understanding and realization of the previous scope, so each is vital. The mind working toward full enlightenment needs to be built on the mind renouncing the whole of samsara—the middle scope. This, in turn, needs to be built on the mind that has realized the preliminary subjects, such as the perfect human rebirth, impermanence and death, refuge and karma—the lower scope. In other words, there is not one single lam-rim topic that we can omit.

It is not like a buffet, where we can pick and choose whatever we fancy. Perhaps meditating on the lower realms is too painful, so we leave that one out. Or trying to understand emptiness seems too intellectual, so we don't bother with that one. No, we can't treat the lam-rim as a buffet. We have to eat the whole feast, otherwise we won't get what we want, liberation or enlightenment. Perhaps we already have a good heart. That is wonderful, but that alone won't get us there. We need to realize bodhicitta. For that, we need complete renunciation of samsara; and for that, we need to see how each and every sentient being is suffering; and for that, we need to understand the nature of suffering. When we explore the lam-rim we will see how each topic leads into the next and how each is therefore indispensable.

The meditations on the perfect human rebirth come right at the beginning of the path, just after relying on a spiritual teacher. We need to understand karma and we need to have refuge, and to deepen our commitment we need to understand impermanence and death. But none of that will happen if we squander this precious and unique opportunity that we now, this one time only, have. That is why the great meditator, Lama Tsongkhapa, who formalized the whole lam-rim structure, broke the lam-rim up into two: appreciation of this life of freedom and richness—the perfect human rebirth—and how to make use of this precious opportunity—the rest of the lam-rim topics from impermanence and death, refuge and karma up to the point where we attain full enlightenment. That is how fundamental an appreciation of the perfect human rebirth is to our Dharma journey.

### The boat to cross samsara

In *A Guide to the Bodhisattva's Way of Life* the bodhisattva, Shantideva, said,

> Relying on the boat of a human body,
> Free yourself from the great river of pain!

As it is hard to find this boat again,
This is no time to sleep, you fool.[11]

Samsara is the endless cycle of birth and death that we are all trapped in due to karma and delusion. It is often described as a river or an ocean in which we are all drowning and liberation and enlightenment are like reaching the other shore. Here, Shantideva, the great eighth century Indian sage, compares this precious human body we now have to a boat capable of crossing the river of samsaric suffering. Only now, only while we have this "boat," can we cross. And as we can never be sure of having this opportunity again, he strongly admonishes us to use this unique chance now, while we have it. To waste this chance—to sleep this time away—is utterly foolish.

This is the whole reason we have this human body. This is the meaning of our life. Imagine that we're in a terrible place but across a wide and dangerous river is a wonderful land, if only we could reach it. However, we have a boat, and so we must push it out onto the water and row across the river, despite any difficulties we might face. How amazing that we have this boat, this chance to save ourselves. How incredibly lucky we are. We should feel extremely happy. Of course, there is no question of being too lazy to make the effort and being stuck in this terrible place forever. We cannot delay for even a second, because if we do, this precious opportunity could be snatched away from us. In the same way, our perfect human rebirth could end at any moment, so there is definitely no time to sleep, to remain trapped in ignorance.

Ignorance is a dark, heavy mind. In many ways it is like sleep. We are unaware of what is happening around us, even if there is danger. If we don't make the effort to wake our mind from ignorance, to gain wisdom, and instead put all our effort into trying to gain the comforts of this worldly existence, all of our actions will create only more ignorance. As long as we work for greed, hatred, pride, jealousy and the many other negative minds, we are working for ignorance.

Because of ignorance of the true nature of the mind, our actions always produce effects opposite to those desired; as long as we are controlled by delusion we will always make mistakes in our physical and verbal actions. No matter how long and how strongly we desire to avoid suffering and attain happiness, our methods will fail. By using our precious rebirth in this

[11] Ch. 7, v. 14.

way, we not only fail to give meaning to our life, we continuously cheat our-selves as well; we perpetuate our imprisonment in samsara.

As we will see, the causes of this perfect human rebirth are incredibly dif-ficult to create. In many, many previous lives we worked tirelessly, practicing perfect morality and generosity in order to receive the body and conditions that we now have, so we really owe it to ourselves not to waste all that hard work. Our goal should not just be a better, more comfortable human exis-tence in our next life, but complete and perfect enlightenment for the sake of all other kind mother sentient beings. Anything less is unworthy of this amazing life we have, and we do have the potential to reach that goal. That is why Shantideva compares this life to a boat. With it we can cross the vast ocean of samsara and reach that distant shore of liberation.

We can also think of this perfect human rebirth as the key to the door of understanding or the medicine that cures all illness.

Because the mind is fundamentally pure—at its core lies what is called buddha nature—and because the defilements that create all our problems are not one with the mind and therefore can be destroyed, we can defi-nitely attain full awakening. No matter how obscured we now seem, no matter what physical or mental problems we face—we might have cancer or AIDS, be paralyzed from a car crash, feel utterly worthless and that nobody loves us—all these problems are temporary. They will not last. They are like fog that is not oneness with the sky. Just as there has never been a fog that stayed forever, our problems cannot last forever either. Impermanence is the nature of all things, and so they must pass. When the day is dark and hor-rible with thick fog, it might seem as if it will never go away but we know it will pass. We must have the same conviction about our problems.

Causes and conditions have come together to create a particular prob-lem, but because of the buddha nature of our mind we can consciously cre-ate other causes and conditions that will cause us not to have it. Not only can we eliminate mental and physical suffering at the gross level, we can also eliminate even the most subtle form of suffering, the pervasive compound-ing suffering that is at the heart of all suffering. And as we do, our life will get better and better. It is not just a matter of some happiness for a short while, but more and more real happiness that goes on and on, life after life. This is due to this precious human body with all its attributes.

Until we reach that other shore there will always be problems. Whether we are reborn as a lower realm being, as a god enjoying the highest pleasures or as another human being, there is always suffering. The Buddha showed that there are three types of suffering: the suffering of suffering, which is what we recognize as suffering; the suffering of change, which we call pleasure but which is in the nature of suffering because it is unreliable and creates attachment and other negative emotions; and pervasive compounding suffering, which is the most subtle suffering of all and is always present as long as we are in samsara.[12] Even formless realm gods, who have no physical body and remain absorbed in perfect meditation for eons, are not free from pervasive compounding suffering; their minds are not free from delusion. And a mind that is not free from delusion will always degenerate, allowing grosser delusions to grow like weeds spreading in a garden.

Therefore, to not waste this perfect human rebirth, we must motivate every action we do with the wish to be free from the whole of samsara, to achieve liberation. But really, that is still not the ultimate meaning of our life. There is one stage further we can go. To achieve liberation for our own happiness, we need incredible wisdom and many other qualities, but by taking the Mahayana path we turn away from our own liberation and motivate everything for others. It is a far harder path, but it has the power to destroy even that last vestige of self-cherishing.

Nothing else will realize our full potential. Every tiny bit of happiness we have ever experienced arose because we created virtuous actions in connection with other beings. Therefore all our past happiness is due to the kindness of other beings. Just as cherishing the self is the source of all suffering, so cherishing others is the source of all happiness. As I often say, happiness begins when we start cherishing others.

The enlightened mind has the ability to take in the suffering of all sentient beings equaling infinite space; it can see immediately and spontaneously how best to help those beings, in accordance with their capacity to be helped. We have the potential to achieve this mind by systematically removing all our delusions and replacing our self-cherishing attitude with the attitude of cherishing others. This is what enlightenment means—freeing the mind of all delusions and their imprints in order to bring all other sentient beings to full enlightenment.

In Tibetan Buddhism we often call sentient beings "kind mother sentient beings." This is to remind ourselves that because we have had infinite lives we have had infinite mothers, and so it is impossible to posit one being who

---

[12] For a full explanation of these three types of suffering, see Rinpoche's forthcoming book on the general sufferings of samsara.

has not been our mother. And if every being has been our mother at some time or other, then they have each been incredibly kind to us. By looking at what our present life's mother has done for us—bearing us for nine months in her womb, giving us life, feeding us, educating us, sacrificing her life for us—we can easily realize the debt we owe every single sentient being. And to see how they are suffering becomes unbearable. It is as if our mother of this life, old, frail and blind, were tottering toward a high cliff, about to topple over the precipice. We would have no hesitation to do whatever we could to save her; we would even risk our own life. So it is with every living being. That should be our attitude, and it is an attitude we can develop. To repay the kindness of all kind mother sentient beings is the aim of a bodhisattva, a being with bodhicitta, and we have the potential to become a bodhisattva.

There is nothing else to do but cherish other beings. That is our life's work; that is the work of all our lives from now on, until we attain enlightenment. And it is this perfect human rebirth that allows us to do such perfect work for all other beings. All we need is the determination.

If the teachings of the Buddha had degenerated, then we could not say that here is the perfect way to lead us to freedom. If the essential points had been lost over the millennia, or if due to misinterpretation by the practitioners the message of the Buddha had been corrupted, then we would have to admit that the Buddhadharma was flawed, and no matter how earnestly we practiced it we could never reach enlightenment. But that has not happened. Within the Buddhadharma that is taught and practiced in Tibet there is not only the lam-rim, which encompasses the entire path, but also the Vajrayana, the esoteric teachings on tantra that show us how to skillfully combine the method and wisdom sides of the path.[13] This all still exists in the holy minds of the great lamas, and it is transmitted from teacher to disciple unblemished due to the great realizations of the teachers. We have the opportunity to tap into this well of wisdom and gain realizations ourselves; we have the possibility to attain full enlightenment quickly, not just at some time in the distant future, but in this very lifetime.

The only factor that is missing is our determination to do it. It is com-

---

[13] Of the two main divisions in Buddhism, Hinayana and Mahayana, and of the two main divisions within Mahayana, Sutrayana (or Paramitayana) and Vajrayana, only Vajrayana has the ability to simultaneously combine the method side of the teachings—developing positive emotional states such as love, compassion and equanimity—with the wisdom side—an understanding of the nature of reality, such as emptiness, in the one mind.

pletely in our own hands. All the conditions are there, waiting for us. We have the teachings, the teachers, the intelligence, the freedom—it's only a matter of whether we choose to follow the path or not. The inner conditions are perfect, with all the attributes we ourselves possess, and all the outer conditions are there, with the teachings existing and having access to the virtuous teachers. But for how much longer?

It is said that there will come a time soon when there will no more qualified teachers to guide us. The teachings will still exist in books, and perhaps our wish to progress on the path will be there, but we will be without guides. And without somebody to lead us to enlightenment it will be impossible, because the most subtle subjects can only really be understood, and more importantly realized, by taking guidance from a fully qualified teacher.

Therefore, we must generate the determination to make the most of every moment. At this time, with this body and mind, in this environment, we have a unique and precious opportunity to understand the teachings of the Buddha and to generate the realizations of the path to enlightenment. If we attempt it, there is nothing we cannot do. We need to see this. We need to understand how limitless our potential is and not block our precious chance with delusions of incapability: "I can't do it! I'm hopeless."

It is time to have big thoughts—huge thoughts! It is time to make vast plans, to lay out the immense project ahead of us and feel happy that we can achieve our goal of developing ourselves to our ultimate potential. We have perfect role models in the Buddha and the numberless great yogis who followed him, as well as the precious lamas we have the fortune to be able to take teachings and gain inspiration from, and we know that we have exactly the same potential as they do. Shakyamuni was once exactly like us; His Holiness the Dalai Lama was once exactly like us. In turn, we can be exactly like them. All the conditions are there. What we now need is the determination to do it.

# 2. The Freedoms

As we have seen, Lama Tsongkhapa and Pabongka Rinpoche divide the topic of the perfect human rebirth into three sections, identifying the perfect human rebirth, understanding its benefits and understanding the difficulty of obtaining such as rebirth. The first part shows exactly what we have that is so precious. There are eight freedoms—states of existence that we are free from—and ten richnesses—qualities that we have that make this situation so special.

The eight freedoms are:

1. The freedom of not being born as a hell being
2. The freedom of not being born as a hungry ghost
3. The freedom of not being born as an animal
4. The freedom of not being born as a long-life god
5. The freedom of not being born when no buddha has descended
6. The freedom of not being born as a barbarian
7. The freedom of not being born as a fool
8. The freedom of not being born as a heretic

The ten richnesses are:

1. Being born as a human being
2. Being born in a religious country
3. Being born with perfect organs
4. Being free of the five immediate negativities
5. Having devotion to the teachings
6. Being born when a buddha has descended

7. Being born when the teachings have been revealed
8. Being born when the complete teachings exist
9. Being born when the teachings are being followed
10. Having the necessary conditions to practice Dharma

Only when we have all eighteen of these extraordinary conditions can we say we have a perfect human rebirth. Only then can we fully take advantage of what we have and develop our mind to its ultimate potential.

The eight freedoms are also sometimes termed the eight "rests"—as human beings, we are "resting" from these restless, sorrowful states, such as the hell or animal realms. Some call them the eight "leisures," but I think "leisure" has too much of a connotation of lazy indulgence, like sitting back, smoking and drinking, so I prefer the term "freedom," because these are unfortunate states from which we are free. And this is more than freedom from suffering; it is the freedom to do what we want.

Are we truly free at the moment? If somebody invites us to a picnic, can we go anytime we wish or do we need to go to work to earn money? If somebody explains a difficult Dharma point, do we have the clarity of mind to understand or is there some block? In our everyday life there are always limitations to completely experiencing what we want to experience, whether it is pleasure or Dharma wisdom. Yet compared to almost every other living being we have incredible freedom. First, we are human and therefore free from the suffering states of the lower realms, which we will look at in the first three freedoms. But we are also not living in the god realms, where there is no chance to practice Dharma, and we are not humans who are totally clouded by wrong views or lacking the ability to understand the truth of the Buddha's teachings. Finally, we live at a time when Shakyamuni Buddha's influence is still present. He lived 2,600 years ago, but Buddhism still exists on this planet and we can benefit from it.

For example, just as many factors have to come together to make it possible to enjoy a picnic, similarly, many factors have to come together to make this human life complete in the freedoms we need to fully actualize our potential. If we're missing just one of the eight freedoms or ten richnesses, we might be able help ourselves in many ways but we'll still be limited.

At present we might feel that there's nothing much wrong with our lives. We have money and friends, we're young and healthy, if we want to go traveling we can save some money and do that; most of our friends are OK, so the world isn't too bad a place. This is very narrow thinking. We are blindly seeing a few temporary pleasures as real and lasting happiness. The very first teaching that the Buddha gave after becoming enlightened was on the four noble truths,[14] in which he explained the nature of suffering. This is because we must realize how unsatisfactory these temporary pleasures are, not only in order to renounce them ourselves but also to see the reality of the situation that the vast majority of other beings are in—that they are overwhelmed by terrible suffering.

I will be explaining just how rare our situation is, but that should not blind us to the suffering of others or to the very real possibility that the situation we are now in will end, possibly quickly and shockingly, and we will be thrown into the same sort of suffering that almost every other sentient being is facing.

When we look at the states that we are free from there might be ideas that we reject because they seem too outrageous to us. We are rational, intelligent people of the twenty-first century. We don't believe in hell. We ran away from the Catholic Church when we were teenagers because of all that hell stuff. But can we really be so sure that what the Buddha said about the lower realms is just make-believe? We don't know everything. We don't remember most of what has happened to us since we were born. We presume we spent nine months in our mother's womb but we only have logic and her telling us as evidence. Defining what is reality and what is myth based on our own very limited understanding is very dangerous.

Moreover, to say that we are right and the Buddha and all the highly-realized yogis who came after him were in error is not only arrogant and wrong-headed, it is also extremely disrespectful to the Buddha. To say, "I like Buddhism but some bits are wrong" will lead to confusion and act as a barrier to real development.

There are many things of which we have no awareness. Our friend might have cancer but we can't see it. Are we to deny it exists? "Show me the X-ray! Give me proof!" There are many things that exist that we don't realize with our limited minds: there are infinite universes, infinite forms of existence—we cannot reject them just because they are beyond our limited

---

[14] The discourse *Setting the Wheel of Dharma in Motion* (Pali: *Dammacakkappavattana-sutta*) is more generally referred to as *The Four Noble Truths Sutra*. It was given at Sarnath, near Varanasi, to the five meditators with whom the Buddha had practiced austerities before. The four noble truths are: the truth of suffering, the truth of the origin of suffering, the truth of the cessation of suffering and the truth of the path that leads to the cessation of suffering.

comprehension. As we progress spiritually and our understanding grows, things we think impossible now will start to seem commonplace. The power of the mind is infinite and so is its ability to understand things, but we need to work on it continuously to increase its power and understanding. Before we achieve the omniscience of buddhahood there will always be things that we don't understand. For example, only a buddha can perceive the most subtle aspects of karma.

Our knowledge is severely limited, while that of the buddhas is limitless, yet when we hear about the hell realms we decide that the wisdom of the buddhas is superstition while ours is superior. This is very deluded thinking. Most probably we find the teachings on the lower realms difficult or impossible because we are scared to let our mind accept them and therefore refuse to believe that there can be such suffering. We need to explore our own limitations rather than reject the teachings. It is painful to have to acknowledge that there is such suffering, but that is the reality of life, that is samsara. We just can't see it now because our minds are so polluted.

In some ways, meditating on the eight freedoms and ten richnesses also becomes a meditation on compassion because we have to think about the problems of the other sentient beings who do not have the opportunity to practice the holy Dharma. When we think about the animals and humans who lack this opportunity, incredible compassion arises for them. By studying this subject we will really start to see how every freedom is so precious and how the loss of that freedom is so terrible, and while all these amazing circumstances have come together for us, they have not done so for the vast majority of other sentient beings. We are free and they are trapped. The only conclusion we can draw from this is that we must do everything in our power to help them as much as we possibly can. From that determination, the precious jewel of bodhicitta arises.

Perhaps, as you study these freedoms and richnesses, you might find that you actually lack one or two. Even so, since you probably have nearly all of them, that itself is the cause for incredible joy. How amazing that you have done so much work in previous lives, living in perfect morality, creating incredible generosity, making pure prayers for such a rebirth, and now here it is. Amazing! It does seem almost miraculous.

If you do find that there is a freedom or richness missing, then that is a very good place to start your practice: "This is what I'm missing; this is what I need to do to get it." In that way you can make a meaningful life even more meaningful.

## 1. THE FREEDOM OF NOT BEING BORN AS A HELL BEING

Of the eight freedoms, the first is having the chance to practice Dharma through not having been born in the hell realms. In Buddhist cosmology there are six realms, the three lower realms of the hell beings, hungry ghosts and animals and the three upper realms of the humans, demigods and gods. Among the six, hell beings have the heaviest suffering. Also, there are infinitely more beings in the lower realms than in the upper realms and there are far more beings in hell than there are in the other two lower realms combined. This is because anger and hatred, the causes of being born as a hell being, are so common and so easy to create.

For the hell being, the suffering is so intense that pain and suffering are what defines its existence. There is no space in that being's mind for anything other than the unbearable suffering that it has to endure for what seems like an infinitely long time without the slightest respite and without any understanding that it will eventually end. Imagine if somebody threw you into a tub of boiling water and held you there. You wouldn't be able to meditate on emptiness, you wouldn't be able to generate compassion—in fact, all you would be able to do would be to struggle to be free from the unendurable pain. Getting free would be all that you could think of. The suffering a hell being has to endure is billions of times worse than this. Therefore, this first freedom is the freedom from that terrible suffering, which means the freedom to practice Dharma and develop positive qualities such as compassion and wisdom.

There is no definite place where the hell realms exist. The texts say that hell beings can be under the earth, on it or in space. Very few human beings have the karma to actually see a hell being, but we do see humans and animals that are suffering hell-like existences: torture victims, people with terrible burns from accidents, people locked in appalling prisons all their lives. Many people have the karma to endure terrible suffering again and again. The vast majority of hell situations, however, are beyond our perception.

As I have said, rejecting the notion of hell states just because they are not part of our limited world is illogical. The reason we cannot see them is because we do not have the karma to see them. We only see the world we have created the karma to see, and fortunately that does not—at present—include the hells.

That is not to say it will never happen. Just looking at situations that occur every day we will see that positive karma can end quite suddenly, negative karma can ripen and, unexpectedly and supposedly inexplicably, people can be thrown into unbelievable suffering. The people in Tibet are living in appalling conditions. Denied the religion that is like air to them, some people might even say that they are in a hellish situation. Eighty years ago, could anybody in Tibet have envisaged such a thing would occur? I'm sure that before the Chinese invasion the average Tibetan lived in his or her own world and it seemed like that would last forever. There was no sense that it could ever be lost. Yet now there is incredible suffering.

In the same way, the Jewish people lived for hundreds of years in Germany as Germans, side by side with their non-Jewish neighbors. How many of them in the early part of the last century had any idea what awaited them with Hitler? If we could go back to pre-Nazi days and tell them to get out of Germany they would think we were crazy. If we described the concentration camps they would probably get furious and beat us up for trying to scare them. Yet it happened. It would have seemed impossible to them, yet it happened. They had no way of seeing the future, just as now, we don't either.

If we consider the assumptions we unconsciously make about our own life we will see that one of them is that nothing bad is going to happen to us. Maybe, logically, we know that we are going to die one day, but that is in the future and so far away it's not real to us. Nothing bad has happened to us so far, so nothing bad will happen to us in the future. Unfortunately, that is not up to us but up to our karma. Meanwhile, we trust in a permanence that does not exist—everything is all right and everything will stay all right. This is foolish thinking because it just makes us more complacent.

Our life is far more precarious than we think it is. Some years ago there was a jumbo jet carrying more than three hundred people. Normally before a plane leaves, the engines and other parts are checked to make sure that the flight will be safe. When this plane was checked, nothing was found to be amiss. The cabin crew were well trained and, of course, knew how to open the doors. Nevertheless, after the plane landed, for some reason they could not open the doors at all. Suddenly the cockpit burst into flames and the pilot shouted for help. Everything inside the plane was completely burned. The airport emergency crews were unable to open the doors because of the heat, and when they finally did they saw that all the passengers had died while trying to escape, their bodies all piled up on top of each other. For forty minutes the whole thing became a hell. I'm sure that none of the passengers had any notion that this would be the outcome of their flight.

Likewise, we have no notion of what awaits us. We could die at any moment from any circumstance, and even if we live our situation could completely change. When karma ripens, that's it. We have to accept what is happening. The only way to ensure that negative karma does not ripen into suffering is to not create any and, by always keeping our mind positive, make sure we stop the negative imprints already on our mindstream from bringing their result and find a way to purify them before they do. That, of course, requires a lot of very positive conditions to come together, which is what this perfect human rebirth is all about. Until then, we cannot say with any certainty at all that tomorrow we might not find ourselves in a situation of such suffering that we would call it a hell.

All these hell sufferings are due to the power of the mind. When our mind is peaceful, virtuous and compassionate we look very peaceful and pleasant. Seeing us gives other people a warm feeling; it even makes them happy. On the other hand, with a very uptight mind, one that is selfish and angry, we look very ugly, even though normally we might be considered to be quite attractive. Even our face changes color; it gets very red, upsetting others just by the sight of it.

The mind has such power that it can not only physically change a person; it can also affect the external environment. Some places have one season that is very violent and wet, with floods and mud and difficulty in getting about, and another season with beautiful weather, sunny, warm and dry. These unpleasant and pleasant seasonal changes are karmic results. Even alone in our room, if we're angry, the whole environment can become very black such that others can find it terrifying to come in.

The atmosphere of a house depends on the minds of the people living in it. When we approach a place where a very pure holy being is living, we receive an incredible blessing that makes our mind very tranquil. Even though we may not see the holy being, just by coming near his or her house, we become very peaceful and happy. The peaceful environment comes from that person living in pure moral conduct.

In *Precious Garland*, the great pandit Nagarjuna said,

From nonvirtue all suffering arises,

As well as the unfortunate realms of the evil transmigratory
   beings.
From virtue all happiness arises,
As well as the happy transmigratory beings.[15]

Nagarjuna also says that all our happiness and suffering come from our
own mind. When we meet a desirable object, a happy feeling arises. When
we meet an undesirable object, a suffering feeling arises. When we meet a
neutral object, a feeling of indifference arises. From morning until night
our feelings fluctuate like this, according to the different objects we meet.
A happy feeling may come, then a suffering feeling, then an indifferent
feeling. Even in one day, a variety of happy and unhappy feelings arise in
dependence upon the different conditions we meet: the place, the food,
the people and so forth. When we meet a friend or are in a beautiful place,
a happy feeling arises; when we meet an enemy or are in an ugly place, an
unhappy feeling arises.

These conditions and the feelings they trigger all happen because karmic
seeds, or imprints, are ripening and we are happy or miserable depending
on whether the seed is positive or negative. At present we are helpless to
prevent being blown about on the winds of these ripening karmic imprints
and so, if we have our purse stolen, for instance, we have little control over
how we react to it. Most of us would be upset. A practitioner of Mahayana
thought-training (Tib: *lo-jong*), however, can change his or her attitude
such that "problems" and "miserable conditions" give rise to happy feelings.

All our dreams also come from our own mind. Frightening dreams of
being caught in a fire, drowned, beaten or killed by others are appearances
of the hallucinated mind. If, before going to sleep, we talk about an enemy
and get angry or read stories and see pictures that cause attachment to arise,
dreams of anger or attachment will come during the night. If, on the other
hand, we practice much virtue during the day, good dreams will come at
night. Dreams come from the impressions planted on our mind by the way
we spend the day.

Can we say that dreams don't exist? Of course they don't exist in the
same way that things in our waking life exist. If you chop off my hand in a
dream, when I wake in the morning I will still have my hand. But can we
say that when, in a dream, we get angry or watch our child die and are dis-
traught, that that emotion is not real? If I wake from a nightmare terrified,

---

[15] V. 21.

while you have just had a beautiful dream, is it right for you to tell me to stop being stupid because everything is wonderful? My reality seems just as real as yours does, even if we are only talking about dreams. The suffering or happiness we experience in a dream seems as real as the suffering or happiness we experience in waking life, and it comes from the negative or positive imprints ripening in our consciousness.

In the same way, we might currently be living in a very beautiful house—the result of positive karma ripening—but tomorrow it might burn to the ground—the result of negative karma ripening. These different experiences are due to different karmas. The difference with the hells is simply that the conditions are much more miserable. The stronger the negativity, the worse the result, and the very strongest negative thought creates the worst hell. This is karma. Within the same situation two people can experience two completely different worlds, one positive and enjoyable, the other terrible, unbearable.

Another way of looking at it is to say that the greater the delusion on the mindstream, the more the suffering we have to experience. If there is no delusion at all—if we have escaped samsara entirely—then there is no sensation of aversion to heat or cold. Very advanced beings may feel heat and cold, but it does not affect them adversely at all. The more deluded the mind however, the more we suffer. And so a pleasantly cool evening for one person might feel unendurably cold to another, or a beautifully warm day for one person might feel like being inside a raging furnace for another. Without having created the causes to feel the suffering of the cold or the heat, it will not be felt, and conversely, if the causes have been created, then it will be felt.

The world the hell being experiences is defined by suffering we could never dream of. The ground is either hotter than the fires at the end of this world system or colder than ice, depending on the karma of the being. These are all projections of the being's mind. Just as the world we encounter every day is the result of karmic seeds ripening in our mindstream, hell beings have created their own world by the countless negative actions they have done in previous lives. That's why in *A Guide to the Bodhisattva's Way of Life* Shantideva said,

> Who created the burning iron ground?
> Where have the multitude of flames come from?
> The Mighty One has said that all this

Comes from the evil mind.[16]

The burning iron ground that the hell being experiences is a product of the deluded, negative mind. But that does not mean it is not real.

There are many different types of environment on this planet that are visible to us. They are all due to the karma of the beings who live there. Some countries are incredibly barren and rocky—the result of past negative actions of the people of that place—and some are green and soft, with a pleasant climate and plenty of water and resources—the result of the past positive actions of the inhabitants.

The world we live in is the creation of our own mind, and for the hell being that world is as terrible as its own mind. The strong negativity that dominates its consciousness has created a world that is horrible and full of suffering, infinitely worse than the worst suffering we could imagine. And because of the weight of its karma, the hell being has almost no chance of escape.

### The hot hells and the surrounding hells

Of the suffering states of hell, there are eight hot and eight cold hells, as well as various neighboring and occasional hells.[17]

Near the time of death, somebody who is going to be reborn in the hot hells will feel unbelievably cold and will crave heat badly. You may have heard about this happening or even seen it yourself. A person starts going through the death process and feels so cold that nothing can warm her enough; the karmic imprint that produces the craving for heat is ripening and becoming stronger, and it is likely that she will be reborn as a hell being. After death, which is like going to sleep, and the intermediate state (Tib: *bardo*), which is like a nightmare, rebirth is like waking up, and it is here that the negative karma to be born in hell manifests fully.

The level of hell into which a being is reborn depends on many factors, but mainly how negative the mind is. If the person has committed a serious nonvirtue, such as killing with hatred, the result will almost definitely

---

[16] Paraphrase of ch. 5, vv. 7 and 8.
[17] For a more detailed description of the lower realms suffering see Rinpoche's forthcoming book on the lower realms or *Liberation*, pp. 322–351.

be the lowest hell, called the inexhaustible hot hell. If the mind is over-whelmed with nonvirtue, but not as strongly, then it could be one of the lesser hells, which have less suffering than the inexhaustible hell but are still more terrible than we can imagine.

It is mentioned in the teachings that the fire that consumes the universe at the end of the eon of destruction is sixty or seventy times hotter than any fire we have on earth today, even the heat from the hottest volcano. How-ever, even one tiny fire spark from the hell realm is said to be far hotter than this—about seven times hotter than all the fires in the universe combined.

I once saw an example of intense fire in Hawaii, when some students took me to a volcano. We saw a stream of molten lava but couldn't get anywhere near it because it was so hot. We think of lava as being incredibly hot, but even that is not hot enough to melt the rocks it runs over. The fire at the end of the universe is far hotter than lava and, as I have just said, the tini-est spark from the hell realms is far, far hotter than the fire at the end of the universe. Putting our hand in molten lava would be like dipping it in icy water compared to having to experience the heat of one of the hell realms. The term the texts use is "oneness with fire." The ground and the hell beings are oneness with the fire.

The body of a hell being seems to have been created to experience the most suffering. Because of all the obstacles gathered, it is huge, like a moun-tain range. Maybe if it were smaller, the suffering would be less, but this enormous body has to endure the intense pain of fire all over its body. And its skin is very, very thin. Perhaps you remember once having a skin infec-tion, where even to put a soft cloth over the wound was agony. This is like the skin of the hell being, only the hell being's is much more sensitive. Fur-thermore, the hell being doesn't die but lives to experience unimaginable suffering for a very long time. This perfect vehicle for experiencing intense suffering is all due to heavy negative karma.

There are various hot hells a being can experience depending on its karma. The length of time a being must spend in the hell realm it first gets reborn into is not fixed but it is an incredibly long period of time. And after finish-ing in the first of the hells, its time in hell has still not finished; it will next be reborn in another hell, such as one of the neighboring or occasional hells.

Even the briefest of the hell lifespans, that of a being in the hell called "being alive again and again" is billions and billions of human years. In the second hot hell, the black line hell, the suffering is doubled and the lifespan is doubled, with the third hell double that of the second and so forth. The last one, the inexhaustible hot hell, has the greatest suffering of all and the longest lifespan.

The first hot hell is the *hell of being alive again and again*. In this hell the beings hack each other to pieces with intense anger. In our human world, if somebody is hacked to pieces they are dead and that's it. An amputated arm is a piece of dead meat with no consciousness. But in this hell, all the pieces of the body retain consciousness and feel the incredible pain of being butchered. Even every drop of the being's blood that splashes on the red hot burning ground feels intense pain. Then a karmic voice tells them that they will revive and the body parts come together and they are alive again. The being sees the other beings and immediately takes up a weapon and they all hack each other to pieces again. This goes on for billions of human years, without respite.

In the *black line hell*, both lifespan and suffering are doubled. There are hell guardians that hold the hell being down, burn black lines over the body with red hot wires like the ones carpenters use, and slice the body up along those lines, like sawing a tree into planks. Like the previous hell, all the parts of the being retain consciousness, even the blood that spills onto the red hot burning iron ground, so every tiny part of the being experiences the most unbelievable pain. This is repeated continuously.

Again, in the *gathered and crushed hell* the suffering is twice that of the previous hell, as is the lifespan. Here, mountains manifest in the shape of beings the hell being might have killed in previous lives. If, for example, the hell being was a butcher who slaughtered sheep, two huge mountains shaped like sheep's heads appear. Or, the hell being might have killed lice, rats, cockroaches and so forth; the mountains assume that shape. The being is trapped between these great mountains, which move together slowly, crushing it completely so that its blood pours out like a waterfall. Then the mountains pull apart, the hell being revives and the mountains come together again, crushing the being to death and reviving it, over and over again.

The next two hells are the *hell of crying* and *hell of great crying*. In the first, the hell being is trapped in an iron house that is oneness with fire, without doors or windows. For an incredible length of time, until its karma finishes, the being has to experience that suffering. In the *hell of great crying*, instead of one house of burning iron, there are two, one inside the other, so the suffering is doubled.

In the *hot hell*, the suffering multiplies. The hell being is impaled on a large skewer that is thrust through its sex organ and comes out its head. It spews molten iron, like lava, from its mouth. In the *extremely hot hell*, which is twice as hot as the previous one, the karmic guardians thrust a trident through the being so that its points come out its head and shoulders, or they lay the hell being out on burning ground that is oneness with fire and roll the being out flat until its body and the fire are oneness too. Like this, there are many tortures inflicted upon the hell being, each worse than the one before.

In the last and worst hell, the *inexhaustible hot hell*, the body of the hell being is like the butter of a butter lamp that dissolves and becomes completely one with the flame. In some texts, the lifespan of a being in this hell is said to be one intermediate eon.

When the karma to experience the hot hell weakens, the being is able to escape, but only into one of the *four neighboring hells*: the fiery trench, the plain of razor-sharp swords, the putrid swamp and the uncrossable torrent. (Some texts list these as six, and there is some slight variation in the way they are described, but the sufferings are the same.) Here, the being suffers terribly every step. It has to escape the fiery trench, a terrible sea of lava-like liquid so hot that the being's legs melt with every step it takes, only to be revived again. Then, trying to cross the plain of swords, it is cut to pieces. Hearing the voice of a loved one coming from the top of a tree, it tries to climb up, but the tree's leaves are razor-sharp knives pointing down and at every movement they pierce the hell being's body. Fierce dogs rip its legs apart and birds swoop down and peck out its eyes. When it finally reaches the top of the tree, it now hears the voice of its beloved calling from below, asking it to come down. It starts the long climb down, but the leaves now point upward and again rip its flesh at every movement.

The putrid swamp is like a cesspit, a swamp of muddy excrement, where worms with long, pointed, needle-like beaks peck the body. Once, when I was making water offerings to the hungry ghosts on a bridge in Tahiti, I saw a fish in the water that had a long, thin, needle-like nose that reminded me of the descriptions of these worms. The being must experience these ordeals for many eons, until the karma finishes.

In the last neighboring hell, the uncrossable torrent, the being must cross this boiling river to be free from the neighboring hells, but just stepping into the liquid dissolves its flesh, like beans that have been boiled too long. It must suffer like this for an unbelievably long time.

If we're in a tropical country without air conditioning it's almost impossible to meditate, yet here we are talking about beings who have to endure heat that is seven times hotter than the fire at the end of the universe. If you have ever slammed your hand in a car door so that it comes up blue and throbbing, you will know that the pain is overwhelming; at such a time I don't think you would be trying to do single-pointed concentration. The hell beings in the *gathered and crushed hell* have this experience billions of times worse, constantly, for an inconceivably long time. What chance do they have to create any virtue at all? It is good to contemplate this every time we have a toothache or some other kind of pain and feel sorry for ourselves.

Even though our life is not perfect, think how much freedom we have compared to a hell being. The worst pain we can suffer is bliss compared to the suffering in the hells; our hottest day is like playing in the snow compared to the hot hells. We have created the causes for this great good fortune, and we must continue to create the causes. By succumbing to greed, jealousy, anger and the other destructive emotions we are getting ourselves ready for a life like the ones I have just described. This body we have is a miracle and we should feel such joy to have it, not just for the pleasure we are able to enjoy but more importantly for the opportunity it gives us to practice Dharma and find real happiness.

## The cold and occasional hells

In the same way as feeling intense cold and craving heat at the time of death can propel a person into the hot hells, feeling like the body is burning up and craving cold can propel a person into the cold hells. If the imprint of previous nonvirtue ripens at that time, then, after the nightmare of the intermediate state, the person wakes to rebirth in one of the cold hells.

As with the hot hells, there are eight cold hells, each one colder than the one before. With the first, the *hell of blisters*, it as if the being is nailed to the icy ground, stuck right inside an ice mountain, with no way to move. There is no sunlight and a terrible wind blows, intensifying the suffering.

From there, the suffering of each cold hell gets worse. The next is the *hell of bursting blisters*, where the blisters from the cold burst and cause intense suffering. Then, in each of the following hells, from the hell called *a-choo* because of the noise the being makes to the *hell of great cracking like a lotus*,[18]

---

[18] The names of the eight cold hells are: the hell of blisters, of burst blisters, of a-choo, of moaning, of chattering teeth, of cracking like an upali, of cracking like a lotus and of great cracking like a lotus.

the time spent gets progressively longer, with billions and billions of years of intense suffering.

Have you have ever been stuck in a snow storm without a jacket? If so, you will know how unpleasant it is, how you start shivering and your hands go numb. The hell being, of course, is completely naked, its skin is far more sensitive than ours and the degree of cold is millions of times greater than we could imagine. Even if we were to put our hand in a freezer and leave it there for an hour, we'd still have no idea of the suffering of a being in the cold hells.

And, of course, with such intense pain there is no way that the hell being can do anything other than suffer. There is no chance to create virtue and no way to practice Dharma, so how can it find a way out of that suffering?

There are also hell environments called the *occasional hells* because they can either be seen on this planet if we have the karma to see them or because the beings don't have to experience them all the time.

There once was a man called Kotikarna[19] who was traveling to find jewels when he came to a desert island where there was just barren sand. All of a sudden he saw a burning house with a man inside being devoured by savage dogs.

When the sun set, however, the whole scene changed and the house that was terrible by day became a luxurious mansion and the dogs turned into beautiful women. The man stopped suffering and enjoyed the most exquisite food and drink, incredible luxury and the pleasure of the women. The next morning, however, the scene changed back again—the house into a burning inferno and the women into dogs devouring the man's flesh. This happened every day.

When Kotikarna asked the man why he had to suffer like that, he replied that when he had been in India before he had been a butcher. He had asked the arhat Katyayana how to keep moral conduct, but because of his occupation of killing animals, he could only take the precepts of not killing at night, not in the day. These he kept purely. For that reason he suffered terribly during the day but at night he had the most incredible pleasure. Each experience was the result of the different karma he created.

He told Kotikarna where a pot of gold and his butcher's knives were

---

[19] Rinpoche uses the Tibetan name (Pagpa Gedun-tso) for the merchant and the Sanskrit for the arhat. We have changed this for consistency. This agrees with *Liberation*, p. 336 and *Steps on the Path to Enlightenment*, vol. 1, p. 380.

buried and asked him to show these to his son with a strong message to renounce killing.

### Our great good fortune to be free from the hells

We have been born in the hell realms numberless times and each time it was almost impossible to escape to another existence. There was never even a chance to hear the word "Dharma," let alone practice it; therefore it was impossible to develop compassion and wisdom.

We should deeply consider just how fortunate we are that this time we have not been born in the hell realms. That is the first freedom of this perfect human rebirth. We don't have to experience the unbelievable suffering that hell beings have to suffer; we don't have to endure those terrible environments. We have the chance to practice Dharma. All the conditions are there for us if we just want to use them.

We live in an environment that is neither too hot nor too cold; we have fans or air conditioners in the summer and heaters and warm clothes in the winter, so we really do not suffer from extremes of temperature at all. We should meditate on how fortunate we are not to be in that state and determine to always create the causes for a perfect human rebirth.

Think of how difficult it is to meditate in extremely hot weather or how it would be impossible to concentrate if somebody were to hold a stick of burning incense against our skin. Think how absurd it would be to put our hand in the freezer for five minutes or sit naked in the snow and try to do our meditation practice. We are free from all these extremes.

Think: "Today, through not having been born in the hells, I have the freedom to practice Dharma. Within these twenty-four hours, within this hour, even within this minute, I have the freedom to obtain whichever of the three great purposes I want—a happy future life, liberation or full enlightenment."

When we contemplate like this we can see how unbelievably precious the freedom to practice Dharma through not being born in the hells is; it is more precious than the most valuable material thing, more precious than a mountain of diamonds. If we want a good rebirth, we can create its cause; if we want the sorrowless state of *nirvana*, we can create its cause; if we wish to attain complete enlightenment, we can create its cause. This is what this freedom means.

We can create whatever merit we want and purify our past negativities completely so that we will never have to experience their suffering results again. We can renounce the very cause of suffering. We should feel incredible joy that we have this priceless gift within us.

If we don't contemplate the suffering of the lower realms in this way we won't be able to see what a miracle this perfect human rebirth is and will be very likely to squander it.

Perhaps we can see that practicing Dharma is worthwhile and that we might become a better person if we do it, but somehow, without the impetus of understanding the lower realms, we will never have the energy to really take on the essence of the Dharma. That is why it is so important to try to fully understand what each freedom means.

## 2. THE FREEDOM OF NOT BEING BORN AS A HUNGRY GHOST

The second of the eight freedoms is the freedom to practice the holy Dharma through not being born as a hungry ghost. Hungry ghosts are beings who live either under the earth or on it, although like the hell beings we normally do not have the karma to see them. Just as the hell being's main suffering is heat and cold, caused by hatred, the hungry ghost's main suffering is hunger and thirst, caused by miserliness and desire, although they also have many other forms of suffering.

Probably you have never been truly starving in your life. Can you remember a time when for some reason you haven't been able to eat for two or three days? Unless you were very sick, the hunger would have been a very unpleasant feeling. Now think what that would be like if you had to go without food for a week. The pain in your stomach would be terrible. It would be almost impossible to think of anything else and certainly impossible to meditate with so much hunger.

As you will know if you have been at one of my courses, I have a bad reputation for teaching past the break times. Were you able to maintain perfect concentration when lunchtime came and I was still teaching? As you got hungrier and hungrier and I was still teaching, were you able to concentrate at all? As the time dragged on and you knew that all that beautiful food was getting totally cold and ruined, could you still follow the teachings? Probably not. When you tried to concentrate, your stomach wouldn't let you; all you could think about was food. And that is when lunch is just delayed for an hour or so. Food and drink are a fundamental need, so when they seem unobtainable, even if there is no danger of starvation, we can still think of nothing else. We certainly cannot meditate on the lam-rim.

This is one of the great advantages of the two-day *nyung-nä* fasting retreat, which is very popular in Tibetan Buddhism. In it, only one meal is taken on the first day and on the second day neither food nor drink are touched. Even though it is only two days and even though the reason for fasting is so beneficial, it is very hard to go without food and drink. By voluntarily putting ourselves in this situation we not only purify much negative karma but we can also appreciate a little of what so many sentient beings must endure all the time.

Any feeling of hunger we could possibly have is nothing compared to what the hungry ghosts have to suffer every moment of their lives. For hundreds and hundreds of years they wander, searching for a scrap of food or a drop of water, unable to find anything. It's impossible to imagine the desperation that must totally overwhelm their lives.

There are some hungry ghosts that are able to find food, but in some ways that's worse because there are always karmic obstacles to their eating it.

The principal cause of being born a hungry ghost is attachment—the desire for worldly pleasure—and the other delusions that arise from it, especially miserliness. When somebody is strongly attached to property and money, jealously guarding everything he has, never giving to charity, never wanting to share it with others, he is certainly creating the cause to be reborn as a hungry ghost.

There are beings in this world who are like hungry ghosts, consumed with miserliness, feeling that no matter how much they might have it is never enough. Even though they are born in a human body, they are never free from an incredible hunger. We see many people like this. They feel they never have enough to give others—even a little small change to a beggar—but their wardrobes are full of expensive clothes, their fridges are full of food and their houses are cluttered with possessions. If we observe them we will almost always see that they enjoy none of this. They buy and buy, yet all their purchases bring them no satisfaction and so they have to go buy some more. It is this needy, miserly mind that goes into the next life as a hungry ghost.

These people are so attached to their house that after they die they can be reborn as a hungry ghost in that area and will try to protect what once was theirs. If somebody steals from that family, the hungry ghost is offended and will make the thief sick. People often say they hear strange noises in their home after somebody in the family has died. This could be that person, now a hungry ghost, unable to leave the home because of attachment.

It is quite common in many countries that mediums have the ability to invoke spirits who are able to give answers to people and even help them in some ways. These can be hungry ghosts. Some hungry ghosts have a little psychic power and can predict the future, but their ability to do this comes from karma, not meditation or merit. They can be very powerful, especially in mountainous regions, and can help people harm their enemies through black magic. But these are not spirits we can trust and we can certainly not take refuge in them. Unfortunately, some people do and can be greatly harmed as a result.

Some humans are able to see hungry ghosts and many high lamas can not only see them but have the power to subdue and help them.

There are many different kinds of hungry ghost but a general description is a being with a huge stomach and tiny arms and legs. Most have enormous obstacles to eating and drinking. Some, after hundreds of years searching, are able to find a scrap of food or a tiny drop of water but are driven away by fierce guardians, who prevent them from reaching it. Others have a mouth like the eye of a needle and can't get any food into it. Some may be able to find a drop of water but can't swallow it because they have three knots in their throat. Others are occasionally able to get a tiny amount of food or water into their stomach but it bursts into flames, like dropping a lighted match into a bucket of gasoline.

Some hungry ghosts have flames spewing from their mouths. This is something I have seen in India. In Buxa Duar,[20] where I first went after Tibet, the monks often told of going into the forest at night for pipi and seeing strange lights moving among the trees. Once I had to go to hospital in the middle of the night and, when coming back to the monastery, I saw a dim light coming from a tree in the forest. Knowing that trees don't have lights, I went closer, but as I approached, the light moved off. It seems that people never get to actually see these hungry ghosts, only the flames that come from their mouths.

Once when Shakyamuni Buddha was living in India, there was one young monk who saw an extremely fearful kind of hungry ghost. The monk was scared and tried to escape but the hungry ghost called out that she was his

---

[20] Buxa Duar is in West Bengal, India. It is the site of an old fort that the British used as a prison camp during their rule and is where most of the exiled monks who fled the Chinese occupation of Tibet in 1959 were sent. Rinpoche stayed there for eight years and Buxa is where he first met Lama Yeshe.

loving mother who had died giving birth to him. She told him how terrible it was wandering the earth as a hungry ghost and how she had not been able to find even a crumb of food or a drop of water for over twenty years, not even a patch of damp earth to suck.

The young monk felt so much compassion for his mother that he went to the Buddha to ask him to dedicate merit for her better rebirth. However, her karma was too strong, so when she passed away from that life the Buddha's skillful means could only secure her a rebirth as another hungry ghost, but this time a wealthy one.

Hearing this, the monk persuaded her to offer a bolt of cloth to the Buddha to dedicate for a better rebirth. Unfortunately, her miserliness was too strong and after she had done it she regretted it. At night she crept back and stole the cloth back. After this had happened several times, the monk cut the cloth in very small pieces and made an offering to each monk. Thus there was nothing for the mother hungry ghost to steal and, due to the skillful means of the Buddha, her next rebirth was a better one.

There was a great yogi called Sangye Yeshe[21] who had psychic powers and could travel to different planets and see other types of sentient beings. Once he visited a city where there were many hungry ghosts, in order to guide them. He saw a hungry ghost, a mother with five hundred children, who could communicate with him. She told him that many years ago her husband had left for the human realm in search of food and she had not seen him since. When the yogi asked for a way of identifying her husband she told him that he only had one eye and limped because of a broken leg.

When Sangye Yeshe returned to the human realm he was able to find the hungry ghost's husband from the description she gave. When he gave him the message the hungry ghost pathetically held up his hand, showing a tiny bit of dried-up spit. He said, "In all the years I have been searching, this is all I could find," and clasped it tightly in his fist so he would not lose it.

He had managed to find this spit when he was around a monastery where a monk who was living purely in the precepts did the practice of dedicating spit, kaka and pipi to the hungry ghosts. Through his prayers they were able to get some sustenance. But there were so many hungry ghosts around the monk all the time that it was a terrible fight to get anything at all and this hungry ghost was lucky to come away with even a tiny lump of spit. I'm

---

[21] In *Liberation in the Palm of Your Hand* Pabongka Rinpoche uses the Sanskrit name, Buddhajnana. See *Liberation*, pp. 343–5.

reminded of this story when I see crowds of beggars fighting for alms at the Mahabodhi *stupa* in Bodhgaya.

There are many practices like this where we can make charity to other sentient beings such as hungry ghosts. The Buddha has given mantras specifically for this purpose and by the power of these mantras the hungry ghosts are able to benefit from the offering; otherwise they can't even see it.[22]

Many hungry ghosts live on the smell of food and the Buddha has shown ways of making charity to help them. There are pujas that involve burning things like *tsampa* that allow the hungry ghosts to get some nourishment.[23] It is common in monasteries for the monks to squeeze a little food from a meal in their hands and say the mantra that enables hungry ghosts to see and enjoy it.[24]

We should take time to really reflect on the suffering of the hungry ghosts and the causes of that suffering—attachment and miserliness—and determine to never create such causes again. We should think, "If I were born now as a suffering hungry ghost, it would be impossible to practice the holy Dharma. How fortunate I am to have the freedom to practice Dharma through not having been born in the hungry ghost realm. With this freedom, within these twenty-four hours, within this hour, even within this minute, I have the incredible freedom to obtain whichever of the three great purposes I want. If I wish, I can continuously create the cause to receive a perfect body in my next life. During each hour, each minute, I have the opportunity to create the cause to attain the sorrowless state of liberation. And, if I wish, I can achieve enlightenment for the benefit of all sentient beings. In this one moment, by practicing bodhicitta, I have the freedom to create the cause of enlightenment."

Thinking in this way, we should try to get a very strong feeling of how precious and important the body that has this freedom is and what a tragedy it is to waste even one moment of the perfect human rebirth. We should determine to make every moment of our life highly meaningful.

---

[22] See Rinpoche's *Practices to Benefit Nagas, Pretas, and Spirits* as well as his forthcoming book on the three lower realms, where he discusses the various practices we can do for hungry ghosts.

[23] See *Aroma Charity for Spirits (Sur Offering)*.

[24] The mantra is *om utsishta pandi ashibya soha*.

## 3. THE FREEDOM OF NOT BEING BORN AS AN ANIMAL

The next freedom is the freedom to practice the holy Dharma through not being born in the animal realm: an animal, bird, fish, insect and so forth.

Unlike the hell or hungry ghost realms, we can see beings in the animal realm and investigate their reality for ourselves. There are many, many kinds of animals, fish, birds and insects, but the suffering common to each is being dumb and foolish, with a mind incapable of understanding anything other than survival, although there are many other sufferings besides. The main cause of being born in the animal realm, ignorance, traps them in a life without choice. Those who must kill to survive do so without choice; their victims are powerless not to be killed by them. Tiny creatures are devoured by bigger ones, who in turn are hunted by yet bigger ones. No matter who they are, there is always an enemy ready to take their life in order to eat their flesh. Others are slaves of human beings.

If we were to suddenly find ourselves in the body of an animal, we'd be terrified. No matter how hard our life as a human is, it is a pure land existence compared with that of an animal. Imagine you are a slug in the middle of the road after a heavy rain or a goat being chased down the street in a village in India by the local butcher. What would it be like? If we look below the surface of the life of any animal to see what it is really like, we will find unimaginable suffering. If you investigate how animals live, you will see that this is true. Overwhelmed by stupidity and dullness, they have no capacity to free themselves from the suffering they must face every day. And, of course, they have no ability to understand and practice Dharma.

Some animals live much longer than humans but that does not mean they can develop any wisdom. There's a turtle in Hong Kong that is said to be thousands of years old. I was invited to meet it but somehow that never happened. Even if I had, I don't think I could have taught it anything. Could I have explained the cause of happiness to it? Even an elephant, which can live for a very long time, wouldn't understand one word.

Our pampered dog or cat might seem to have a leisurely life, sleeping all day and eating better than we do, but if we think it is fortunate we're judging only its external appearance. If we could understand our pets' minds we would see how ignorant they really are. For example, when they are sick from having eaten bad food, they can't tell us about it so that we can find the right medicine.

Our cat can live with us its whole life and we can try to teach it mantras every day but it won't be able to utter one syllable. This is because it has the body of a suffering transmigratory being and a mind that is incapable of that sort of understanding.

We can explain emptiness to pigs for years and they would be none the wiser. We can scream bodhicitta in the ears of those pitiful sheep or goats all day and there is no way they could understand. We can teach chickens that compassion is the true path to happiness but this won't stop them eating insects in the ground.

Once while teaching at Stanford University in California, His Holiness the Dalai Lama said, "You should not be like an animal," meaning we should not accept everything at face value without question. Here he was talking about conventional and ultimate truth, how we suffer because we thoughtlessly accept the appearance of things, which seem to be truly existent, and as a result are overwhelmed by negative emotions. In that, we are like animals.

Animals simply do not have the capacity to understand how to get out of the suffering they are in, and so, whereas they may be quite cunning in other ways, in this most fundamental and important way, they are stupid. Seeing this will make us glad we are not an animal.

But in fact, this is what we could well be by this time tomorrow. We simply do not know when we will die or what our next rebirth will be. We could soon be living in a glass tank full of water in a restaurant, a tasty lobster or a fat fish, waiting for a customer to choose us for her meal. We could soon be a fish struggling on the end of a line with a hook in our mouth or a worm being eaten alive by thousands of ants. We just don't know. If we *did* know, we would then really value this most precious of things, the human life.

Would you want to be born as any animal? Even a pet. Would you want to have hair all over your body and have to fight the other dogs or cats in the neighborhood and always rely on your human owners for every bit of food that you get? We have been born as dogs and cats countless times. We have had infinite lives, so there's not one animal that we haven't been. We have been monkeys and tigers, cows and zebras, cockroaches and mosquitoes, many, many times. Even the Buddha's omniscient mind cannot see how many times we have been a cockroach or a mosquito. That is life in samsara, endlessly cycling from one suffering body to another.

As centipedes, we have been stepped on while crossing the road. As moths, we have been squashed against a wall. Perhaps we went straight from being the squashed centipede to the life of the moth, only to be squashed again. Poor us! Whenever we see an insect trapped in a spider web or a small animal run over by a car, they are telling us that we have been saved from such a terrible end by being human and we had better practice Dharma and do nothing but practice Dharma or we ourselves might well be destined for a spider's web or the wheel of a car.

Thinking on the suffering of animals we can start to appreciate how there is no escape as long as we are in samsara. It really is unbearable and terrifying and we need to do whatever we can to be free from it.

Only the practice of virtue can free us. This is something no animal can understand. But we are not an animal; we are human and we have the capacity to understand this. This is an amazing freedom. Therefore we should think, "How fortunate that I am not an animal. I have found this perfect human body, qualified with eight freedoms and ten richnesses, and have the freedom to practice Dharma." We should feel this deeply from our heart, but we should also feel that there is no certainty that it will last—it might even finish today—therefore we need to make the most of this most precious opportunity.

My root guru, His Holiness Trijang Rinpoche,[25] used to say that if we could fully understand the suffering of the lower realms and how many times we have been there, we would be so terrified that we would never want to sleep or eat; food would be of no interest to us. All we would want to do would be to meditate and practice Dharma in order to create as much merit as possible every moment. Therefore it is vital that we study the teachings on the four noble truths, especially the truth of suffering, and the lower realms and karma if we are to truly appreciate our perfect human rebirth.

How amazing, how wonderful that we have the freedom and ability to study such great teachings and to live our lives according to them.


## 4. THE FREEDOM OF NOT BEING BORN AS A LONG-LIFE GOD

The next freedom is that of not being born as a long-life god. "God" in this context does not mean a buddha, one free from ignorance. These are worldly beings who are still ignorant, and although their lives are full of

---

[25] His Holiness Trijang Rinpoche (1901–81) was the junior tutor to His Holiness the 14th Dalai Lama and root guru of both Lama Yeshe and Lama Zopa Rinpoche. He edited Pabongka Rinpoche's *Liberation in the Palm of Your Hand*.

pleasure that we could not even imagine, they are still not free from suffering. They are called gods because their enjoyments are so much greater than ours. For example, desire realm gods can have thousands of goddesses. They live on nectar; their food is not like ours, which must be harvested and makes kaka. Their bodies shine with light and their clothes are exquisite. They live in unbelievably beautiful palaces made of lapis lazuli with beams made of jewels and so forth. Even the ground is like lapis and they can see their own reflection in it as they walk. Their possessions are so precious that one earring is more valuable than the combined wealth of our world system.

The gods of the form and formless realms have renounced the sense pleasures of the desire realm and have attained great peace through profound concentration. The gods of the formless realm don't even have a body, just a consciousness. There is no suffering of suffering or suffering of change, but they are still not free from pervasive compounding suffering. They live for eons but are really only aware twice: as they are being born they have the thought, "I am being born as a god," and when they die they have the thought, "Now I am dying and leaving this rebirth as a god." In between they stay in a concentration that is like a deep sleep, lacking in any wisdom or discrimination, so it is virtually impossible to practice any Dharma at all.

The world of the desire realm gods is free from the problems that we experience—having to work to feed ourselves, having to expend energy being comfortable and happy. Every pleasure comes to them effortlessly. With all this luxury, their minds are constantly distracted by sense pleasure and they have no thoughts other than what to experience next. We can see this a little bit in our own life, where we can easily be distracted from meditation by thoughts of the new car or computer we want to buy or the movie or restaurant we're going to that night.

The gods are so overwhelmed by pleasure that they have no way of knowing the nature of suffering and no way to practice Dharma. Kopan students often say that when they return home their ability to practice Dharma slips and can even get lost altogether because of the distractions that once again fill their lives. But these distractions are nothing compared to those of the gods.

There is the story of one of Shariputra's disciples, a doctor who became a long-life god.[26] Before his death he was very devoted to Shariputra. If he

[26] Shariputra was one of the two principal disciples of the Buddha. In *Liberation* the doctor is referred to as the "king of doctors," Kumarajivaka; see p. 272.

was riding his elephant and saw the arhat walking along the street he would immediately jump off and bow down before his teacher with much love and devotion. After the doctor died, Shariputra saw with his psychic power that he had been reborn in the god realms and went there to give him more teachings. However, when the doctor saw Shariputra this time, he was so intoxicated by the pleasures of the god realm that he simply raised a finger in recognition and then ran off to play with his friends. He had no time to listen to Dharma and no time for his old guru.

The main problem, of course, is attachment. Material possessions bring with them attachment, and with attachment comes the mind that always wanders to the object of attachment. This becomes a huge distraction when we try to practice Dharma. If, however, we could be free from attachment, it wouldn't matter how many wonderful possessions we had; they would not be able to distract us.

This is the problem of the god realms. Even if the gods could hear the Dharma, they would not be able to make use of it because they are so obsessed with pleasure. It is said that a few gods in the Thirty-three Realm at the very top of Mount Meru[27] do actually get to hear the Dharma by hearing a big drum that is beaten on certain days. Just as animals benefit from the sound of mantras without understanding anything, the gods respond to the sound of the Dharma drum and receive some limited benefit. Other than that, most gods have no opportunity to hear the Dharma at all.

Seven days before a god's death—and each day in the god realm is fifty human years—a karmic voice tells the god he is going to die. Then everything decays. For the whole of the god's life there has been no dirt, no unpleasant smell, nothing in his world that was anything other than pleasure. Now, suddenly, things change. His body gets dirty and smells; it loses its radiance and becomes quite ugly. He becomes dissatisfied with his bed and, no longer able to relax, is unable to sleep in it. The flowers around him, which have remained perfect his whole life, wilt and die. His friends, who have always only been there to amuse him and give him pleasure, are repulsed by these changes and shun him. He is terrified and totally alone.

Due to karma he is then able to remember past lives and, even worse, see his future life. He sees that his karma to be a god has finished and that within seven days he will be reborn in the lower realms. The suffering he

---

[27] The Thirty-three Realm is the second of the six realms of the gods of desire on Mt. Meru.

experiences as a result of this knowledge is worse than actually experiencing the hells.

It is easy to see that as a hell being, hungry ghost or animal it is almost impossible to create any virtuous action, but also as a long-life god—either in the desire realm distracted by pleasure or in the form or formless realm absorbed in concentration—it is extremely difficult to see the nature of suffering and therefore extremely difficult to practice Dharma. Unless we see its faults, how can we renounce samsara? The gods have no chance to practice morality or generate the mind renouncing samsara, so no matter how long and pleasurable their lives are, their next rebirth is surely in the lower realms.

It seems that compared to human beings, the gods have unbelievable pleasure and freedom, but they lack the most important freedom, the freedom to practice Dharma. That is why not being born a god is considered one of the eight freedoms of this perfect human rebirth.

Contemplating the suffering of the gods, even with their unbelievable pleasures, helps us appreciate how precious this human life is. Only with this perfect human rebirth can we practice the Dharma—no god can, no animal can, no hungry ghost can and certainly no hell being can. Therefore we should think, "How fortunate I am not to be a god. I have found this perfect human body qualified with eight freedoms and ten richnesses and have the freedom to practice Dharma." We should feel this deeply in our heart and determine never to waste even a second of this life.

## 5. THE FREEDOM OF NOT BEING BORN WHEN NO BUDDHA HAS DESCENDED

The previous four freedoms pertain to being free from undesirable non-human states; the next four are about being free from the four types of human existence that prevent us from developing our full potential.

The first of these is the freedom to practice Dharma through not having been born at a time when no buddha has descended. Even if we were born human but in a dark age where there was no buddha and therefore no Dharma—no teachings leading us from nonvirtue to virtue—what would be the point of our human existence?

Try to imagine such a place. There would be no teachings at all, so no opportunity to understand the route out of suffering. What could we do? It would be the same as being born as a dog. Think, "How fortunate I am to have the opportunity to practice Dharma through not having been born at a time when no buddha had descended."

## 6. THE FREEDOM OF NOT BEING BORN AS A BARBARIAN

The sixth freedom is not being born as a barbarian, the literal translation of the Tibetan term *la-lo*, which refers to somebody living in a border region or irreligious country and therefore has no chance to hear or practice Dharma. Another term for the country itself is "outlying" in the sense that a country that has Buddhadharma is central and those countries that are irreligious are outlying or on the edges, beyond civilization. They are completely dark, with no sense of morality.

The "barbarians," the people of that country, have no understanding of what is a positive action and what is a negative one, what is the cause of happiness and what is the cause of suffering. Like being shut in a dark room with no light, there is no chance to understand any of this. Like a dark night without moon or stars, completely foggy, there is no sun of Dharma and the beings stumble from one suffering to the next. Without any concept of karma, how can they know why they suffer or what to do about it? Therefore their whole lives are spent in chasing happiness in the wrong places, mistaking the cause of suffering for the cause of happiness.

Because there is no understanding of karma and also no faith in refuge, no thought to purify negative actions can possibly arise. Such people have no opportunity to become better people, to purify the obscurations and negative karma accumulated in the past, no opportunity to practice the holy Dharma. Even if you show worldly people teachings on karma and refuge or give them purification methods such as Vajrasattva, they cannot understand or accept them. With no understanding of karma they have no idea that nonvirtuous actions create suffering. Put yourself in their place. Imagine what it would be like with no opportunity at all to practice Dharma. Try to feel how awful it would be to stumble blindly though life with no sense of right and wrong. How unfortunate they are.

Being a barbarian is much worse than being blind, because even if we are blind we can still understand and have faith in karma and take refuge in Buddha, Dharma and Sangha. Of course, these days with many sophisticated tools, blind people have very little disadvantage, but even in India and Nepal before, when being blind meant having no education and being illiterate, blind Tibetan lay people still did many practices, such as reciting

OM MANI PADME HUM, the mantra of Chenrezig (Skt: *Avalokiteshvara*), the Compassion Buddha, and were able to accumulate a great deal of merit because they had faith in refuge and karma. Even without much understanding of the lam-rim, they could make their life meaningful. This makes a big difference. The physical eye cannot see things, but the mind is rich, not poor. On the other hand, even though they may have perfect senses, barbarians are actually poorer because they have no opportunity to practice Dharma.

The great pandit Chandragomin[28] uses a very effective example to explain the nature of such beings. A cow sees a small bunch of grass growing right on the edge of a precipice and runs toward it thinking that if she can eat it she will be happy. Out of attachment, she tries to reach the grass and falls over the precipice, killing herself. Her attachment brings her suffering instead of the happiness she sought. Chandragomin says that worldly beings seeking only the happiness of this life are just like the cow. They are so attached to pleasure that they run toward it without seeing the danger, fall down and die. Everything barbarians do to try to obtain happiness is wrong and only results in problems and suffering. Think of all those people in the West, the people busy in the cities trying to make a living, people who have no understanding of Dharma, no faith in refuge and karma, and so no opportunity to create merit or purify the obscurations that cloud their minds. Even though, like everybody else, they are only looking for happiness, the result of their actions is only rebirth in the lower realms.

The terrifying thing is that we can be a practicing Buddhist today and become a "barbarian" tomorrow. Unless our understanding and faith are strong, we can lose our belief in reincarnation and karma. Somehow, due to a lack of merit, we start thinking that what once seemed logical and true is now false and superstitious. We can wake up one morning and suddenly karma doesn't seem feasible any more. Then, even though we continue to call ourselves "Buddhist," somehow things slip away and we find ourselves further and further from where we want to be. We should never take our present great good fortune for granted.

When we consider the causes needed to have faith in Buddha, Dharma and Sangha, we will see that is takes a lot of merit and, if we don't con-

---

[28] A famous seventh-century Indian lay practitioner who challenged Chandrakirti to a debate that lasted many years. His writings include *Twenty Verses on the Bodhisattva Vows* and *Letter to a Disciple*.

stantly collect more by creating virtuous actions, the accumulation of merit we have could very well run out.

Without that firm basis, even if we study Buddhist philosophy for a long time and can meditate single-pointedly, something can happen and we can *totally* lose faith; we can become a barbarian. It is a question of both lack of merit and failing to purify past negative imprints of heresy, of believing things such as karma don't exist. One day we wake up as if from a pleasant dream. Our life as a Buddhist is there in the past, something remembered like a dream, which has no relevance to our life any more.

Therefore, in this life, we need to be very careful with our mind and take great care to create only positive actions and never leave negative imprints on our mindstream. Even small negativities can cloud our mind, making it easier for us to create heavy negative actions and much harder to gain realizations. We have the freedom to practice Dharma now but that freedom is very easy to lose.

How amazing and precious is this time when we do have faith in Buddha, Dharma and Sangha and the wish and opportunity to practice Dharma. Knowing this can change and that life is like a water bubble and can end any moment, we should determine strongly not just to practice Dharma but to practice Dharma *continuously*, from this moment on.

Think like this: "If I were a barbarian I would have neither the wish, the chance nor the freedom to practice Dharma. However, because I have found this perfect human rebirth and have the freedom to practice Dharma, how fortunate I am; I have the freedom to practice Dharma any time I want. I have access to the teachings of the Buddha, I have some wisdom and I can distinguish right from wrong. How incredible that is." Thinking like this, we should feel great joy in our heart that this is so.

## 7. THE FREEDOM OF NOT BEING BORN AS A FOOL

The next freedom is the freedom to practice Dharma through not having been born a fool. Although the Tibetan, 'on-pa, literally means "deaf," it has the connotation of somebody utterly unable to understand or communicate. Being deaf and mute in old Tibet meant having no education and no way of communicating, and so, of course, no way of hearing and understanding the Dharma. This is where the connotation comes from. Of course, just being deaf and mute is not nearly such a disadvantage now, although the deaf are unable to receive oral transmissions, which is definitely a significant shortcoming.

With this freedom, we are not just talking about people who have trouble understanding things; we are talking about people who have no way of taking in anything at all, people who have such extreme mental difficulty that their minds are incapable of functioning above a basic motor-function level. They are unable to be of any help to themselves and obviously can't help others. They must be tended constantly and fed and clothed. We can see this with severely mentally handicapped people. Perhaps we can think of severely autistic people in this category, people who even as adults are unable to communicate or understand basic things. There are many organizations that try to help them but, despite years and years of effort, these people make no progress.

This is not necessarily something we are born with. Karma can ripen at any time and we can lose the ability to understand or communicate. A car accident can leave us in a coma, a disease can turn us into a human vegetable, even age can rob us of our wits. These days, Alzheimer's and dementia are big problems for many old people. Think of how terrible it would be if you had started to study the Dharma and then, a few years later, were unable to remember even one syllable of a mantra because your memory had failed.

At the moment, we really are very fortunate. If we had such severe mental problems, life would have very little meaning. Even worldly pleasures like eating and drinking would have no meaning. Not only would we be of no benefit to others, we would also be a huge burden on our family and society. People would try to help but we would be unaware of their kindness.

We are not like that at all; we are free from that. We have a reasonably good body, a mind that is capable of understanding and there is no limit to our potential. Think, "How fortunate I am not to have been born as a severely disabled person unable to understand or communicate, unable to understand even one word of Dharma. I have found the perfect human rebirth and have the freedom to practice Dharma. This freedom can be lost at any time, so without wasting even an hour, even a minute, I must practice Dharma."

## 8. THE FREEDOM OF NOT BEING BORN AS A HERETIC

The last freedom is the freedom to practice Dharma through not having been born a heretic. If barbarians are people who live in an irreligious country, heretics are those who are irreligious no matter where they live. The Tibetan term is more precise than the English; the Tibetan is *log-ta-chän*, which means literally a person with wrong view. In Buddhism, heresy is the belief that something that exists does not exist. There is such a thing as karma but a heretic will deny that. Similarly, to a heretic, the Buddha, enlightenment and the other important topics within Buddhism are just lies or fantasies; the self is permanent and independent; impermanent phenomena are permanent. Heretics also deny that there is such a thing as reincarnation; they believe that the consciousness stops at death. With no karma and no life after death, there is no base upon which to develop morality. There is no cause and effect, therefore harming somebody will not bring future suffering and helping others will not bring future happiness.

Following such wrong doctrines, heretics not only create the cause for heavy suffering but such wrong views become deeply entrenched, blocking any acceptance of the Buddhist path, no matter how often it is heard. Accepting mistaken views creates the cause to hear them again, in this or a future life, and so the chances of understanding the Dharma become even more remote.

There are many people who, by the Buddhist definition, are heretics— all the people who have no belief in what Buddhism holds as key tenets, for example. It is not necessarily true that having no understanding of the four noble truths makes somebody a bad person, but it is very sad for people to live lives opposed to the causes of happiness in the deluded belief that they are making themselves happy.

There are people who call themselves religious, yet regularly kill in the belief that it will make them happy. Some think that animal sacrifice appeases the gods and brings them what they want; others believe that killing people who oppose their religion is the easiest way to get to their heaven. Certain ascetics deliberately mutilate themselves in order to attain liberation; other people reject all religion, seeing religion as superstition while believing that material possessions are the cause of happiness.

Heretics mistake poison for medicine and medicine for poison. They are completely hallucinated, as if they're tripping on drugs; the world appears as a fantastic place, which has no connection with reality. Where there is a precipice they see a beautiful garden; they run toward it as fast as they can, only to plunge headlong into the incredible suffering of the lower realms.

Heresy is one of the greatest hindrances to ultimate peace because it prevents the holder of wrong views from creating merit. Heretics cannot think beyond immediate pleasure because they believe that this life is the only one they'll have; there seems very little reason to practice virtue. Unable to distinguish between positive and negative actions, they create the cause of suffering thinking that it's the cause of happiness, harm themselves and others in the process, and ruin countless future lives. Even if heretics eventually manage to find another human body, because of their habituation to wrong views they will continue to hold wrong views in that life.

Heresy is a very ignorant mind. Imagine being a heretic. Imagine thinking that there is no such thing as cause and effect, that Buddha, Dharma and Sangha don't exist, that impermanent things are permanent and relying on them for happiness. Think how wonderful it is that you have met the Dharma and now have the opportunity to learn these profound subjects and turn your life around.

Think: "How fortunate I am that I am not a heretic, a person filled with wrong views with no chance to practice Dharma. Now, having received this perfect human rebirth, I must practice Dharma while I have this freedom."

# 3. The Richnesses

JUST AS THERE ARE the eight situations from which we are free that give this life great meaning, there are also ten things that we have received that enrich our life enormously. These are called the ten richnesses, or endowments. The first five are personal richnesses, things that we have within ourselves that make life so full. The second five are richnesses that relate to others, such as the support of a teacher.

## 1. BEING BORN AS A HUMAN BEING

The first of the ten richnesses is birth as a human being. A human being is generally defined as a being who is able to speak and understand. But, from the Dharma point of view, the *real* human being is the person who prepares for the happiness beyond this life, up to enlightenment. This entails much more than just being able to speak and understand.

Without this richness, there would be no opportunity to practice the holy Dharma, therefore think, "How fortunate I am that at this time I have been born as a human being. Furthermore, I have received the freedom to practice Dharma. With this richness I can create the cause of any of the three great purposes I wish, at any time—within these twenty-four hours, within this hour, within this minute. This richness is much more precious than diamonds equaling the number of atoms of this earth. Wasting this opportunity by not practicing the holy Dharma for even a minute is a greater loss than losing that many precious diamonds."

## 2. BEING BORN IN A RELIGIOUS COUNTRY

The second richness is being born in a central, or religious, country.[29] Think like this: "Even though many times I was born as a human being, I was not fortunate enough to be born in a religious country. But now I have that great good fortune." Rejoice.

If we had not received this richness, if we had not been born in a place where Buddhism exists, there would be no opportunity at all to receive teachings or to practice Dharma. There are two ways to think of this: in terms of the place and of the existence of the teachings.

The first way a place is considered religious is because it is where the thousand buddhas of this fortunate eon have descended. That is why places like Bodhgaya are so incredibly holy.

A country is also considered religious if there is an established Sangha there, which means both novice and fully-ordained monks and nuns purely observing the thirty-six vows for novices or the 253 vows for fully-ordained monks or the 364 vows for fully-ordained nuns; a place where the lineage of the ordinations is still alive, where it's still possible for those who want to get ordained to do so. Ordination is an important means of protecting the mind from committing nonvirtuous actions. Without this intact transmission going back to the Buddha himself, even if somebody knew the teachings of the lineage he or she would be unable to give the vows to others, so we are incredibly fortunate that this precious lineage has not been broken and still exists.

Some people may think that this has nothing to do with them, that it is only a custom, but people who receive ordination are very fortunate, because keeping the different levels of ordination is a quick way that leads to enlightenment. They are in the safest place; it protects them against both outside enemies and their own harmful actions, like a protective fence surrounding them.

Having Sangha in a country is extremely precious. Not only does it give the members of the Sangha the opportunity of giving vows to others, but the mere presence of a spiritual community such as a monastery or nunnery is important for the welfare of the whole country. The positive effects of the energy generated by pure Dharma practitioners cannot be exaggerated.

---

[29] This may not mean a country in the current geographical sense. Often translated as "land" or "place."

Happiness arises from observing karma, from avoiding harmful actions and doing positive ones. Of course, people who keep their vows purely benefit themselves greatly, but they also benefit the beings around them as well. There is a big difference between a country that has a monastery and one that doesn't. If we are a monk or nun living in a monastic environment, we ourselves are nurtured and inspired by others working for the same goal, but we also nurture the surrounding lay community and inspire them to always keep pure morality.

In a religious county, the weather, the economy, the degree of happiness of the people and many other things are indirectly affected by the practice of the Sangha. This is illustrated by the story of the four harmonious brothers, the four animals who helped each other and helped the kingdom in which they lived.

There once was a kingdom in ancient India that had terrible droughts and famines and much fighting and disharmony among its people, but then, strangely, things changed. Rains came at the right time, the crops grew well and peace and happiness were restored. The king was very pleased and thought that it was his leadership that had caused this, but many of the ministers also thought that they were responsible. Nobody could agree who caused this newfound prosperity and everybody wanted to claim responsibility, so the king called in a famous clairvoyant to settle the argument.

After checking, the sage told the king and his ministers that in fact it was none of them but four brother animals who lived in harmony in the forest, keeping the five precepts and spreading the precepts to other animals—an elephant, a monkey, a rabbit and a bird who were actually embodiments of Shakyamuni Buddha and three of his disciples. The elephant took the responsibility of spreading the five vows to the other elephants, the monkey led other monkeys to live in five precepts and so forth, and in this way the whole forest became a place of great harmony. This harmony spread to the entire country and created the good weather, the wealth and the peace and happiness that the people were enjoying.

In the same way, a monastery or nunnery might not be actively trying to change laws or improve the climate, but the atmosphere of harmony created by monks and nuns living in the vows purely brings peace and harmony to all around.

Besides a country being considered religious because of the existence of the Sangha, it is also considered religious because of the existence of the teachings in that country. Actually, the two are closely related because one definition of the existence of the teachings in a place is if the lineage of the ordinations still exists there. Here we are mainly talking about the Sutra and Vinaya teachings. The Buddha's 84,000 teachings are divided into Three Baskets (Skt: *Tripitaka*): the Vinaya, the Buddha's teachings on moral discipline; the Abhidharma, his teachings on psychology and the mind; and the Sutra, all the other discourses he gave. Although there is also the Vajrayana, the Buddha's teachings on tantra, this is not considered essential for a country to be called religious.

Because of the existence of both the spiritual community and the teachings, those who can explain the teachings exist and as a result we are able to actualize the Dharma. Happiness arises by observing karma, by avoiding harming ourselves and others; but to observe karma we must understand it. To understand karma we need to study the teachings on it and have them explained to us. This is only possible because of the existence of the great masters and those who live in pure vows. Also, seeing such pure practitioners inspires us to follow their direction. Without such role models it would be very difficult to have the determination to follow the path. So there is a big difference between a country that has Sangha and one that does not.

Therefore think, "If I were not in a religious country, where all the teachings exist and where ordination is still held purely, without the slightest degeneration, there would be no opportunity to practice the holy Dharma. Even if I wished to keep moral conduct by taking ordination, if its lineage did not still exist I would have no chance to do so. How fortunate I am having received the richness of being in a religious country. With such a richness I can achieve the three great purposes and in particular I can practice bodhicitta."

## 3. BEING BORN WITH PERFECT ORGANS

The third richness is being born with perfect organs. Think like this: "Even though many times I was born as a human being in a religious country, I was not fortunate enough to be born with perfect organs. But now I have that great good fortune." Rejoice.

As we have seen with the seventh freedom, if we are incapable of understanding or communicating, we are unable to practice Dharma, so this richness traditionally includes not being a deaf mute. Again, it is the inability to understand that is the problem. In the West there are many deaf mute people who communicate perfectly well and can have as rich a life as some-body who has perfect hearing and vocal powers. I have even seen groups of deaf people at His Holiness the Dalai Lama's teachings receiving the teachings through a signer. This is wonderful. Such amazing mudras! And there is also Braille and audio for the blind.

Imperfect organs also include missing limbs. This may be because this is one of the reasons a person may be refused ordination. A person who is deaf, missing a limb and so forth cannot be granted the thirty-six vows or higher ordinations. According to the Hinayana, such a person does not have the requisite body for the *pratimoksha* (individual liberation) vows. This is also true of hermaphrodites.

This is part of the monastic code established by the Buddha, who could see that there must be certain restrictions on who is eligible for ordination. He saw that imperfect organs would be a hindrance for both the individual and the community. An abbot cannot grant ordination to somebody with imperfect organs.

Of course, it is possible to attain enlightenment without becoming a monk or a nun, but that is exceptional. In general, to make good progress down the Dharma path, we need to follow the clear guidelines laid down by the various levels of vow, and taking robes is a vital aspect of that. It is so much easier to practice virtue purely within the framework of ordination. There are far fewer distractions and it is much easier to discipline the mind.

We should explore this to see how having perfect organs gives us many opportunities and think how fortunate we are to have this richness.

## 4. BEING FREE OF THE FIVE IMMEDIATE NEGATIVITIES

The fourth richness is not having committed any of the five immediate negativities (also called the five uninterrupted negative karmas). Think like this: "Even though many times I was born as a human being with perfect organs in a religious country, I was not fortunate enough to be free from having committed any of the five immediate negativities. But now I have that great good fortune." Rejoice.

The five immediate negativities are:

- ▸ killing your mother
- ▸ killing your father
- ▸ killing an arhat

- maliciously drawing blood from a buddha
- causing disunity in the Sangha

They are called "immediate" because, unlike the results of other nonvirtues that can be interrupted, postponed or purified, these nonvirtues are so heinous that when we die we immediately get reborn in the lower realms, specifically in the lowest hells. Our state of mind is paramount at the time of death, and dying with a positive mind can influence a generally negative mindset and allow us an upper rebirth, but with these five actions this can almost never happen. Only if we are able to do intensive purification can we escape their results.

Furthermore, a person who has committed any of these extreme actions cannot receive monastic ordination. At the beginning of the ordination ceremony, one of the questions candidates are asked is whether or not they have committed one of these actions. If they have, the abbot cannot grant ordination. Refusing ordination in such cases is not without purpose. An ordained person must benefit the teachings in some way and that is impossible if there is such a heavy imprint on his or her mental continuum. It creates serious obscurations and becomes a great hindrance to generating realizations.

That is the general definition of the fourth richness. There is also a stricter one, which is often found in the Nyingma tradition and says that this richness is not having committed any of the ten nonvirtues.[30] This is very strict; it means we would have to be creating virtue every moment—while eating, sitting, sleeping and so forth.

I first heard this interpretation of the fourth richness from His Holiness Trijang Rinpoche. It was the very first lam-rim teaching I heard, in Sarnath, where Buddha turned the first wheel of Dharma. I don't remember much of the teaching, but this point really stood out. It is similar to the interpretation given by Rongphuk Sangye, Trulshik Rinpoche's root guru, in his commentary on Thogme Zangpo's *Thirty-seven Practices of the Bodhisattva*.[31]

---

[30] The ten nonvirtues are: killing, stealing, sexual misconduct, lying, slandering, speaking harsh words, idle gossip, covetousness, ill will and heresy. See Rinpoche's forthcoming book on karma for a full explanation.

[31] Trulshik Rinpoche (1923–2011) was one of Lama Zopa Rinpoche's gurus and briefly head of the Nyingma tradition. He founded Thubten Chöling Monastery in Nepal, where Zina Rachevsky passed away in 1973. His root guru was Ngawang Tenzing Norbu (1867–1942), who also known as the Buddha of Dza Rongphuk, after the monastery he established on the

We should therefore rejoice that we have this richness of being free from having created any of these five immediate negativities.

## 5. HAVING DEVOTION TO THE TEACHINGS

The next richness is having devotion to the teachings. Think like this: "Even though many times I was born as a human being with perfect organs in a religious country and had not committed any of the five immediate negativities, I was not fortunate enough to have devotion to the teachings. But now I have that great good fortune." Rejoice.

Simply knowing about the different subjects within Buddhism is not enough. We need to fully trust that they are our way out of suffering and we must have devotion to them. The Three Baskets of the Vinaya, Sutra and Abhidharma relate to the trainings of morality, concentration and wisdom and having devotion to the teachings means following each of these three practices.

Essentially, however, devotion means having refuge in the Three Jewels in our heart. With that, even if we hear advanced teachings, such as those on the Vajrayana, and don't understand them, we have complete faith in the Buddha and know that our lack of comprehension comes from our obscurations rather than any failings in what the Buddha taught.

We need faith and devotion not just in the Buddha but in the Dharma and Sangha as well. There are many people who have great faith in the Buddha but dismiss aspects of his teachings, such as the Vajrayana teachings or even the entire Mahayana canon. It is not a matter of not practicing them because it does not suit them; they actually feel that these teachings are wrong in some way. To have complete devotion we need to examine all the teachings and have a sense of their infallibility; that requires a strong relationship with a spiritual teacher, otherwise we will never be able to overcome the obstacles to understanding the more esoteric subjects. This is why there are so few of us who can honestly say that we have devotion to the teachings in their entirety.

With much devotion to the lam-rim and the inspiration to practice it, our mind changes. If we don't have this devotion and inspiration, we become thick-skulled and careless. When we hear different lam-rim sub-

---

northern slopes of Mt. Everest at the foot of the Rongphuk Glacier. Thogme Zangpo's text is found in Geshe Sonam Rinchen's commentary (see the bibliography).

jects, we think: "Oh, yes, yes, I know that! I've heard that a hundred times!" No matter how much we listen, the teachings don't move our mind; our mind is like a rock in the ocean, which can stay there for a billion years without changing. The outside gets wet but not much else happens.

Another analogy is the leather bag that Tibetans use to store butter. Normally butter is used to soften leather, but this leather gets so permeated by butter that it gets rock-hard. We should not get so casual about the Dharma that it no longer affects our mind. There's a saying, "The evil one can be subdued by the holy Dharma but the thick-skulled one cannot." If we dismiss any Dharma teaching because we've heard it so often, we can lose our devotion for the Dharma in general. That is being thick-skulled; it's very dangerous.

Just being in a place where the teachings are widespread does not mean we will naturally have devotion to them. In Tibet and Nepal there are numberless holy beings with realizations on the path, like stars on a clear, moonless night, and the teachings have spread across the entire country, but there are still many people who act like Buddhists, who say they are Buddhists, but who have no devotion in their heart and beneath their "Buddhist" activities there is self-interest and worldly concern.

Think how fortunate we are to have devotion to the teachings, especially the lam-rim, which gives us much energy and determination to practice the Dharma.

## 6. BEING BORN WHEN A BUDDHA HAS DESCENDED

The first five richnesses are qualities that we possess; the next five are richnesses that we have in relation with others.

The sixth richness is being born at a time when a buddha has descended. Think like this: "Even though many times I was born as a human being with perfect organs in a religious country, had not committed the five immediate negativities and had devotion to the teachings, I was not fortunate enough to be born when a buddha had descended. But now I have that great good fortune." Rejoice.

Of course Shakyamuni Buddha is no longer alive, but to say that therefore no buddha has descended is too narrow a definition of this richness. During the Buddha's time his disciples could receive teachings directly from him, but ever since then there has been an unbroken lineage, which means that the teachings have remained pure. The Buddha is still here in the aspect of our spiritual teacher. The guru is the pure representative of the Buddha and to receive teachings from him or her is to receive teachings from the Buddha.

To realize how rare it is to live at a time when there is a buddha, we need to have an overview of the four great eons of the evolution of the universe. Although I will talk about this in more detail later, I will give a brief explanation here.

There are said to be four great eons in one cycle of a world system's existence: the great eons of evolution, when the world system comes into being, existence, decay and emptiness. Buddhas appear only during the eon of existence, when there are beings who have the karma to benefit from them.

Furthermore, during each of the twenty lesser eons that comprise the great eon of existence, the human lifespan fluctuates from 80,000 years down to ten and then back up again, and it is only when the lifespan is decreasing that the buddhas appear, and then only at certain times. It is said that there will be a thousand buddhas in this eon. Guru Shakyamuni Buddha was the fourth, and one of only three who will reveal the Vajrayana, which means that it is incredibly rare that the entire Buddhadharma exists in this world system.

But the time of Shakyamuni Buddha's teachings existing and, therefore, his influence is almost over. It is like the very last flickering of a candle flame, just before it goes out, or like the last rays of the sun once it has set over a mountain range. We have the great fortune to have been born as a human during this extremely rare time and to have met a guru who can transmit and explain the complete Dharma. How lucky we are to have received this most precious gift before it is too late.

How fortunate we are to be alive in a time and a place where the rich treasure of the Dharma is still alive and being taught as it was in the Buddha's time, without fault or distortion. If the Dharma were no longer alive or if it had been corrupted, what could we do? That will happen, and soon, so we need to do everything possible to develop ourselves fully while we still have this precious opportunity.

## 7. BEING BORN WHEN THE TEACHINGS HAVE BEEN REVEALED

The seventh richness is being born when the teachings have been revealed. Think like this: "Even though many times I was born as a human being with perfect organs in a religious country, had not committed the five immediate negativities, had devotion to the teachings and was born when a buddha has descended, I was not fortunate enough to be born when the teachings had been revealed. But now I have that great good fortune." Rejoice.

For a buddha to descend in this universe is rare, but for a buddha to reveal the teachings is much rarer. Of course, buddhas work only for the benefit of sentient beings and the best way of doing that is revealing the Dharma, but most of the time people don't have the capacity to understand the teachings, so the buddha has to benefit them in other ways.

It is said that when human life expectancy is a mere ten years, the next buddha, Maitreya, will appear. At that time people will be very small, like children in size, and Maitreya will appear huge to them, with a glowing, golden body. Although they will not have the ability to understand the Dharma, by his appearance and by showing the twelve deeds,[32] he will inspire them to collect merit by having loving kindness to each other and this will trigger the new cycle of increasing lifespan, where their bodies will gradually become bigger again.

Sometimes, due to the obscurations of the beings around him, all a buddha can do is send light rays from his holy body to bless them. He does not give verbal teachings and there is no chance to practice Dharma in the way that we can now. Sometimes, immediately after enlightenment, a buddha may show the aspect of passing away into the sorrowless state, so no teachings are given. If Shakyamuni Buddha had passed into the sorrowless state immediately after he became enlightened under the bodhi tree at Bodhgaya rather than stay to bring the teachings to all sentient beings, Buddhism wouldn't exist for us and there would be no way we could create virtue or benefit ourselves and others.

At the time the Buddha was born, four other Indian kings also had baby sons and the whole earth was filled with brilliant white light. Each king thought that this incredibly auspicious sign was because of his own son, but a very wise old Brahmin who could foretell the future saw that it was the son of the king of the Shakyas who had caused the light. Not only that; when he checked further he saw that Prince Siddhartha would become a buddha,

---

[32] Each buddha of this eon is said to manifest on this world system and do twelve deeds, which are: 1) descent from Tushita heaven; 2) conception in the womb; 3) birth; 4) training in the arts and sciences; 5) enjoying palace life; 6) renouncing the life of leisure; 7) practicing austerities; 8) sitting under the bodhi tree at Bodhgaya; 9) victory over the maras; 10) the attainment of enlightenment; 11) teaching the Dharma; 12) passing into *parinirvana*.

with the thirty-two major marks and eighty minor signs[33] of an enlightened being, and be a great spiritual leader. When he told the prince's parents this, however, he was crying, which caused them great concern. They asked him why such good news would upset him and he explained that by the time the prince became enlightened and started teaching he himself would be dead and therefore unable to see this future buddha. In other words, the sage was alive when a buddha had descended but would not live to see the teachings revealed. He did not have this richness.

The sun has almost set and it is becoming darker and darker. But for the moment we have the opportunity to study the holy Dharma because the teachings exist and, because fully qualified teachers are still alive, we have the opportunity to realize the teachings. At this time, not only has Buddha descended but he has also revealed the teachings, so we have this wonderful richness. How fortunate we are.

## 8. BEING BORN WHEN THE COMPLETE TEACHINGS EXIST

The eighth richness is being born not just when there are teachings but when the complete teachings of the Buddha still exist. Think like this: "Even though many times I was born as a human being with perfect organs in a religious country, had not committed the five immediate negativities, had devotion to the teachings and was born when a buddha had descended and revealed the teachings, I was not fortunate enough to be born when the complete teachings existed. But now I have that great good fortune." Rejoice.

If it is rare that people have access to the Buddhadharma, it is much rarer still that all the various vehicles of the Buddhadharma exist: Hinayana and Mahayana, and the two Mahayana vehicles, Paramitayana (Sutra) and Vajrayana (Tantra).

We have just made it. Like arriving at the airport moments before they close the gate and the plane takes off. We haven't arrived too late and missed it completely. If we had been born too late to receive the teachings—when all the Tibetan lamas had passed away and no one could reveal the complete path to enlightenment—it would be extremely difficult to even plant the seed of the entire path to enlightenment in our mind let alone hear the complete teachings. We have *just, just* made it. If we had born into this world

[33] See the online glossary at LamaYeshe.com for more on these.

later, then taking a human body wouldn't have had any special purpose. Our existence would have been no higher than an animal's.

However, the existence of the complete sutra and tantra teachings means more than just the existence of Dharma books explaining these teachings. If we go to the big university or public libraries in the world we will see rooms filled with teachings of the Buddha, commentaries by the great pandits and famous scholars' theses on those commentaries. That does not mean that the teachings exist. For the teachings to actually exist, they have to exist as realizations in the minds of accomplished practitioners.

There are two levels of the teachings, the external Dharma and the internal Dharma, the words and the actualization of the meaning of the words. The Dharma we study is the external level; the realizations are the internal level, the Dharma that lives inside the mind. That is the actual definition of the existence of the teachings. Intellectual understanding alone is worthless. The real understanding is the heart understanding we get when we successfully put the teachings into practice. It is pointless to know everything that has ever been taught on bodhicitta but to have no love or compassion for anybody.

At Guru Shakyamuni Buddha's time, realization meant having achieved the *arya* path, having a direct understanding of emptiness and a profound experience of bodhicitta, but perhaps in these degenerate times we should modify that a bit to say that the teachings exist when genuine, sincere practitioners with a profound understanding of the Dharma work diligently to put that understanding into their lives.

In *Liberation in the Palm of Your Hand*, Pabongka Dechen Nyingpo explains just how rare this richness is and how many unique factors need to come together for it to happen.[34] Not only does a buddha have to descend, which is very rare, but he has to reveal the teachings, which is rarer, and not just that but the complete teachings—much rarer—and there need to be highly qualified teachers to reveal the essence of those teachings, which is rarer still. And rarest of all is that we must have the karma to meet those highly qualified teachers and have devotion to them so that we can receive the essence of the great truths they teach. We have actually met His Holiness the Dalai Lama, the embodiment of Chenrezig, the Compassion Buddha. How many people can say that? And how amazing it is that we

---

[34] See *Liberation*, p. 274–275.

have had the karma for this to happen. This is extremely rare in this world system.

From my side, I have very little of benefit to say. However, one thing that makes me very happy is that somehow I have been able to introduce many students to many great masters. Although I have no qualities myself, I have been able to send students to receive teachings from gurus such as His Holiness the Dalai Lama, Kirti Tsenshab Rinpoche, His Holiness Tsenshab Serkong Rinpoche, His Holiness Song Rinpoche, Denma Lochö Rinpoche and many others. This, of course, is all due to the unbelievable kindness and love of Lama Yeshe. For that, I am very happy.

This richness involves being in a country where there are not only teachings that will lead to nirvana, such as those in the Pali canon, but where there are also the two Mahayana paths, the Paramitayana teachings and the quick path of Vajrayana, where we can achieve enlightenment for the sake of all sentient beings. If seeing how rare it is to have any exposure to the Buddhadharma makes us appreciate this precious gift, then seeing how much rarer it is to have access to the entire teachings of the Buddha, especially the very esoteric tantric ones, is like discovering a mountain of diamonds in our own back yard.

Just as the very basic teachings of Buddhadharma do not fit everybody's interest or propensity, so those who can benefit from the Mahayana are much fewer than those who can benefit from the Hinayana. This is logical. The path of the individual liberation practitioner is a simpler path that does not require such a sharp analysis of the nature of reality and a commitment to helping not just many but *all* sentient beings. And of the two main aspects of the Mahayana, the Paramitayana and the Vajrayana, the gradual path of the Paramitayana suits many more people than the esoteric, quick path of Vajrayana.

Even though this is the quick way to enlightenment—allowing us to attain it in one lifetime rather than the three countless great eons it takes through the Paramitayana—very few people have the capacity to benefit from Vajrayana practice. It is also called "secret mantra" because initiates are not allowed to reveal details of the practice. This is not because there are any cult practices but because the understanding needed to undertake Vajrayana practice is so subtle that unless the person is completely ready, terrible misunderstandings can arise. Therefore Vajrayana practices are revealed only to the highly intelligent and fortunate few whose minds suit such practices.

Even today we hear people criticizing the Vajrayana, saying that these are not the teachings of the Buddha but a later invention by teachers like Nagarjuna. This is completely wrong and shows how through misunderstanding they have come to reject a crucial side of Buddhism. Moreover, such criticism creates a huge amount of negative karma.

We are just too clouded with obscurations to see. In the *Heart Sutra*[35] we read that the Buddha gave this precious teaching to hosts of buddhas and bodhisattvas on Vulture's Peak at Rajgir, but if we go there today all we will see is a barren rock. We might even think that the *Heart Sutra* is a myth and all those bodhisattvas couldn't have fit onto that rock. We are simply too deluded. Actually, if we had the eyes to see, we'd see that there's still a lot of activity on Vulture's Peak.

When Shakyamuni Buddha revealed the secret mantra teachings, he manifested as the deity, transformed the place into that deity's mandala and then revealed the teachings to those highly fortunate beings. To deny the Vajrayana and even the Mahayana, as some people do, is to suggest that there is only one level of sentient being, one level of mind. As the Buddha taught for different levels of understanding, that is to suggest that the Buddha was unskillful in his approach. There are many levels of mind and many different propensities; the various levels of the Buddha's teachings were given to benefit beings at every level.

Shakyamuni Buddha is the first buddha of this eon to reveal the Vajrayana, and of all the thousand buddhas who will descend in this fortunate eon, only two more will teach it. It is said that in a much later time the seventh buddha, an embodiment of Lama Tsongkhapa called "The Sound of a Roaring Lion," will descend and give some tantra teachings. Then the very last of the thousand buddhas will also teach tantra because he prayed, "Whatever the previous buddhas did for sentient beings, I will do the same."

Not only are there very few human beings of this world system with the karma to practice Vajrayana but of the countless other sentient beings in the countless other world systems, none have the karma to practice it. Other than in this world system at this point in time, Vajrayana just does not exist.

---

[35] The *Heart of Wisdom Sutra* (Skt: *Prajnaparamita-hrdaya*) is the best known of a series of sutras classified as *Prajnaparamita (Perfection of Wisdom) Sutras*, wherein the Buddha explains emptiness.

## 9. BEING BORN WHEN THE TEACHINGS ARE BEING FOLLOWED

The ninth richness is being born when the teachings are being followed. Think like this: "Even though many times I was born as a human being with perfect organs in a religious country, had not committed the five immediate negativities, had devotion to the teachings, was born when a buddha had descended and revealed the teachings and the complete teachings still existed, I was not fortunate enough to be born when the teachings were being followed. But now I have that great good fortune." Rejoice.

The teachings being followed can be defined as people taking refuge in the Three Jewels. There are two causes of refuge, the door to the teachings of the Buddha. The first is a healthy fear of the sufferings of samsara, which naturally leads us to look for a way to escape that suffering. The second is faith in Buddha, Dharma and Sangha, which arises through understanding that they have the true method for putting an end to suffering forever. To say that people are following the teachings because they have read and understood Dharma books is not at all what this richness means.

In fact there are two Buddha refuges. One is the historical Buddha, Shakyamuni, the external refuge, the external Buddha, the external guide—the causal refuge that leads us to the path. The other is the inner refuge, the internal Buddha, our own buddha nature—the resultant refuge, or the buddha we will eventually become.

The ninth richness shows us that not only are the entire teachings available, but that people are following them, are practicing them. Because of that, we also have the possibility of following them. It is like before we were standing at the gate to a beautiful park looking in but now we have entered the park and can fully enjoy it. We have been born in countries where Buddhadharma existed before and we might have even been aware of it, but we never really entered into the practice and that is why we have not yet been able to gain realizations or control our delusions.

There are many places on earth where people want to practice Buddhadharma, but even though they might have found some Dharma books in a bookshop, there are no other people around them following the teachings, so they have no way of getting the guidance they need. No matter how inspired that person might be to study and practice, without an infallible guide and fellow practitioners it is very difficult to make much progress toward goals such as bodhicitta and emptiness.

In Tibet before the Chinese invasion there were many great lamas and most of the people were very devoted to the Dharma, but there were still many people who didn't live within the teachings or who weren't even Buddhist—for example, there was quite a big Muslim community—and of the vast majority who did have devotion, very few had more than a superficial understanding. Therefore this richness shows us that we need more than the existence of the teachings. We can have the best, most expensive medicine in the world for our illness but if we don't take it we will never be cured. If we have not created the karma to hear and integrate the teachings it will not happen. Even if there is a buddha teaching in the room next to us we will not bother to go and see him. These days His Holiness the Dalai Lama teaches in many countries but that does not mean that everybody in the world attends his teachings.

We can see this clearly in India, the birthplace of Buddhism. This is where the Buddha lived and taught, and for over fifteen hundred years after he passed away the great universities flourished with highly realized beings meditating and expounding the Dharma, setting out the whole path with great clarity. Even when it declined in India, the Buddhadharma spread to other countries and places like Tibet were able to preserve the whole of the Buddha's teachings.

Now, thanks to the Chinese who took over Tibet, great teachers are back in India and the teachings are freely available again to the people of India. At the Library of Tibetan Works and Archives in Dharamsala there are ongoing classes by some of the greatest Dharma teachers in the world. Perhaps a few Indians attend the teachings there but the vast majority are Westerners. We can see the different karmas involved here. Getting Tibetan teachers to the West is extremely complicated and costly—it sometimes takes years of work to negotiate passports, visas and so forth—and there are many hardships for the Western students coming to India. On the other hand, the Buddhadharma and great Buddhist teachers are everywhere in places like Dharamsala yet few Indians are interested. How many Indians study Buddhism? How many get ordained? Even though the teachings exist in their country, very few follow them. Because of that they do not develop their understanding and their minds do not progress from stage to stage along the path.

My first impression of Westerners was completely wrong. When Lama Yeshe and I began teaching in Nepal the students were mostly hippies, with long hair and beards and dirty bodies and clothes. At that time they were everywhere in Kathmandu, with their pale skins and lost looks. Sometimes there seemed to be more hippies than Nepalese. They were strange and simple, but the ones that got to Kopan had enquiring minds and Lama and I enjoyed being with them. After some time, however, I think some of the Western countries told the Nepalese Government not to allow the hippies to stay and when the visa laws changed they became fewer and fewer.

Before going to other countries I did have some idea of the West from talking to students and reading *Time* magazine. Our first Western student, Zina Rachevsky, had lots of friends and they talked about life in the West. Some lived like peasants with their animals; some lived like worldly gods. Their lives seemed to me to be extremes, incredibly poor or incredibly rich.

Somehow it seems natural that the hippies came to Kopan to hear the teachings. But when people invited Lama and me to go to the West to teach, I got a huge surprise. The West wasn't full of ragged hippies living in broken down hovels like in Nepal. Looking at the richness of the West and the material possessions that everybody seemed to have, at the pace of life and at what people considered important, I was even more amazed by the hippies of Nepal. The West was like another planet. It seemed impossible that anybody born in such an environment could ever consider the Dharma. For these young people to reject that materialism and comfort and live as they did in Nepal for the sake of finding the truth impressed me very much after seeing the West. It was like a dream of the gods turning their backs on the god realms, but it was actually happening.

After Geshe Rabten[36] returned to Dharamsala from his first trip to the West he jokingly told his students that he always thought of Tibetans as worldly and complacent, idly saying mantras as they made business or drank *chang*, but after seeing Westerners in their own countries he realized that Tibetans weren't as empty as he had thought. At least the Tibetans were doing something constructive. They had devotion and some belief, and even though their understanding of karma was slight they did have some understanding of it. We just have to look around to know that even though he was joking there is a good deal of truth in what he said.

We have the potential to differentiate virtue from nonvirtue, and we have the potential to purify our minds, all the way to enlightenment. The

[36] Geshe Rabten was an eminent scholar who was very influential in teaching Westerners.

complete Mahayana teachings, including the entire Vajrayana, the lightning quick route to enlightenment, are still available. And only humans of the southern continent[37] can benefit from the Vajrayana because the Vajrayana practices involve moving the psychic winds into the central channel of the body, which is impossible for a nonhuman.[38] It requires a body that has the three elements from the mother and the three from the father that only a human birth in our continent provides.[39]

We should feel great joy that we have this richness. We have not only found the Dharma, which so few people have, but we also have a degree of devotion and are able to follow the entire teachings. As we continue to study the Dharma we will come to see more and more how this richness is precious, and how fragile it is. We have only a short time so we must put all our energy into developing this precious gift.

## 10. HAVING THE NECESSARY CONDITIONS TO PRACTICE DHARMA

The final richness is having the necessary conditions to practice Dharma. Think like this: "Even though many times I was born as a human being with perfect organs in a religious country, had not committed the five immediate negativities, had devotion to the teachings, was born when a buddha had descended and revealed the teachings, the complete teachings still existed and the teachings were being followed, I was not fortunate enough to have the necessary conditions to practice the Dharma. But now I have that great good fortune." Rejoice.

The focus here is on the help we need to receive in order to succeed in our spiritual quest. In some ways, this is the rarest of all the richnesses.

There are so many factors that must come together before we can encounter and follow the Buddhist teachings that it sometimes seems a miracle that anybody is able to do it all. Not only do all the external conditions need to be in place, such as having support from our family or kind benefactors,

---

[37] See p. 111.
[38] The winds (Skt: *prana*; Tib: *lung*) are psychic energies upon which the consciousness rides. They travel along defined channels (Skt: *nadi*) paralleling the physical nervous system, the three most important being the central channel and its two side channels that run in front of the spine. There are concentrations of channels, called channel wheels (Skt: *chakra*), at various points in the body, notably the heart, throat and crown.
[39] Skin, flesh and blood from the mother and sperm, bone and marrow from the father.

but most importantly of all, we need the compassion and concern of a spiritual friend, a guide who can show us the infallible path.

Traditionally the lay community in Buddhist countries supports the Sangha and so monks and nuns rarely have to think about food or shelter, giving them great freedom to practice Dharma. In Tibet the great monasteries relied on the generosity of the people, and even today in places like Thailand and Laos, monks walk through villages as they did in the Buddha's time, collecting alms.

In the West it is not that easy. If we live in our own country that usually means we have to work full time and stay involved with society. If we go to Asia to study and meditate we have to save beforehand or rely on the generosity of family and friends. It can be quite hard. Many students who go to India or Nepal with the sincere wish to study Dharma are unable to stay long because they don't have the necessary support. And it's not only a question of money—visas can also be difficult to get and are often of much shorter duration than desired.

Basically, we need a huge amount of merit to receive all the conducive conditions that we need to practice Dharma. It also requires, for many of us, a change of attitude. We need to prioritize and understand what is important and what is not. If we need to find sponsorship to help us stay in a long retreat or go on a long course, it is not shameful or foolish to ask others to help; it is only the Western preconception that makes it seem so. Begging in such a way, with a pure mind free from attachment to temporal things and free from laziness, can bring great advantages. It can enable us to practice Dharma, which certainly enriches us, but is also enriches our benefactors.

The other and most important aspect of this last richness is receiving the kindness and compassion of a spiritual friend willing to guide us. Not just a teacher to show us how to achieve worldly success, not just somebody to help us find the happiness of future lives or even individual liberation, but a guru who can reveal the whole path from where we are now all the way to enlightenment.

This is extremely rare and extremely precious. I have heard many stories of Western students who have searched for a guru and found it extremely difficult to find one. There are so many "gurus" out there, but who has the infallible method to lead us out of suffering? People rely on self-help books and experts in worldly happiness and it doesn't help; people try exotic Eastern trips and it doesn't help. Even if somebody introduces them to Buddhism and takes them to see a great master, they find fault with him or her. They simply do not have the karma to meet the right teacher at that time.

There are many people who want happiness now and in the future, who want to follow a spiritual path. They see a charismatic teacher and are drawn to him, but has that teacher transcended his ego? Has he developed his compassion enough to give himself totally to his students? Does he have enough wisdom to skillfully guide them? Looking for a virtuous friend, many people find a nonvirtuous one. Even to attain a human body in our next life we need near-perfect morality, but there are teachers who neither practice it themselves nor inspire their students to practice it. Such teachers cannot save us from the lower realms let alone lead us on the infallible path to enlightenment.

However, this time we *have* met a virtuous friend who can show us the infallible path to achieve the body of a happy transmigratory being and develop all the way to enlightenment, a teacher who has great compassion and great understanding and the skill to lead us according to our level of mind. How incredibly fortunate we are to have met a such a virtuous friend.

## THE PURPOSE OF MEDITATING ON THE EIGHT FREEDOMS AND TEN RICHNESSES

The eight freedoms and the ten richnesses are not just a list of ideals that cannot be matched. We already have most if not all of them. We have already come a long way on our journey to enlightenment. We should rejoice that this is so but must never be complacent. We have created the causes to get this far, to have this degree of freedom and these qualities, but we must continuously keep on creating such causes, otherwise we could easily lose our hard-won freedoms and richnesses. The final goal of enlightenment is a long, hard journey away from where we are now. We need to understand that and prepare for it properly.

Lama Tsongkhapa emphasizes that we must take the best care by being aware of everything we do at all times, creating only positive actions and never negative ones. Not only that, we also need to diligently purify our mental continuum of negative imprints by using the four opponent powers and other methods of purification.[40]

---

[40] The four opponent powers refers to a four-part practice that counteracts and thereby purifies negative karma. The four powers are: the power of the object (taking refuge in the Triple

It is extremely worthwhile to constantly remind ourselves of how precious this life of freedom and richnesses is. When we're feeling down and depressed we should think of the suffering of the hells and realize that although we are not in those realms at the moment, the delusions that are currently troubling our mind can lead us there. When we are overwhelmed by desire we should think of the hungry ghosts who are tormented with unfulfilled craving caused by the strong attachment they had in previous lives and see how destructive it is. If we are bitten by a mosquito we should not get angry but reflect on the story of that mosquito—what caused her to take that body and need to drink our blood—and realize how amazing it is that, despite having created exactly the same causes to take a mosquito body, in this life we're human with the freedom to do anything we want.

It is like a dream. It is like a dream that we have been saved from the suffering of the hells, that we are not at this moment tormented by hunger and thirst like hungry ghosts are, that we are not that mosquito or that cockroach, unable to do anything but eat and try to survive. Only in this human body can we practice the holy Dharma. No hell being can do this, no hungry ghost, no frog, elephant, cat or worm. Hardly any other human being on this planet can practice Dharma either. And yet, somehow, miraculously, we can.

We can look at every freedom and richness in this way. We can take every experience every day and relate it to the freedoms and richnesses we have. Anything that happens in our daily life can be a Dharma teaching, telling us how incredible our life is and how rare these freedoms and richnesses are. Every experience we have can remind us that we must make the most of every opportunity to practice Dharma and destroy the delusions that still plague us. There is not one minute to waste and, conversely, if we use it wisely, every minute can bring us closer to enlightenment.

Perhaps in checking we find that we have one or two freedoms or richnesses missing or not as strong as they ought to be. It is then time to consider how to go about securing that freedom or richness. Perhaps we are studying Buddhism but don't have the strong devotion to the teachings as described in the fifth richness. What is missing? How do we acquire it? Maybe our worldly life still has too much of a pull on us and so we don't have the con-

---

Gem and generating bodhicitta), the power of regret (for having done a specific negativity), the power of resolve (never to repeat the negativity) and the power of remedy (a specific practice such as Vajrasattva mantra recitation).

ducive conditions for practicing Dharma as described in the tenth richness. How can we change our life so that those conditions will be fulfilled? We should not feel depressed if we find that one or two of the eighteen are missing. We definitely have the vast majority and that is a cause for incredible rejoicing. It means that our life is extremely meaningful, that we have the power to do whatever we want with this perfect human rebirth.

# 4. Thinking About the Great Benefit of the Perfect Human Rebirth

After explaining the freedoms and richnesses, traditional lam-rim texts next look at the great advantages of the perfect human rebirth. In *Liberation in the Palm of Your Hand,* the great yogi Pabongka Dechen Nyingpo divides this subject into three topics:

- the temporal benefits
- the ultimate benefits
- how the perfect human rebirth is useful in every moment

This perfect human rebirth is unbelievably useful in these three ways, bringing us the temporal benefits of happiness in this and future lives, the ultimate benefits of liberation and enlightenment and the benefit of allowing us to make every moment of this life highly meaningful.[41]

Whatever happiness we wish for can be ours. The temporal benefits—eons as a long-life god, future lives in pure lands and so forth—are called temporal not only because they are not the ultimate meaning of life but also because they are experienced while we are still in samsara and one day will end.

On the other hand, the ultimate goals, liberation or enlightenment, will not end. By making our motivation as vast as possible, by doing everything we do with the deep wish to attain enlightenment for the sake of all sentient

---

[41] This is a slightly different way of appreciating our spiritual path from the three great purposes, which are happiness of future lives, liberation and enlightenment. See *Liberation,* pp. 275–278.

beings, we are in fact ensuring the other two great purposes are attained effortlessly along the way. And by creating the cause for happiness in our future lives we are also making our current life meaningful and thus ensuring the happiness of this life as well.

When our mind is imbued with bodhicitta, even if we aren't consciously doing a Dharma activity, we're still creating the causes for enlightenment. And when we make a light offering or burn a stick of incense, for every moment that that candle or incense burns we're creating the causes for enlightenment; with every breath, every mouthful of food, every step, every action, we're bringing ourselves and all sentient beings closer to enlightenment.

Keeping the ultimate goal in mind gives us the energy to undertake whatever practices we need to do and overcome any obstacles that arise in our quest for enlightenment. Unless we keep pure morality, we will still harm others, even unintentionally, and this will disturb our mind and make it difficult to develop perfect concentration. Without concentration, we can never develop a deep understanding of the nature of reality. With pure morality, however, our concentration, compassion and wisdom can develop quickly. And, as we develop these qualities, we are making the most of every moment of this life. This is why it's important to understand the temporal and ultimate benefits of the perfect human rebirth.

## THE TEMPORAL BENEFITS

Whether we want to be born as a human being, a wheel-turning king or a long-life god, we can choose our rebirth when we have a perfect human rebirth. Even if we want to be reborn in a pure land to hear the teachings of the bodhisattvas and buddhas and quickly attain enlightenment, that is possible. Through having, in previous lives, kept pure morality, practiced great generosity and made stainless prayers to be born with these conditions, we have now received this perfect human rebirth. By doing the same in this life we can ensure another perfect human rebirth in the future.

Just as this life is the gift of the hard work we did in previous lives, our future lives are determined by what we do now. It is entirely up to us. We prayed strongly for a long time to have this opportunity; now we have to pray for the opportunity to continue this good work. Whatever rebirth we want is there waiting for us if we create its cause.

*A favorable human rebirth*

One result whose cause we can create with this perfect human rebirth is another human body suitable for practicing Dharma. Ideally, such a rebirth has eight ripened qualities, as mentioned by Pabongka Dechen Nyingpo in *Liberation in the Palm of Your Hand.*[42] These are eight conditions most conducive to practicing Dharma:

- a long life
- a handsome or beautiful body
- a noble caste
- wealth
- power and fame
- trustworthy speech
- a male body
- a strong body and mind

Each of these qualities makes practicing Dharma that much easier, so we should do our best to cultivate them.

The first is to have a long life. If we spend our life chasing worldly happiness, then no matter how long we live it will be totally wasted. The longer we live, the more we will harm others, and when we die we will experience great suffering. A long life gives us more time to practice Dharma and thus derive greater benefit from our perfect human rebirth.

The second ripened quality, a handsome or beautiful body, gives us the power to attract and influence others and thereby be of more benefit to them.

The third ripened quality, a high or noble caste, might sound a bit strange to Westerners, but even today in India and Nepal people's caste is important and determines their social standing. The purpose for wanting to be of noble caste is not for the wealth it often brings (there are also many poor high caste people in India) but for the respect that others show those of higher caste. This is not to have a good reputation for its own sake but because it is easier to influence people if they respect us, and as our job is to benefit others as much as possible, it is that much easier when we have their respect.

[42] *Liberation*, pp. 414–419.

Even in the West, if somebody is a butcher, for instance, a job involved in killing, people see that person as somebody creating negative karma and therefore not a good influence. And so, in India and Nepal, high caste people command respect. The great teachers like Shakyamuni Buddha and Lama Atisha chose to be born into high caste families so that many people would listen to and be benefited by them. By giving up all the wealth and power of the noble lives they led and devoting their lives to practicing the Dharma, both the Buddha and Lama Atisha were giving us teachings by example. Seeing a beggar meditating doesn't inspire us to meditate, but when somebody like a king, who has wealth and power, begins to meditate, millions of people are inspired to try to meditate too.

The West does not have a caste system as such but still we are influenced by the rich and famous. Celebrities like Richard Gere, for example, are known to young and old, and people try to emulate the way they dress and the way they live. They become examples for worldly people. If that example is a good one, then they become a very powerful positive influence.

In the same way, the next two qualities, wealth and power and fame, are not for worldly pleasure but for the ability they give us to influence others and bring them into the Dharma. A king or a dictator has a huge influence over the people he controls. Mao Zedong ruled China as head of the Communist Party for many years, telling people what to do and how to think. His influence caused millions of people to suffer. The mistake the Chinese people made was to not analyze his philosophy, to not check what he said, but to just follow him blindly because of the great power and fame he had. Because of that he could control the army and the people.

The sixth quality is having trustworthy speech. That means people trust us and our words have weight. His Holiness the Dalai Lama is the perfect example of this. With just a few words he can have a very positive impact on people's minds. We can explain the same thing in great detail and numerous times and nobody will listen, but when somebody like His Holiness simply mentions it briefly, everybody listens. Every word he utters has the power to benefit other sentient beings extensively.

If we want to be able to influence people verbally in the same way we must create the causes of trustworthy speech. Just as a wife won't listen to an untrustworthy husband, if our words don't have power, other people won't listen to us. To be able to influence others—even a few, let alone thousands—we need to create those causes. Whatever we say to others, our main aim should always be to bring them into the path to enlightenment.

The seventh point, having a male body, often causes Western students some consternation. We don't need a male body to achieve enlightenment; both men and women are equally able to achieve enlightenment and there is nowhere in Buddhism that says otherwise.

I remember a long time ago in Root Institute in Bodhgaya, the question of why a male body was important was put to Kirti Tsenshab Rinpoche[43] by Venerable Karin, the wonderful Karin, the pillar of Kopan monastery, who always stays at Kopan, never going anywhere or needing anything.[44] The question and answer were translated by Venerable Tsenla, Yangsi Rinpoche's sister,[45] who helped found the Kopan Nunnery[46] and who has done incredible work for decades. She is Tibetan, but even so I sensed she was a little disturbed by what Kirti Tsenshab Rinpoche had said. Rinpoche did not answer directly but asked instead why there were so many more male leaders in the world than female ones.

This quality relates to overcoming obstacles in the outside world, although I think it can also relate to which kind of body has the most obstacles. Even though there are more and more female heads of state emerging these days, there are still far more male leaders, but that has no bearing on the qualities of the women.

The texts mention that it depends on the form—male or female—in which a person wants to benefit other sentient beings. There is no difference in the potential of either sex; both men and women can attain enlightenment in exactly the same way. If a man doesn't practice Dharma, nothing happens, and it's the same for a woman. Just as there have been innumerable male yogis who have gone on to attain enlightenment, there have also been innumerable yoginis who have done the same thing. Tara is probably the most prominent example of a person who attained enlightenment in female form. So why do we count having a male body as an advantage?

[43] Kirti Tsenshab Rinpoche (1926–2006) was a highly respected ascetic yogi who lived in Dharamsala and was a guru of Lama Zopa Rinpoche. He was one of the great proponents of the Kalachakra tantra.

[44] Ven. Karin Valham, a Swedish nun who first attended the seventh Kopan course in 1974 and was ordained in 1976. She has been Kopan's resident teacher since 1987.

[45] Yangsi Rinpoche (b. 1968), a *lharampa* geshe from Sera Je Monastery in south India, became the director and resident teacher of Maitripa College in Portland, Oregon, at its inception in 2006. His sister, Ven. Tsenla, is a well-known and much sought after interpreter, having learned excellent English at a school in Darjeeling.

[46] Khachoe Ghakyil Ling, founded next to Kopan in the 1980s, is now the largest nunnery in Nepal and home to more than 400 nuns.

Every day, many people do Tara or Vajrayogini practice and gain incredible benefit from it. There is also Machig Labdrön[47] who spread the practice of *chöd* in Tibet. This is a quick way to realize emptiness, a hero's bodhicitta practice on exchanging self with others by totally making charity of one's whole body to others. Often performed in a terrifying place like a charnel ground, practitioners transform their flesh and bones into nectar and offer it to the Three Jewels and the sentient beings of the six realms, particularly the spirits.

So, there are many practitioners who have become enlightened in female aspect. It depends on our own motivation. If we see that we can benefit others more in a female body than a male one, we can ensure that we get one. And vice versa, of course.

The English nun, Venerable Tenzin Palmo, is a great inspiration. Like the wonderful stories we hear of French and Spanish Christian nuns living in isolated places or the great Tibetan yoginis, she lived in an extremely remote place for twelve years, sacrificing her life to the practice and facing great hardships. We need inspiring stories like that.[48] To get results from our practice, the main thing we need is continual renunciation, so examples like hers are very, very good. Just as the places in India and Nepal where yogis achieved the path hundreds of years ago are to this day places that inspire others to practice, by being a living example, she is an inspiration to the Western world.

The last ripened aspect is having a strong and healthy body and mind. Some translate it as "powerful body." When we are sick, we can't function properly, don't think clearly and have no space to think of others. It also means having a body and mind that are strong and resilient enough to withstand the hardships that can come with Dharma practice.

Milarepa is the perfect example of this. He had an incredibly strong mind, with iron-clad determination. Nothing could deter him from practicing Dharma every second of the day. And with that, he put up with starvation and intense cold. He lived in conditions we could not even imagine. Though his body was stick-thin and blue-green from the cold and his diet of nettles, he developed an amazing resilience and was able to withstand any condition. Through his devotion to the Dharma he vanquished all thoughts of comfort and the other eight worldly dharmas.

---

[47] Machig Labdrön (1055–1149), literally "Unique Mother Torch of Lab," was a great tantric practitioner and teacher who developed several chöd practices.
[48] See *Cave in the Snow* for Ven. Tenzin Palmo's story.

In addition to the eight ripened qualities, a favorable rebirth also includes the four Mahayana Dharma wheels: relying on holy beings, abiding in a harmonious environment, having supportive family and friends and collecting merit and making prayers.

We need a Mahayana virtuous friend to guide us, the support of family and friends and a conducive environment. That does not simply mean meditating in a place where we are not liable to be harmed or get sick, as mentioned in the instructions for a calm-abiding retreat, but also that where we live—the place, our family and so forth—are harmonious and supportive of our Dharma practice. Collecting merit and making prayers seems very obvious to me. Of course we need to do that.

### The potential to become anything we want

With this perfect human rebirth we have the potential to become anything we want. If the motivation for what we do every day is to become a long-life god, then we can become one. We can become a desire realm god, with unbelievable sense pleasure, or a form or formless realm god, spending eons in perfect concentration. We can become the king of the god realms if we want. This perfect human rebirth is like a ticket to any place we want to go.

Even in this life, the things we want and need come naturally and easily. Other people struggle to attain the comforts of this life, but we seem to come by them without putting any effort into it. Whatever clothes, food or possessions we need or want we can have. Without obstacles, we can become successful in whatever field we want. We can have wealth and fame and be able to create great art. We can use that talent for anything we want, such as making beautiful Buddha statues.

While others struggle and rarely succeed, all these things come easily to us and we can do anything we want with them. Of course we can squander them if we wish, but we can also use our wealth, fame, talent and other worldly benefits to develop our love, compassion and wisdom and really help others.

If we want to become a wheel-turning king, a *chakravartin*,[49] we can, by making prostrations to holy objects. When we prostrate, with every atom that our body covers—and there are billions of atoms—we create that many merits to be reborn as a wheel-turning king for a thousand lifetimes. To be

---

[49] A universal emperor who rules over the four continents with love and ethics, according to the Dharma.

born a wheel-turning king just once requires inconceivable merit, so imagine how much merit we must be creating when we prostrate to holy objects to be born a wheel-turning king a thousand times.

When we have a perfect human rebirth that we don't squander, our mind is relaxed and happy all the time. We have the perfect conditions, we are making the most of them and when we die we will die with a happy and peaceful mind. This is extremely important. When death shows up one day, whether we are eating, walking, partying, working on a project—whatever we are doing—we won't feel at all upset, regretting all the things we haven't done and experiences we haven't had. We will have done what we needed to do and even though we may not have gained deep realizations on the path we will be confident that we are going from one perfect human rebirth to another and will have time in our next life to realize all the lam-rim topics.

By observing moral conduct and practicing generosity with this rebirth, all these temporal goals can be achieved easily, and the vital temporal goal, receiving another perfect human rebirth, will happen naturally if we pray for it, giving us the chance to continue our Dharma practice and develop further on the path. Then, again, the conditions conducive to practicing Dharma will be there waiting for us—the eight freedoms and the ten richnesses, the supportive environment, the loving family and friends, access to the teachings and so forth.

On the other hand, if we don't strongly practice morality and generosity now, those conditions will not all be there in our next life, even if we do manage to be reborn human. We might have a comfortable environment but lack harmony with our family; we might have access to the teachings but be too poor to do anything other than work hard every day just to survive and thus have no chance to study the Dharma. There will be something missing in the conditions.

### Rebirth in a pure land

With a perfect human rebirth, we can do the practices for transferring our consciousness to a pure land at the time of death (Tib: *pho-wa*). If we have not been able to attain enlightenment in this life, rebirth in a pure land gives us a quick way to complete the path.

As with a perfect human rebirth, the principal causes for being born in a pure land are practicing morality and generosity, but in addition we have to strongly dedicate our actions and make fervent prayers to get such a rebirth.

With those causes in place, there are many special Vajrayana techniques that will help us find rebirth in a pure land. However, the essential method is to renounce attachment and purify negativity as much as possible—this is what rebirth in a pure land depends on. At the time of death we need to be completely free from any clinging to worldly pleasure—possessions, family, friends or body. Any clinging whatsoever will simply ensure another samsaric rebirth.

There is a famous story about Longdöl Rinpoche, a very high Tibetan lama. He really wanted to be reborn as the king of Shambhala in the pure land of Kalachakra and therefore made every effort to renounce attachment. He lived in a hermitage and relied on people bringing bags of tsampa for his food, and one of his practices was to never think about whether the food would be there for him the next day. Like this, he renounced even attachment to the food that kept him alive.

One day he asked the third Panchen Lama, Palden Yeshe,[50] whether he would succeed in his desire to be king of Shambhala. The Panchen Lama made an observation and sent a message to Longdöl Rinpoche, saying, "The old monk is very greedy. You will succeed in your aim."[51]

Through the special techniques of consciousness transfer, rebirth in a pure land does not depend on having parents. We are born in a lotus in a kind of rebirth called an "entering rebirth."

A pure land body is not a gross physical body made of flesh, skin and bones like the one we have now; it is a spiritual body, a body of light. And there is no such thing as suffering—the sufferings of rebirth, sickness, old age, the body becoming decayed and wrinkled and so forth. Pure lands are incredibly beautiful, with breathtaking scenery all around, exquisite wish-granting trees and many beautiful flowers covering the ground. There is nothing that is not sublimely beautiful.

Many of the animals there are actually bodhisattvas manifesting in that aspect, there to guide us. We constantly hear the sound of Dharma; even the sound of the birds singing and the wind blowing through the trees is the sound of Dharma.

---

[50] The Panchen Lamas are a lineage representing incarnations of Amitabha Buddha. The Dalai Lama and the Panchen Lama are the two highest spiritual leaders in Tibet. Panchen Palden Yeshe (1738–1780) was the third Panchen Lama. In 1995, when he was six, the current Panchen Lama, the eleventh, recognized by His Holiness the Dalai Lama, disappeared, presumed kidnapped by the Chinese authorities.

[51] Of course, this is "greedy" in a good way.

Whatever we wish for is there. Pure land sense pleasures are millions of times greater than the best on earth, the food is exquisite and the drink is nectar but, even though there are sense pleasures that we can't even imagine, we don't develop attachment to them; they don't become a condition for developing the unsubdued mind. The incredible pleasures of the god realms only increase the gods' attachment and delusions; this does not happen at all in a pure land.

There are different pure lands—those associated with Amitabha, Chenrezig, Tara, Heruka and other deities—and through strong prayers and motivation we can choose which one to be reborn into. The greatest benefit of being born in a pure land is that we can actually communicate with and receive teachings from the buddha of that pure land and thus complete the Vajrayana path that we were unable to complete in our previous life and attain enlightenment.

## THE ULTIMATE BENEFITS

This perfect human rebirth is extremely useful because it gives us the chance to achieve not only temporal goals but, far more importantly, the ultimate goals of liberation and enlightenment.

Of the three great purposes of the perfect human rebirth, the greatest meaning is the opportunity we have to attain full enlightenment. We have already seen just how rare and precious it is to have all eighteen attributes. The rarest of all is to have met a fully-qualified Mahayana virtuous friend who can show us not just some of the path but the whole path, without one single mistake. Only when we set our mind to attaining enlightenment in order to benefit all other sentient beings can we say we are truly using the full potential of our perfect human rebirth.

With the entire Buddhadharma at our fingertips and a pure guide to show us the way, we have the perfect conditions to go beyond this limited existence and eliminate all obscurations from our mind, developing the selfless wish to help all beings. This is possible. The road is there ahead of us: taking refuge, developing renunciation, cultivating compassion and bodhicitta and realizing the nature of reality. All it takes from our side is the determination to take that road. And using the techniques taught in Vajrayana with bodhicitta motivation, we can reach the end of that road very quickly, without having to wait the eons it would take following the Sutrayana path.

*We can achieve nirvana and become an arhat*

Individual liberation, nirvana (Skt: *pratimoksha*), is possible with this perfect human rebirth. *Prati* means "individual" and *moksha* means "freedom" or "liberation." This shows we ourselves are the cause of it, not some other being. When we attain liberation we become an *arhat* (Tib: *dra-chom-pa*), a foe-destroyer—one who has destroyed the foe of the afflictions and is therefore no longer in samsara.

We have been suffering in this samsaric body since beginningless time; we have already experienced an infinite number of times in previous lives every problem, pain and misfortune we have had in this life and will have until we die. The one crucial difference now is that for the first time we have the possibility to eliminate all suffering, no matter how small, forever.

If there were no suffering mind there would be no suffering body. But this mind, with all its propensities and qualities, also gives us the ability to cut through the delusions that keep us trapped in samsara. This is why we have such a mind. Just as a plane is meant to fly in the sky and not taxi through thick jungle, the purpose of this life is to destroy the delusions that keep us from perfect happiness and to develop our positive qualities to their utmost. We are the pilot; it's up to us.

We have the potential to realize the three higher trainings of morality, concentration and the penetrative insight that realizes emptiness. Penetrative insight into emptiness, which is what ultimately frees us, depends on calm abiding meditation, perfect concentration. And it is impossible for us to gain perfect concentration while our mind is confused because we lack pure morality. So these three higher trainings are all necessary for individual liberation.

With individual liberation we destroy all our delusions except for the very subtle ones—the obscurations to knowledge[52]—and free ourselves totally from samsara. This is an incredible thing. It is a wonderful motivation and being able to achieve liberation is truly unbelievable, but it is still not the ultimate purpose of life.

---

[52] The two obscurations (Skt: *dvi-avarana*; Tib: *drib-nyi*) are deluded minds that block the attainment of liberation and enlightenment. They are the gross kind, called disturbing-thought obscurations, or obscurations to liberation, and the subtle obscurations, the imprints left when the gross ones are purified, called obscurations to knowledge, or obscurations to enlightenment.

*We can become a bodhisattva*

The ultimate potential of this perfect human rebirth is beyond even liberation, as remarkable as that feat is. Only when we have the motivation to attain full enlightenment can we say we are making the optimum use of every second. The key to enlightenment is bodhicitta. If we generate bodhicitta, then just like the Buddha, we become a source of temporal and ultimate happiness for all other sentient beings. With our perfect human rebirth we have received the best possible life in which to generate loving kindness, compassion and bodhicitta. In *Letter to a Student*, Chandragomin said,

> It is only with a human life that you obtain the most powerful
> mind [bodhicitta].
> That is the basis of the sugatas' path leading all beings to freedom.
> That path cannot be attained by gods, nagas, demigods,
> Garudas, wise spirits, ugly spirits or snakes [nagas].[53]

We can easily generate this ultimate good heart that brings all temporal and ultimate success for ourselves and others because we live as human beings in this southern continent, where there is a mixture of happiness and suffering. Seeing the nature of suffering without being overwhelmed by it, we can renounce samsara, and seeing how all other sentient beings are trapped in the cycle of suffering, we can generate compassion for them and then develop that into great compassion and ultimately bodhicitta. This is not possible in any other continent.

Bodhicitta is the heart of the Mahayana and to be a bodhisattva is to practice its essence. This is the whole purpose of meditation. With a good heart we can approach this incredible mind, and once we have attained bodhicitta we can practice the six bodhisattva activities, the six perfections of generosity, morality, patience, joyous perseverance, concentration and wisdom.

Even if this is not possible in this lifetime, by meditating diligently on the lam-rim with bodhicitta motivation we ensure that in future lives we will become a great bodhisattva and then attain enlightenment. It all depends on the strength of our practice with this perfect human rebirth.

---

[53] Cited by Geshe Sopa in *Steps on the Path to Enlightenment, Volume 1*, p. 254.

*We can become enlightened in this very lifetime or within a few lifetimes*

As a Mahayana practitioner, as long as we keep purifying the negative imprints on our mindstream, stop committing any negative actions and do only virtuous actions, and as long as our motivation is to attain enlightenment for the sake of all sentient beings, there is no possibility that we will not reach our ultimate goal.

How long that takes depends on how determined we are and the vehicle we use to get there. Taking the bodhisattva path without relying on the profound practices contained in the Vajrayana will take a very long time—three countless great eons. They are called countless because they are so long, beyond ordinary human comprehension. But that doesn't mean they are countless for the omniscient mind; the omniscient mind can count them.

According to sutra, there are five paths through which we progress to reach enlightenment: the paths of merit, preparation, right-seeing, meditation and no more learning (which is enlightenment). There are also ten bodhisattva stages (Skt: *bhumi)* through which we progress. From the time we enter the Mahayana path on the path of merit, it takes one countless great eon to reach the right-seeing path. It takes another countless great eon from there to the eighth bhumi, which falls within the fourth path, the path of meditation. And from there to enlightenment takes the last countless great eon.

Of course, this depends on individual practice—how strongly we purify negativity and accumulate merit. Great practitioners who have strong guru devotion are said to be able to complete the paths in two countless great eons or less. In only seven years, the great bodhisattva called "Always Crying" created merit equivalent to one eon of normal practice by perfectly following his guru.[54] This perfect human rebirth gives us the possibility of attaining enlightenment in eight ordinary eons.

However, for a bodhisattva who feels the suffering of every living being as if it were his or her own, it seems unbearable to be unable to effectively help all other kind mother sentient beings for that length of time. Therefore the Buddha taught the Vajrayana so that such deeply compassionate bodhisattvas could attain enlightenment in a much shorter period of time, within

---

[54] Bodhisattva Sadaprarudita was called "Always Crying" because of his great compassion for all suffering sentient beings. See *The Perfection of Wisdom in Eight Thousand Lines*, p. 277 ff. for his story.

seven lifetimes, or even two. If all the cooperative conditions are there we can even attain enlightenment in this very brief lifetime of this degenerate age.[55] It is even said that a meditator can achieve enlightenment within three years, three months and three days. It all depends on the strength of the practitioner's commitment and the profundity of his or her practice.

If an advanced practitioner is unable to attain enlightenment in this lifetime, it is also possible to attain enlightenment within the intermediate state by making use of the cooperative conditions of both Vajrayana and Paramitayana. So, although it seems that enlightenment is a long way off, if we have strong enough guru devotion and a very pure Vajrayana practice, there are several ways we can get there more quickly.

There are many stories of great yogis who attained enlightenment in one lifetime, achieving the rainbow body, where just the fingernails and hair are left behind. It is very inspiring to think that this can be done. The stories also reflect how much dedication and determination they had and the difficulties and dangers they faced in order to practice so purely. Yogis like Ensapa[56] or Milarepa are inspirations to anybody wishing to take the Vajrayana path seriously.

They were ordinary people, just like us, although probably even uglier. People would visit Milarepa because of his incredible reputation, expecting to see an angel, but what they saw was a skinny, hairy, dirty beggar, his skin blue from his nettle diet. But that was just his external appearance due to years of continuous meditating, disregarding all physical comfort. Inside was another story. His mind had perfect control, perfect bodhicitta and pure realizations.

Knowing how all the great yogis started where we presently stand, we can see that we have everything we need right now. The teachings that helped them achieve enlightenment still exist as purely as they did when they were alive and there are still great beings actualizing them. This is not some ancient myth but a present reality.

However, when we read the life story of Milarepa we will see that it is not easy. If we want to achieve the profound results that the great yogis got as

---

[55] See p. 97.
[56] Gyalwa Ensapa (1505–1566), who achieved enlightenment within a few years, was a predecessor of the Panchen Lamas and a guru of Khedrup Sangye Yeshe. His story is told in *Enlightened Beings*.

quickly as they got them, we will have to endure many hardships, keep every precept absolutely purely and maintain incredibly strong guru devotion.

The secret is Vajrayana, tantra. By being initiated into a deity by a fully-qualified vajra master we can actualize this profound practice, which combines the method and wisdom sides of the path with such skill that realizations come much more easily and quickly. The Vajrayana teachings and practices exist, fully-qualified teachers are still with us and we live in where we can receive empowerments. These empowerments ripen our mind and allow us to practice the Vajrayana, like water poured on the ground allows the seeds it contains to germinate and grow.

The power of Vajrayana is that it purifies our impure body and mind and prepares our subtle mind and subtle body to become a buddha's wisdom and form bodies.[57]

That is not to say that Vajrayana practice is easy or that we can do it without a proper foundation. It must be based on strong refuge, strong morality, strong bodhicitta, deep concentration and a firm understanding of emptiness. If any of these elements is missing our Vajrayana practice will not work. Worse than that, because it is such a powerful practice, it will increase our delusions, strengthen our self-grasping and make us capable of doing great harm to ourselves and others. Trying to practice Vajrayana without that strong foundation is very, very dangerous.

We have this perfect human rebirth with its eighteen attributes, and in particular we have this precious human body. A human body of the type we have is a necessary prerequisite to the practice of tantra. The gods have divine bodies, far more beautiful than the most beautiful human, but not only are there no Vajrayana teachings in the god realms, their bodies are not conducive to tantric practice—because they are not born from parents their bodies do not contain the red and white seed that ours do. Even though humans on the other continents[58] are also born from parents, they have problems that prevent them from practicing the Mahayana in general and the Vajrayana in particular. For one thing, it is difficult for them to generate renunciation and, therefore, bodhicitta.

In Vajrayana, the practitioner utilizes the winds that reside in the body, moving them to the central channel and dissolving them into the central chakra, exactly as happens naturally at the time of death. When a practi-

---

[57] The dharmakaya and rupakaya respectively.
[58] See p. 111.

tioner can do this in meditation he or she can experience what is called the clear light. By combining this with the illusory body that is the focus of the deity practice done in a tantric meditation session, the two bodies of a buddha can be actualized and enlightenment attained.

This can only happen with a body that has these physical attributes. It must have been born from a womb, conceived through the union of the father's sperm and the mother's egg. When that happens the embryo receives three substances from the mother—skin, blood and flesh—and three from the father—sperm, bone and marrow—and these form the basis of the subtle drops that are vital for completion stage tantric practice, the only way to attain enlightenment in this lifetime.

Of course, such a body is useless unless Vajrayana practices exist, but the Vajrayana teachings and practices do still exist, if only just. Only here, on this southern continent, at this particular time, with this body with its six substances and our perfect human rebirth can we actualize the generation and completion stages of a tantric practice and so attain enlightenment in this lifetime.

## How every moment is beneficial

This perfect human rebirth is highly beneficial every minute, every second. In every moment we can create extensive merit and do extensive purification; in every moment we can create the cause for liberation and enlightenment.

When we light a stick of incense with bodhicitta motivation we are fulfilling our incredible potential because at that moment we are doing what we need to do to attain enlightenment. As that incense burns we are fulfilling our potential and as it finishes we are fulfilling our potential. Every action we do with bodhicitta motivation helps us fulfill our ultimate potential of enlightenment. If it were form, the merit we create by the charity of giving a crumb of food to an ant with bodhicitta would encompass the whole of space. We can do this because we have this perfect human rebirth.

Of course, we create incredible merit by meditating on bodhicitta or emptiness, making offerings and studying Dharma, but we can create just as much if not more by doing even mundane, everyday activities with bodhicitta. In that way, not one hour, minute or second ever gets wasted.

In one second we can do what no hell being can do, even in the entire length of time it spends in hell, all those long, long eons. Even if a hungry ghost could generate merit, the amount it could create in eons would still be less than what we create in the second it takes us to light a stick of incense and offer it with bodhicitta. It is extremely difficult for animals to create any merit, no matter how long they live. And, as we have seen, worldly gods are too immersed in pleasure to create virtue.

Other people might have the leisure and the mental ability that we do but they lack the other conditions, especially the understanding and determination that allow them to see the value of the Dharma and so they are trapped in nonvirtue. We, on the other hand, have an understanding of these vital subjects—we have been inspired by bodhicitta; we have faith in the teachings of the Buddha and great respect for the holy beings on this planet, and so for us, creating merit is as easy as breathing.

By motivating every action of our day with bodhicitta, we create more merit than we would by giving universes full of jewels equal in number to the grains of sand in the Ganges to infinite buddhas. One second of bodhicitta is worth far more than eons of other positive minds and we can generate that mind second after second after second. And every second of bodhicitta purifies eons of negative karma.

It doesn't depend on the size of the action but on the mind behind it. We can make charity of a universe of priceless jewels to countless sentient beings for eons and that will still be nothing compared to offering a grain of rice to a tiny insect with bodhicitta. No matter how valuable the offering is or how much we offer, no matter how long we offer it for—for billions and billions of eons—or how many beings we offer it to—even if we offer it to billions and billions of buddhas—any tiny action done with bodhicitta creates far more merit.

This perfect human rebirth gives us the incredible chance to do highly meaningful actions very, very easily, even in such a short time, without depending on having many material things. A bowl of water, a few grains of rice, a flower—offering such things with bodhicitta creates skies of merit.

At present this is an aspiration, but we can make it a reality. At present we are obscured by ripening imprints from past negative actions; they dull our mind like clouds block the sun. But with bodhicitta we can purify even the heaviest of negative karmas. Bodhicitta has that much power.

Therefore we should start our day with bodhicitta—with a strong motivation as we wake up—and continue generating bodhicitta throughout the day. Every sip of tea should be taken with bodhicitta, every morsel of food eaten with bodhicitta, every word spoken with bodhicitta. In that way, we are making the very most of our incredible potential every day, every hour, every minute, every second. As Khunu Lama Rinpoche[59] says in *The Jewel Lamp: A Praise of Bodhicitta,*

> When you walk, walk with bodhicitta.
> When you sit, sit with bodhicitta.
> When you stand, stand with bodhicitta.
> When you sleep, sleep with bodhicitta.
>
> When you look, look with bodhicitta.
> When you eat, eat with bodhicitta.
> When you speak, speak with bodhicitta.
> When you think, think with bodhicitta.[60]

Thus we should do everything with bodhicitta. Every moment, we have this choice. We can do whatever we have to do with an ordinary mundane mind full of worldly concern and capable only of keeping us trapped in samsara, or we can do it with bodhicitta. The choice between meaningless and meaningful, between suffering and happiness, between samsara and liberation and enlightenment is ours to make every second. That is what makes every second of this perfect human rebirth meaningful.

---

[59] Khunu Lama Tenzin Gyaltsen (1894–1977) was a renowned bodhisattva and Sanskrit scholar and one of Lama Zopa Rinpoche's gurus.
[60] Vv. 338 & 339. Published as *Vast as the Heavens, Deep as the Sea.*

# 5. How the Causes Are So Difficult to Acquire

## THIS LIFE IS PRECIOUS BECAUSE THE CAUSES ARE DIFFICULT TO ACQUIRE

WHY IS THIS perfect human rebirth so precious? Why do so few beings enjoy such an existence? Because the causes of a perfect human rebirth are so difficult to acquire. Without creating the cause the result cannot happen. That is the most basic fact about karma. We have created the causes for this perfect human rebirth, so now we are enjoying it. Realizing how incredibly difficult is it to acquire such causes makes us appreciate the hard work we did in the past and generate the determination not to waste it now.

The causes of a perfect human rebirth are morality, generosity and making stainless prayers to receive a perfect human rebirth in the future in order to benefit others. In our previous lives we were not just moral, we observed *pure* morality by keeping the various levels of vows. In addition, we were incredibly generous. Furthermore, we saw that we could best advance on the path with a perfect human rebirth, so made many prayers for such a rebirth. Doing all this takes a very strong and determined mind, but we obviously must have created all the right causes and conditions, because now we are experiencing the result.

Understanding karma is not easy, so to see the link between our present happy situation and a previous act of generosity or morality might be beyond us now, but it is crucial that we study the teachings on karma and come to see how the laws of karma are profound and definite. To be in this situation we *must* have created its causes in the past. There is no way around karma. When we plant the seed of a poisonous plant, a poisonous plant will grow and not a medicinal one, and vice versa. The result has to match the cause. To expect a crop of medicinal plants from sowing poisonous seeds is ridiculous. This present life is the result of the incredible merit we accumulated in previous lives—positive results coming from positive causes. Therefore, if we want another perfect human rebirth like this one in the future, we have to create the same kind of causes now. We can't simply expect that because we have it now we will continue to have it without creating any more causes for it.

We need to check to see if we are continuously creating the causes for a future perfect human rebirth. Perhaps we know a little about karma and meditate every morning. It is easy to think that because we pray and do a few good things that we don't have to worry about anything; in fact, we might even feel proud of being a good person. We need to look deeper and see whether whatever we do during the day is propelling us toward a better rebirth or a worse one.

Until we reach a quite advanced stage, creating virtue is like pushing a huge boulder up a steep slope. One slip and it rolls back to the bottom and we have lost all that hard work. We can't get tired now. Think of how demoralized and frustrated we would feel if we let that boulder slip, knowing of all that wasted effort and how we would have to start from the very beginning again. We can't let that happen with this perfect human rebirth.

We need all three causes to have a perfect human rebirth: morality, generosity and prayers for such a rebirth. Without generosity, with just very strong morality, we can take a human rebirth, but it will not be a perfect human rebirth. It needs both prime causes. The Buddha said,

> The being who has a missing leg cannot follow the road.
> Similarly, you cannot attain liberation without practicing
>     morality.

Practicing morality alone is not enough. It might get us a human rebirth, but one that is overwhelmed with poverty, and this will give us no time to think of anything other than survival. Generosity without morality does not even ensure an upper rebirth. The result of generosity is wealth, but beings other than humans can be wealthy. If we have maintained morality in a previous life, but that slipped—say we had taken vows but broke them—but at the same time have been very generous, the likely outcome is to be reborn as a naga. Many nagas, the snake-like beings that inhabit many places including the ocean floors, are incredibly rich but they are still in the lower realms and still have to endure great suffering. Therefore it is essential that we practice both morality and generosity.

### The difficulty because of lack of morality

In Buddhist cosmology, it is said that the age in which we are now living is a degenerate age. We will discuss the five degenerations when we look at the evolution of the world system, but briefly, the last two are the degeneration of view and the degeneration of sentient beings. That means we have reached a point in the evolution of life where the view has degenerated and it is extremely rare that people can understand the nature of how things and events exist. Because of that, the negativities of sentient beings become ever-increasing and their delusions get increasingly grosser. This is the degeneration of sentient beings. Our delusions are so gross and overpowering that it is rare to find somebody who is not self-obsessed, not bound by the chains of self-cherishing. If we look around we will see that most people are living for only this life and the pleasure it can bring.

As the world around us becomes grosser and more materialistic, it becomes more difficult for us to remain outside the influence of society, and so practicing morality becomes more difficult. Greed, jealousy and taking care of oneself at the expense of others seem to be condoned by society and what we see around us: the television we watch, the books we read and even the way our government runs the country.

This is where we need to be totally honest with ourselves, to look at everything we do and see whether it is a moral action or not. We do many actions each day, most very trivial but some not so; how many of them can we truly say are moral actions? How many are meaningful? The answers to these questions tell us whether or not we are using our perfect human rebirth wisely and creating the causes for another one.

The Buddha gave us guidelines to follow, specifically advising us to avoid the ten nonvirtues, ten actions that harm others and create the cause for future suffering:

- killing
- stealing
- sexual misconduct
- lying
- harsh words

- ▸ divisive speech
- ▸ idle gossip
- ▸ covetousness
- ▸ ill will
- ▸ heresy

Check up. Has any action you have done been more moral than the actions of the birds in the tree? Have you done anything more worthwhile than your cat or any of the other animal sentient beings around you, doing their activities of eating, drinking, sleeping, walking and so forth? You are a hardworking human being, but check your daily actions. Every day you eat, drink, sleep, work, walk and so forth. Is any one of those actions ever done without attachment to sense pleasure and hence in any way different from the actions of the flying and crawling sentient beings around you? When you really investigate you'll probably find that you have a lot of work to do on your mind before you can honestly say yes, but this is the sort of honest investigation you need to do to see if your perfect human rebirth is being wasted or not.

Lying, stealing, engaging in sexual misconduct, slandering, gossiping, speaking harshly, in big or small ways—are any of these part of your normal day? How about the nonvirtues of the mind, covetousness, ill will and heresy? Do you ever act as if there were no past and future lives or no need for refuge in Buddha, Dharma and Sangha?

Remaining mindful of your actions and maintaining your moral discipline for just one day is a cause for great rejoicing. But I think you will find that generally, it is far easier to lie, gossip, slander, harbor ill will and so forth than it is to do their opposites.

By following nonvirtue, we are ensuring the most terrible suffering in the future. Even if we know this logically, following virtue is still extremely difficult. If we could really see the results of our lack of morality, there would be not a moment's laziness. Nothing else would matter; we would only ever think of creating purely virtuous actions.

The essence of morality is keeping precepts. That is why, in Buddhism, there are the various levels of vows that we can take, the various pratimoksha, bodhisattva and tantric vows. But even though we take them in front of a spiritual master and at the time are strongly determined never to break any of them, they are still very hard to keep. There are many obstacles; all sorts of hindrance arise. We are controlled by such thick delusions that our mind reacts and we find that we are unable to keep our vows. This shows just how difficult it is to practice morality in these degenerate times and, consequently, just how rare a perfect human rebirth is.

Each set of vows is based on an increasingly subtle form of morality, from the five lay pratimoksha vows to the bodhisattva and tantric vows. If receiving a perfect human rebirth depends on keeping pure morality, then we need to keep not only the pratimoksha vows but the bodhisattva and tantric vows as well. To say we are keeping vows purely when we are breaking the higher vows is clearly not right. Therefore, seeing how difficult it is to keep the tantric vows, we can understand how difficult it is to obtain a perfect human rebirth.

The thing about vows is that the more you keep, the better; the longer you keep them, the better; the more purely you keep them, the better; and the more quickly you recognize and purify transgressions, the better.

Of all the people living in your country, how many are keeping all the bodhisattva and tantric vows purely? How many are keeping the vows of the fully-ordained monk or nun or even the novice vows purely? How many are keeping the five lay vows purely? The number of people keeping five vows is smaller than the number keeping four. The number keeping four is smaller than the number keeping three. There are fewer people keeping three than two, and fewer still keeping two than one. The number of people keeping the thirty-six novice vows is much smaller than the number keeping one vow, and the number keeping the vows of full ordination is much smaller still. Then, of course, there are fewer people keeping bodhisattva vows than there are keeping pratimoksha vows, and the number keeping tantric vows is the smallest of all.

So, if we look at all the people in the world today and ask how many are keeping even one vow, the vow not to kill, properly, we will understand how few are looking at an upper rebirth. And among those who do keep vows, how conscientiously do they recognize and purify breaks? How seriously do they take their vows? Do they even remember what they all are?

You will see in depictions of Lama Atisha that he always had a small stupa with him. He used to say that he kept his pratimoksha vows perfectly and rarely transgressed his bodhisattva vows, but broke his tantric vows like rain falling. (I don't think he did but that's what he used to say.) So the moment he noticed he'd broken a vow he would jump down from his horse or stop whatever he was doing, make prostrations to his stupa and apply the four opponent powers right away. That's how seriously he took his vows and that's how seriously we need to take ours. And that's the kind of morality we need to practice in order to ensure another perfect human rebirth.

Even in a country like Tibet before 1959, where there were so many monks and nuns keeping all the levels of ordination, there was still a big majority of people *not* living in the vows. And so, looking at the entire population of the world and comparing those who live in any form of vow and those who don't, the former is immense and the latter is tiny.

Why do so few people in this world live in ordination? Why do so few people observe karma and live in pure morality? Because it is so difficult. Even when there is the wish to live morally, there are many outer and inner hindrances to doing so.

## The difficulty because of lack of generosity

There are also many hindrances to creating the other main cause of a perfect human rebirth, generosity. Even when we want to give we find that there are reasons we can't or people who interfere with what we are trying to do.

Generosity is the wish to give, rather than the actual act of giving, so we don't have to be rich to attain another perfect human rebirth; we just need to have a generous heart. Also, material giving does not mean that sentient beings have to receive material help from us. If it did, we would not be able to complete our practice of generosity until there were no beings in need left. And because the perfection of generosity is a practice needed to attain buddhahood, that would then mean that there are no buddhas. No, what we need is the generous mind. Fully developing our generosity means completely eliminating our clinging to things such as possessions, body, merit and so forth. We can be completely generous even if we have nothing material to give. Generosity is a state of mind.

There is the famous story of the small boy who was playing with his friends when he saw Shakyamuni Buddha coming along the path. He wanted to offer the Buddha something but all he had was sand, so, standing on the shoulders of his friends like a circus act—the Buddha was very tall—he offered the sand into the begging bowl imagining it was gold. As the result of that act of generosity he was reborn as Ashoka, the great wheel-turning king who was able to build a millions stupa throughout India. Even though he didn't offer real gold, just sand, he received the karmic result of offering gold.

There are three kinds of generosity: material giving, the giving of fearlessness and giving the Dharma. Giving fearlessness includes saving lives and helping people in difficult situations. For instance, taking a fly from a web that is about to be eaten by a spider saves its life and thus is the giving of fearlessness. (In this act, we are saving the fly from death and the spider from killing. Of course, this does not help the spider's hunger or her need to kill again, but just because one positive act cannot stop all problems does not mean it is not worth doing.) Giving the Dharma is the best kind of giving, because the recipient not only receives comfort now, she also has the knowledge to go all the way to enlightenment.

Usually we cling to our possessions, thinking of them as "mine," but even when we give them away, we rarely do it purely. When we make offerings, which is part of the practice of generosity, we can very easily pollute the offering with a nonvirtuous thought. What pollutes an act of generosity is the evil thought of the eight worldly dharmas, the wish for comfort, reputation and so forth. If it is not the wish for reputation or praise, it can be the expectation of getting something back in return.

As long as we harbor clinging in our mind we will find it very difficult to practice Dharma and will encounter many hindrances to developing the causes for a future perfect human rebirth. The degree of generosity we are talking about here—not a bodhisattva's perfection of generosity but at least a very pure state of mind—is incredibly difficult to realize. It is very, very rare that somebody can live with material things all the time, as we do, and have no sense of attachment and be able to freely give what others need without any sense of clinging. But that is the mind we need to develop.

### The difficulty because of anger and other delusions

Besides the lack of morality and generosity, a thousand other delusions plague our mind and block our chances of attaining another perfect human rebirth. And the worst of these is anger. As Shantideva says in *A Guide to the Bodhisattva's Way of Life*,

> Doing virtuous actions
> Such as charity or making offerings
> Accumulated for a thousand eons
> Is destroyed by one second of anger arising.[61]

[61] Ch. 6, v.1.

These are very tasty teachings. Shantideva is pointing out to us very forcibly just how difficult it is to create the causes for a perfect human rebirth and how easy it is to create the causes for a rebirth in the suffering lower realms.

It is no exaggeration to say that a moment of anger destroys eons of virtue. A flash of anger can wipe out all the merit we have accumulated over eons, causing us to be reborn in the suffering lower realms. Any action we do, including making offerings to the buddhas, will be destroyed if anger arises in our mind, and this anger need not be prolonged or even strong. A little anger for a short time is enough to destroy the positive imprints on our mental continuum. And if we get angry with a realized being, we destroy so much more good karma, karma that has been painstakingly collected for eons.

Getting angry at a bodhisattva has terrible consequences, but getting angry at a buddha or our own guru is even more terrible. It is said that every second of anger toward a holy being results in an eon in hell. Just one second. That is why, of all the deluded minds, anger is the one we need to avoid most.

If we had clairvoyance and could see into the minds of other beings, we might be able to judge who is a holy being and who isn't. Then, perhaps, we could feel it was a little safer to get angry at this person and not that one. But we simply don't know. Anybody could be a holy being. An animal could be. Buddhas manifest in countless ways to best guide sentient beings, sometimes as a sage, sometimes as a beggar, sometimes as a crazy person, and we simply don't have the ability to know. Therefore, it is very dangerous to feel we can get angry at anybody because he or she appears to be lower than we are.

Here, Shantideva speaks of one moment of anger, but our anger usually manifests for much longer periods. Say we are unable to sleep because of the buzzing of a mosquito. At first we try to ignore it, but it bites us and we lazily try to slap it away. But it persists and we lie there awake, getting angrier and angrier. It bites, we slap, but it has moved. Hour after hour, it seems. And then—slap!—we get it. We feel incredibly happy. That little bug was making our life a misery and now we have killed it. Now we have peace. But what in reality we have done is kill with all the four conditions required for it to be a complete negative karma of killing—the motivation, anger; the object, the mosquito; the action, slapping it; and the completion, the mosquito dying before we do. Such actions become throwing karmas, which ripen at the time of death and throw us into our next life, in this case, hell. Not only have we powerfully created a very negative karma; by rejoicing over instead of regretting this nonvirtuous action, we have strengthened it, making it likely to ripen sooner rather than later.

In the same way, we can look at the other negative emotions that plague our mind at present—jealousy, resentment, prejudice and so forth—and see how they can so easily rob us of the chance of a perfect human rebirth. Shantideva said,

> An eon in the deepest hell may result from one moment's evil.
> Therefore, because of all the negative karma accumulated
> Since beginningless time, what need to mention
> Not being able to attain the state of the happy transmigratory
>      being?[62]

When we truthfully check our mind we will probably see how weak our virtues are—we have done them without strong motivation and have failed to dedicate them properly—and how strong our nonvirtues are. *Those* were done with strong motivation and rejoiced over at completion. Because our nonvirtues are so much more powerful than our virtues, is there any wonder that it is so difficult to attain an upper rebirth, let alone a perfect human rebirth?

## The difficulty because of wrong view

As we have seen when we looked at the freedom of not being a heretic, holding wrong views is a barrier to attaining a perfect human rebirth. Again, we can explore this and see how rare it is that people in this world are free from this affliction. Denying what exists means that they are unable to see reality and so whatever they do is mistaken and leads to suffering. Denying reincarnation, karma, the existence of buddhas and bodhisattvas and other fundamental concepts in Buddhism, people try to find happiness in things that will only harm them. It is like drinking poison believing it to be nectar. Believing the I to be independent and inherent leads to a sense of separation between I and other, which in turn leads to attachment and aversion and all the other delusions. Confusion and darkness cloud the mind and only suffering results. Even if such people try to do good things, like helping

---

[62] Ch. 4, v. 21.

others, their minds are confused by wrong views and the results can never be satisfactory.

Having wrong views does not stop people from looking for happiness. For most of us, our principal wrong view is equating sense pleasures with happiness, but if we look around we will see many faulty philosophies. From nihilism to materialism and everything in between, teachers are telling students that their path is the true path to happiness. People are so desperate for happiness that they follow these mistaken teachers and go in entirely the wrong directions. People travel to Asia looking for guides and meet teachers who sound convincing but who can only teach them suffering. They return to the West dissatisfied and even more confused, having completely wasted their money and maybe even on the brink of a nervous breakdown. It is incredibly rare that we can meet somebody who can show us the right path. And yet, without right view, how can we hope to attain a perfect human rebirth?

## SOME ANALOGIES FOR THE DIFFICULTY OF ACQUIRING IT

Buddhist texts use many analogies to explain just how difficult it is to attain a perfect human rebirth and because of that just how rare it is. The most well known analogy is that of the blind turtle surfacing through a golden ring. In *A Guide to the Bodhisattva's Way of Life*, Shantideva said,

> The Buddha has said that it is more difficult
> To attain a human state,
> Than it is for a blind turtle to stick its neck
> Into a ring floating in a vast ocean.[63]

There is a blind turtle that lives in the ocean, only coming up to the surface once in a hundred years. On the surface of the ocean is a golden ring, con-

---

[63] Ch. 4, v. 20. The footnote for verse 20 in Stephen Bachelor's translation has the sutra citation: *Yang dag-pat den-pä lung.* Thog. p. 61 seq., 'O monks, suppose that this great earth were to become an ocean upon which a single yoke were being tossed about by the wind and thus being moved from here to there. If under that ocean there were a blind turtle, do you think it would be easy for it to insert its head into that yoke when it rises to the surface only once every hundred years?' 'No Lord, it would not,' replied the monks. The Lord then said, 'In a similar fashion, O monks, it is extremely hard to obtain the human state.'

stantly moving with the wind and tides. The blind turtle surfaces in a different place every hundred years and the ring is never in the same place, so imagine how remote the chance is that the turtle would surface at exactly the right place and slip its neck through the ring. Such a thing is almost impossible, isn't it? In the same way, attaining a perfect human rebirth is equally unlikely.

The ocean is vast and there are an infinite number of places that the turtle can surface. Being blind, it has no way of seeing what is on the surface, even if it were looking for the ring. And the ring could be anywhere on that vast ocean. Even if the turtle surfaced every day, let alone once a century, its chances of coming up near the ring are very remote, and its chances of putting its head through the ring are remoter still.

Each of the elements in this story has a meaning. Of course a golden ring is heavy and would not float; perhaps the Buddha should have said it was a plastic ring. However, the ring signifies the teachings of the Buddha and gold signifies their preciousness and purity.

That it moves about the surface of the ocean signifies that the teachings are not always to be found in the same place. Where they appear depends on the karma of sentient beings. Just like before in Tibet, in ancient times, the country was very evil—it was jungle, forest, a very mischievous place. When Buddhism moved from India to South-east Asia and China, and then to Japan, it seemed like it would not get to Tibet, but somehow it did, and now, while it is weak in some countries, it is still strong for the Tibetan people, even though it is suppressed in Tibet itself.

The turtle represents sentient beings and living at the bottom of the ocean signifies always having to take rebirth in the lower realms as a hell being, hungry ghost or animal. Being blind signifies being ignorant of the Buddhadharma, blind to what is virtue and what is nonvirtue. Just as the blind cannot see visual objects, ignorant sentient beings can't understand the meaning of the Buddha's teachings.

Just as the turtle swims helplessly around the vast ocean, the samsaric being constantly circles through the suffering realms. After eons as a hell being it might take rebirth as an animal; then, after an unimaginably long time, the karma might ripen for it to be reborn as a hungry ghost. Like this, it takes one unfortunate rebirth after another, with no way of creating virtue. So, with every action it ties itself more tightly to incredible suffering.

Only once in an inconceivably long period does the samsaric being happen to obtain an upper rebirth. This is symbolized by the turtle surfacing once every hundred years. But perhaps it comes up where the ring was but now has moved, in the same way that we can receive a human rebirth after a buddha has descended but is no longer there. Or sometimes it comes up near the ring but does not put its neck through it, in the same way that we can be born at a time when there are the teachings of the Buddha but in an irreligious country. So, even though we are close to the teachings, we cannot benefit from them. Obtaining a human rebirth is not enough, we must obtain a perfect human rebirth, represented by the turtle actually being able to surface and put its neck through the ring.

Just as we are blown around by our karma, in the same way the turtle surfaces entirely at random. So how rare it is that we can obtain not just a human rebirth but one with all the eight freedoms and ten richnesses. When we observe the people around us in all the different countries, we can see just how rare the perfect human rebirth is.

It is as rare as grass growing on a roof as opposed to the grass that grows all over the ground in the countryside. The perfect human rebirth is as difficult to obtain as trying to balance a grain of rice on the tip of a needle, or throwing a grain of rice against a windowpane and having it stick to the glass. Receiving a perfect human rebirth is as unlikely.

There is the story of a blind man who stumbled over a sleeping *kyang*, a kind of wild ass found in Tibet. The frightened *kyang* jumped up and ran off, but the blind man had grabbed hold of its ear and pulled himself up onto its back, so galloped off on the animal. He was so happy he sang out, "How amazing for me, a blind man, to get to ride on the back of a *kyang*! This can only ever happen once!" When a Kadampa geshe saw this, he laughed and used it as an example of how we receive this precious body only once and must make full use of it to practice Dharma when we do.

In most areas of Tibet, fish is very rare. So there's the story of a man from Tsang who managed to get hold of an entire fish. It was such a treat that he gobbled the whole thing down so quickly that he started to vomit it back up again. Realizing he was about to lose his precious fish, he pulled his belt off and tied it around his neck tightly to stop from vomiting. When people asked him what he was doing he told them that it would be such a pity to waste such valuable food.

There is a very special food made out of butter and tsampa called *mar-zen* that is eaten by Tibetans at New Year. It is a kind of cake made with lots of butter and because it is expensive, poor families consider it very precious. Once a father in Penpo gave some to his son, who loved it so much that he stole some more off his father's dish. So that his father would not see what he'd done, the boy hid it behind his back, but the family dog came up and stole it from his hands. The boy was so upset he started crying, which surprised the father, who thought that he had eaten the *mar-zen* he had been given and so should be very happy.

We have this very precious thing in our hands at this moment—our perfect human rebirth—but if we don't make full use of it, the dog of death might steal it away before we can, something a billion times more terrible than losing the most valuable material thing.

The point of all these stories and analogies is to show us just how incredibly rare this perfect human rebirth is, thereby inspiring us not to waste one moment of it. Only with a perfect human rebirth can we achieve the three great purposes: a better future rebirth, liberation or enlightenment. Whatever we want can be ours if we develop the determination to make the most of this amazing opportunity.

# 6. It is Difficult by Nature to Acquire

## THE RARITY OF THIS LIFE

THIS PERFECT HUMAN REBIRTH is extremely rare. When we consider all the causes and conditions that need to come together to create this wonderful opportunity we will quickly see that the chances of this happening are exceptional and, furthermore, that this situation is so fragile; it could finish at any moment. If we don't do whatever we can to attain enlightenment in this life, then when? When will this opportunity to practice happen again? In *Hymns of Experience of the Graduated Path*, in which Lama Tsongkhapa describes his own spiritual progress, he explains,

> This body qualified by freedoms and richnesses
> Is more precious than a wish-granting jewel.
> Finding such a perfect body will happen just this one time.
> It is very difficult to find and easily decays, like lightning in
>     the sky.
>
> By reflecting on the nature of life,
> Realize that all worldly activities are like a husk,
> And take the essence all day and night.
> I, the yogi, practiced this way.
> I beg you who are seeking liberation also to practice this way.[64]

---

[64] Vv. 13 & 14. This is Rinpoche's translation. The text is more commonly known as *Lines of Experience* or *Songs of Experience*. Geshe Thupten Jinpa calls it *Songs of Spiritual Experience: Condensed Points of the Stages of the Path* (Tib: *lam rim nyams mgur*).

Lama Tsongkhapa shows us the uniqueness of the perfect human rebirth by explaining it is more precious than a wish-granting jewel, as brief as a lightning flash and highly meaningful, unlike the worthless "husk" of worldly activities. In a few short words he summarizes all the teachings on the perfect human rebirth, emphasizing four very important points:

- how precious this human body is
- how rare and fleeting it is
- how meaningless worldly affairs are
- how, because of all this, we need to take the essence of this life right now

It is like a miracle that we have found this perfect body but Lama Tsongkhapa's words are not to be taken literally. He does not mean that we have never before had a perfect human rebirth in our infinite previous lives. He means that is so rare and it has been such an unbelievably long time since our last one that it is as if this were the only time. When we look at the causes we needed to create in order to have such a life, we will see how miraculous it is. Every one of Lama Tsongkhapa's words has a very powerful meaning.

### The evolution of the human world

As we have seen, a perfect human rebirth needs not just a human body but the presence of the entire Buddhadharma and this is incredibly rare. To get a better understanding of what a unique position we are in, it would be good to consider further what was mentioned in the freedoms and richnesses, how humans with the eight freedoms and ten richnesses are extremely rare compared with other beings.

According to Buddhist cosmology, the period of the existence of a world system is divided into four great eons, each consisting of twenty intermediate eons. The first period is the great eon of evolution, where the whole universe—the three lower and the three upper realms, including our southern continent and the realm of the worldly gods—comes into existence. The second great eon is the eon of existence, where things have evolved and exist for a period. Then follows the great eon of decay, the period in which the universe is destroyed, and finally there is a great eon of emptiness, where things exist only in potential. There are no sentient beings and no physical environment.

During the eons of evolution, decay and emptiness there is no Buddhadharma at all. It can only exist during the eon of existence. And even then, the Buddhadharma does not exist the whole time.

Buddhist cosmology also describes four continents: northern, eastern, western and southern. Our world system is the southern continent (Skt: *Jambudvipa*).[65] The humans who exist in the other continents have different attributes, created by their past karma. For instance, beings of the western continent have a fixed lifespan of a thousand years and experience great enjoyment, making it almost impossible for them to renounce samsara—their great wealth and enjoyment become an obstacle to developing renunciation. They fail to see the various problems of samsara, so it is difficult for them to realize how samsara is in the nature of suffering.

Likewise, what we experience in the southern continent is the product of our karma. We created this world system and all the myriad things and experiences that make it up. This earth comes from the karma—the minds—of all the beings, including all the animals, humans and holy beings, who use it. It is only on this southern continent that the lifespan varies so much and where there is such a mixture of suffering and happiness. This means we can easily see the impermanence of life is and the nature of suffering without being overwhelmed, thus giving us the chance to renounce samsara.

The very first humans evolved from the form realm gods and were god-like in that they did not have the physical bodies that we do, but just as their transition from god to human resulted from a degeneration of their mindstreams, even then these first humans were subject to a series of five degenerations that made them grosser and grosser, evolving into what we are today:

- ▶ the degeneration of disturbing thoughts
- ▶ the degeneration of lifespan
- ▶ the degeneration of time
- ▶ the degeneration of view
- ▶ the degeneration of sentient beings

As the early human beings' minds became grosser, their lives became increasingly dominated by delusion—the degeneration of disturbing thoughts—which shortened their lifespan—the degeneration of lifespan. As the karma created by these disturbing thoughts ripened, the world they experienced became harsher and more difficult—the degeneration of time. This was

---

[65] Literally island or continent (*dvipa*) of the rose-apple tree (*jambu*).

compounded by their minds becoming more and more immured in wrong views—the degeneration of view—which in turn caused their behavior to degenerate such that they began to harm each other more and more—the degeneration of sentient beings. These five degenerations are still happening.

The lifespan of the original humans is 80,000 years but it gradually shortens all the way down to about ten years. From ten the lifespan climbs back up to 80,000 years and then drops down to ten again. Like a series of waves, in a great eon there are twenty of these cycles, each considered to be one small eon.

The point is this: while the lifespan is increasing from ten up to 80,000 years, no buddha descends to give teachings. Those times are called dark eons. There are teachings only when the lifespan is degenerating from 80,000 years down to ten. During this present eon, a thousand buddhas will descend to give teachings. When the life span was 40,000 years, the first buddha, Krakucchanda, appeared; then came Kanakamuni and then Kashyapa. Shakyamuni is the fourth buddha and Maitreya will be the next. It is said that he will appear when the lifespan is ten years and his appearance will be the inspiration for humans to start practicing virtue and so make the lifespan increase again.

Only when the human lifespan has decreased to around a hundred does Buddhadharma appear. Our average lifespan now is now around eighty years so we are at the very end of the period where the Dharma is revealed.

Having evolved from the gods, even though their bodies were different, the very first humans enjoyed many of the pleasures of the gods. They lived for an incredibly long time—not just thousands but tens of thousands of years. Their bodies were ethereal, made of light rather than the gross physical matter that ours are made of, and they could fly. There was no such thing as day and night. They were born spontaneously rather than through the union of sperm and egg of parents, as we were.

At first their food was natural and very pure, not gross material at all, but as they slowly degenerated various crops started to grow. These were grosser, but materially still very subtle and they grew effortlessly. Later, when they did need to be grown, they could be planted in the morning and eaten in the evening. So even as the early humans became grosser, there was still no major discomfort and no problem in finding sustenance. It was almost as if with the thought of hunger came the food to appease that hunger, with no effort from their side.

The main cause of this degeneration was the ever-increasing attachment within the minds of the humans. As they degenerated, their bodies, although still finer than ours, became gross physical bodies instead of the light bodies they had at the beginning, and sex organs began to develop.

The sexes were now differentiated, male and female, and sexual attraction manifested. It is not as if sexual attraction arose from nowhere. It had always lain latent in the minds of the form realm gods and the early humans who came from them, but with light bodies there was no way for sexual desire to manifest. Now, with the grosser bodies and differentiated sexes, it could do so.

Gradually, more effort was required to get food, so crops were grown and harvested. There was still no such thing as "me" and "mine," where different humans owned land and possessed crops, but slowly, grosser negative thoughts arose and jealousy of somebody else's "better" crop created bitterness and competitiveness. Other delusions such as attachment and miserliness also developed, although at this stage the delusions were still more subtle than the ones we face today. People started to claim things as their own and protect them from others. Rivalry grew and, with it, the desire to possess what others had.

Similarly, although there was mild aversion and attraction as their bodies became grosser, there came a time when they felt heat and cold and needed shelter from it. So they formed mud into walls and built the first houses, and a sense of privacy began to emerge as their lives became more and more isolated. They started to become ashamed of their bodies and cover them with clothes.

With ownership, disputes and quarrels arose, and with that, laws were needed and life became more and more complicated. With the sense of need came the worry that they would not have enough, so people started to collect things and protect them.

Dissatisfaction, miserliness, pride, jealousy and all the delusions grew and grew and problems became correspondingly more frequent. There became the need for a leader to settle disputes that the people themselves could not, and from that arose the need for a king. At first the king was a servant of the people, there to serve them with wise counsel, but slowly the idea of king became somebody who had power and could dictate what was right and wrong.

And so it has degenerated to the present, where we live for about eighty years, power determines what is right and wrong and gross delusions prevail.

Perhaps you might think that things are getting better, that life is better than it was a few hundred years ago, but that's a very narrow view. Physically, things might have improved temporarily for a small section of the planet, but in general, not only is the lifespan decreasing but material conditions and human mentality are definitely degenerating.

This is the degeneration of time, when the world is seeing more and more fighting, more and more famine, more and more trouble and more and more fear. Instead of becoming more peaceful, the world has become more violent. And as the delusions of the sentient beings that inhabit the planet increase, so does the incidence of natural disasters. Everything is becoming less and less harmonious.

Although we might have more education than we have ever had, that does not mean we are wiser. In fact, there is a degeneration of view. People place more faith in material things, see external possessions as the cause of happiness and are unable to understand the Dharma. Thinking that happiness is something that can be taken, they steal and even kill to get what they want. That is the last degeneration, the degeneration of sentient beings.

It is becoming more difficult to subdue the mind by means of the holy Dharma. People are becoming more "thick-skulled," their minds stubborn, like iron or rock. They think that Dharma is superstition and if they ever hear about emptiness it doesn't make any sense to them. People actually have aversion to religion and get frightened by its message. The degeneration of sentient beings is like this and that comes from the degeneration of disturbing thoughts.

Looking at this evolution of beings from form realm gods to the earliest humans to where we are now, we can see that there is little time in all this where sentient beings' minds would be open to the Buddhadharma. Understanding this process of degeneration helps us appreciate how special and precious this time is. Only now do we have the chance to break free from this terrible cycle of suffering. The Dharma exists for such a short time that we must make the most of it while we can. Neither in the other three great eons nor in the periods in this great eon of existence when the lifespan is increasing are there any teachings; even when the lifespan is decreasing and the Buddhadharma exists for a short time during that period, it is extremely rare for anybody to be able to hear and benefit from it. And as I just mentioned, the period of the existence of the Buddhadharma has almost finished.

The teachings still exist but their time is almost up. There are still great teachers but for how long will they be around? The time is fast approaching where it will be totally impossible because the teachings will no longer exist on this planet. The path before us is illuminated by the light of Dharma but it is the last flickering of a dying candle. While it is still there we have the chance to create the cause for real happiness, to follow the method that cuts ignorance and delusion, to attain full enlightenment. That is why this human rebirth is so precious.

### The rarity of this life compared to other realms

Not only is this perfect human rebirth very rare in terms of time—now we are here at the very end of the existence of Dharma—but it is also rare in terms of numbers. Countless other sentient beings exist with us on this planet at this time, but how many are able to benefit from the teachings of the Buddha? Very, very few. The Buddha explained that compared with number of beings in the lower realms, the number of beings in the upper realms is like the amount of dirt under a fingernail compared with the amount of dirt on earth. The number of lower realm beings is unimaginable. And as small as the number of beings in the upper realms is, the number of human beings is far, far smaller. And, of course, the number of human beings with a perfect human rebirth is far, far smaller still.

This is the rarest rebirth of all, the one that is hardest to receive. Without looking at the difficulty of creating the causes, without seeing the rarity of the existence of the Dharma, just considering numbers, this perfect human rebirth is extremely rare.

Perhaps we think that in fact there are already too many people in this world. In *Liberation in the Palm of Your Hand*,[66] Pabongka Dechen Nyingpo tells a story of when a Mongolian lama was giving teachings on how hard it is to be born human, a Chinese person in the audience said that he was only saying that because he had never been to China. On the surface it might look like this, but humans are only one part of the sentient beings that make up this world system, and compared to all the others, we are so few. And seeing as we are migrating from one realm to another all the time depending on our karma, just based on numbers the chances of our receiving another rebirth in the upper realms is quite remote.

Of the lower realms, most sentient beings are in the hells, with fewer in the realm of the hungry ghosts and fewer still as animals, so we can start to

---

[66] P. 279.

see how vast those numbers are if we consider the lower realm beings we can
see around us all the time, the animals.

Consider the great herds of animals in Africa, or the millions of birds
that fly in the sky. If you have swum in the ocean you will know that it is
teeming with fish. Perhaps you have watched those wildlife documentaries
that show the great migrations of fish from one ocean to another in unbelievable numbers. From the tiniest fish to the biggest, from dolphins and
sharks to whales, so many varieties and such huge, uncountable numbers.
Yet there is even more life in the ocean when we look at the ocean bed.
There are billions and billions of tiny creatures in every part of the ocean.
We can see that at the seashore, where there are shellfish on every rock, and
crabs, starfish and all sorts of other creatures on the sand.

UNKNOWN

*Rinpoche on the beach in New Zealand, 1974.*

I remember once in New Zealand seeing the rocks sparkling when we were
down on the beach one evening. Wondering what it was, I went closer and
saw that there were millions of tiny creatures, all sorts of shellfish, in each
crack and crevice in the rocks, just waiting for the seagulls to send them to
their next rebirth. And the sand was so covered by them where they had just
been washed off the rocks that it was impossible to avoid stepping on them.

Just stand on a piece of ground and look down. How many sentient
beings are there below your feet? On one stem of a plant, hundreds of tiny

insects are rushing about; on the ground, lines of ants are marching from one place to another, beetles are flying or crawling to their various destinations; spider webs are everywhere, with spiders waiting for one of the millions of unlucky flies or moths. Cows and sheep graze in the fields, birds fly from tree to tree. We might not normally notice it, but everywhere we look is alive with millions of nonhuman beings. And these are just the animals we see. Beneath the earth there are far more, and those too small to see are far more still. The people of this planet are nothing compared to just one species of insect.

Even in the city, which seems to be just streets and houses, there are far more animals than humans. Under every road is a city of insects; every tree has its population of sentient beings; in every rotting piece of wood there are countless living beings; and anybody who has lived in Kathmandu knows about the flies—it's difficult to count the number of them in one room, let alone the whole city.

We think our house is safe from pests, but they can be there in their millions. Lice and fleas can infest a house or a dog. Ants eating the wood, moths eating the clothes, fleas making the carpets jump—so many beings sharing our living space with us. Even our body! There's an itch and when we look we see a little red mark that tells us a kind mother has used us for dinner. And that is not to mention the living beings that make their homes inside our body, the microbes and other beings so tiny that they can only be seen by microscope.

Every moment, millions of animals are dying and within a day their bodies are crawling with maggots and other insects feeding off their flesh. Left alone, as often happens in India, a dead dog will have thousands and thousands of maggots all over its body within days, which shows that at any time there are millions and millions of intermediate state beings waiting for rebirth as maggots to feed off that animal. When the conditions are there, in a flash, the consciousness can enter a new body and the cycle can continue.

Between death and rebirth, sentient beings spend time in the intermediate state, driven by karma to find their future mother and father in union, where the mind of the being joins with the sperm and egg and a new life begins. When two animals are mating, there are countless intermediate state beings that could be born to those animals. Which one finishes up doing so depends on karma.

When we don't wash our clothes or hair properly, the warmth and dirt can become the conditions for lice, fleas and the like to be born. In the same way, tiny beings are born in rotting flesh or rotten wood. If there were not that many sentient beings in the intermediate state waiting for a body, there would be no reason for those creatures to get born so quickly.

There are countless billions of beings suffering in the animal realm. How did they get there? It certainly was not free will. A person didn't look at an ant and think that maybe in his next life he would be an ant to see how it felt. There was no decision involved. Every animal was pushed into that rebirth; controlled by the poisonous minds of ignorance, hatred and attachment, it had no choice—animals are suffering because of past ignorance. And having no concept of karma or any sense of morality, they have almost no chance of escaping that cycle of suffering.

Do we have the karma to become a dog or one of the maggots that live in the corpse of a dog? We just have to look honestly at the causes we are creating every moment of the day to answer that question. Perhaps it seems inconceivable that a human being could become an animal. It might seem that once we are human we will always be human, but that kind of thinking comes from a narrow perspective, from misunderstanding the nature of the mind and the relationship between the mind and the body. Even within this one life our body can change radically due to the power of the mind, but when our mind leaves our body at death, the body to which it attaches itself to next depends entirely on the throwing karma that ripens at that time. If we have the karma to be reborn as an animal, that is what will happen. Considering how difficult it is to create the causes of a human rebirth and how easy to create those to be reborn an animal, it's no wonder that there are so many more animals than humans.

*Even compared to other humans this life is rare*

If it is almost impossibly difficult to create the causes to be reborn human, it is much, much more difficult to create the causes to be reborn a human with the eight freedoms and ten richnesses. Just because we manage to find another human body does not mean we will be able to meet the Dharma or that, if we do, we will be able to understand or practice it.

Of the four continents, the northern, southern, eastern and western, only humans in the southern continent—ours—have the right conditions to meet and practice Dharma. We are currently living in the only continent, with the only type of body, where we can not only overcome suffering but attain enlightenment in one lifetime.

But even of the human beings of this southern continent, the people of our world, how many can practice Dharma? Human beings have the capacity to understand the Dharma but so few have the merit to even meet it. Most people don't have enough education or money to do much more than survive. Look at how few places in the world are free from drought and famine, how few are free from war and terrorism. Look at how few people are not dominated by gross ignorance.

We don't have to look much further than the people we know to see that having education, intelligence and even opportunity does not mean that a person will naturally want to meditate or will have the wisdom to distinguish between what is virtuous and should be practiced and what is nonvirtuous and should be abandoned.

Of those on any religious path, and of those who are Buddhists, how many have the opportunity to follow the entire path? Even in places like South-East Asia, where the people are devoted Buddhists, they still have little notion of what is needed to get beyond their present situation. They have devotion but no access to the lam-rim and no way of seeing that this is what is really needed.

Most people, however, don't follow any religion very much. Even those who say they are religious spend most of their time chasing sense pleasure in the same way that non-religious people do. Normally people have some sort of notion of improving themselves. Western people seem to have a sense that life should get better and better the more they work and the more things they acquire. If we ask them to look back to their childhood and assess whether from then until now they have acquired any calmness, humility and compassion or just more agitation, pride and anger, I think they would have to say by those criteria, their life has become worse. Developing worthwhile, positive qualities is the real definition of improvement. Forget about striving for enlightenment or liberation, it is very rare to find somebody just trying to become kinder. So of course, normal worldly people are not going to appreciate the perfect human rebirth. Thinking that because we are human we can relax and won't slip into the suffering realms is deceiving ourselves.

I hope you have already heard about bodhicitta and realized what an amazing mind it is and therefore developed the strong determination that everything you do will lead you to realize it. If you have, how wonderful! However, it is said that merely hearing the word "bodhicitta" requires an incredible amount of merit, let alone receiving teachings on how to actualize it. How few people in the world have this great fortune and how incredibly lucky we are that we do.

We need to realize how incredibly rare it is that we have met the Dharma and have access to the entire teachings of the Buddha, and how tragic it is that so few people, let alone other beings, also enjoy this amazing opportunity. Just this understanding should cause compassion to arise. This thing that is more precious than skies full of wish-granting jewels is there for everybody, yet so few can see it.

## THE BREVITY OF THIS LIFE

### So little of our life is spent practicing Dharma

We can die at any moment, but even if we were certain of living for a hundred years it would still be a tragedy to be complacent. We don't have long to practice Dharma, and if we don't make the most of this chance while there's still time, we will surely lose it. Even if we were to live for a hundred years, which few of us will, half of that is lost in sleep. Can we practice Dharma while we're asleep? Can we transform sleep into virtue? And of the remaining fifty years, over fifteen is lost in childhood, where we lack the wisdom to make our life meaningful. It is full of play and grabbing at whatever we think will make us happy. In the same way, as we finish our hundred years we can safely say that the last fifteen at least will be lost to old age, where our memory and health will have gone and all we'll be able to do will be to sit around waiting for people to feed and wash us. Studying the Dharma, meditating, thinking of others first and so forth will all be impossible.

Of the remaining twenty years of our life, how much is Dharma? So much time is spent eating and drinking, working for the essentials and luxuries of life and going to work and back. Then we waste more time gossiping, talking, quarreling and fighting. We get sick and can't practice Dharma, but even when we're not sick we still somehow can't find the time to practice Dharma. And so in our long, hundred-year life, if we really look at how much time we give ourselves to practice Dharma and make the most of this perfect human rebirth, we will find it is very, very little; maybe a year at the most.

Our life is very short and, moreover, we can never tell when it will end. I say a hundred, but few of us will make even eighty. Children and babies die; people just reaching adulthood die. Many people die from illness or accident in their middle age. The causes of death are many and the conditions for staying alive are few. When, in this fleeting moment we call life, do we have the time to practice Dharma?

I remember during the first lam-rim course that Lama Yeshe and I ever did in Australia,[67] there was one young man who was very keen to become a monk. Lama agreed to ordain him but asked him to return home to get his parents' permission. He had bought new robes and made all the preparations, but after he left we never saw him again. Something changed in his mind, obstacles to practicing Dharma came up and apparently he went to India and jumped off the roof of a building and killed himself. It looked like he had a life of Dharma ahead of him, but then something happened.

This is why understanding all these points about a perfect human rebirth is vital. We need to know how rare and difficult it is to obtain in order to see how urgent it is that we practice Dharma as conscientiously as we can while we have it. Seeing the qualities of the perfect human rebirth and the worthlessness of worldly life gives us the energy to renounce sense pleasure and to only ever do things that are full of meaning. As Lama Tsongkhapa said,

> Understanding that the precious freedom of this rebirth is found
>     only once,
> Is greatly meaningful and difficult to find again,
> Please bless me to generate the mind that unceasingly,
> Day and night, takes its essence.[68]

The more we understand the great value of the perfect human rebirth, the more energy we have to do only meaningful actions. We move from a mind that wants to be virtuous but finds virtue difficult to one that effortlessly and joyfully creates only virtue. Not only do we not dare to create nonvirtue, we have absolutely no wish to create nonvirtue. How wonderful it would be to spend every single moment of our life meaningfully. Then, even if death were to take us tomorrow, we could truly say we have made the most of this perfect human rebirth.

[67] In 1974, at Diamond Valley, ninety minutes north of Brisbane, Queensland. The first FPMT center in the West, Chenrezig Institute at nearby Eudlo, resulted from that course.
[68] V. 2. V. 3. From the *FPMT Prayer Book: Essential Buddhist Prayers, Volume 1*, p. 139.

*A flash of lightning and life is gone*

In the beautiful lam-rim prayer, *The Foundation of All Good Qualities*, Lama Tsongkhapa said,

> This life is as impermanent as a water bubble;
> Remember how quickly it decays and death comes.
> After death, just like a shadow follows the body,
> The results of black and white karma follow.[69]

These words have much taste. They are like medicine when we're sick, like a cool drink when we're thirsty. A water bubble is extremely insubstantial and lasts a very short time. Our worldly endeavors, all the things we strive and work tirelessly for, are no more substantial than a water bubble, and before we can enjoy them, just as a water bubble pops, our life is gone. In the sutra teaching called *The King of Concentration*, the Buddha said,

> The three worlds are impermanent like an autumn cloud. Look
> at the dance of the sentient beings, birth and then death. It is
> same—how the sentient being's life is here and then gone, like
> lightning in the sky.

Autumn clouds roll across the sky constantly changing with the wind, reforming and disappearing. This is our life. It never remains the same for one moment. The three realms of desire, form and formlessness are the same. There is nothing constant, nothing permanent in any of the three realms. An autumn cloud looks substantial but it is nothing but vapor, and in a second it is gone. This is our life.

We believe we are not going to die. Of course, logically, if we're asked if we're immortal we deny it, but we act as if we are. And then, when it happens, it is always a big surprise, as if somebody had cheated us in some way. In fact, as Lama Tsongkhapa says, life is as short as a flash of lightning, is extremely difficult to find and very easily decays. It arises suddenly and just as quickly is gone.

If our life lasted a long time and was always perfect and if we could be

---

[69] Ibid, v. 3.

assured of finding another good rebirth easily, we could relax and think about practicing Dharma sometime in the future, but that is not the case. Life is extremely short and starts to decay from the moment of birth.

Say we are a jewel thief looking for a priceless diamond but the night is pitch black. Suddenly there is a lightning flash and there on the road is that diamond. We only have a second to pick it up before it becomes too dark to see it again. Taking the essence of our life is like picking up that diamond, something we can only do in this lightning-short life we have.

We can also use the lightning analogy to explain emptiness in a very simple way. Imagine we are walking on a road, unable to see anything. When it's completely dark we don't label anything because we can't see anything. Then there is a flash of lightning. In the brief flash we see a tree and another person on the road. The two bases appear because of the sudden light and we label them "good," "bad," "ugly," this and that. Even during this short period attachment and aversion arise. As soon as there's the appearance of the base, we label it.

It is just like this in real life it. From birth until death we see objects and label them, assigning them to roles of "friend," "enemy" or "stranger," with no more evidence than a fleeting appearance. If we knew how little time we had left we would know how foolish such discrimination is. Following attachment and anger, we are blinded to what is really there. And then we die full of delusions, pushed and pulled by the attachment and anger that dominate our life.

We waste the precious time we have assigning positive and negative attributes to people and things that they don't in reality have, and so we set up patterns that feed our delusions and make our life miserable. Our "real" friends, our "real" enemies, the "real" places we love and hate, the "real" things we love and hate to do, when we die they will all disappear in a flash, the help and harm they gave us no longer there. Only the delusions we held onto concerning those objects remain as negative imprints on our mental consciousness to determine our next rebirth. So how pointless it is to cling to these delusion while we are alive. They seem so real now, while lit by the lightning flash, but they will be gone in an instant.

### Death can happen at any moment

Fear of death can be morbid or healthy. Being so terrified by the thought of death that we freeze is useless, but reflecting on how even now we are growing older and inexorably moving toward a death that might occur at any moment can inspire us to make the most of every second by practicing Dharma and renouncing any thought of worldly concern.[70]

This is not something that we don't need to worry about until we reach middle age. Life is impermanent and transitory. From the moment of conception we are moving toward death, minute by minute, second by second, split second by split second, forever moving closer to it. From the moment a flower blooms, it starts to wilt and die, yet we are still surprised when it happens. And so it is with our life. Like a river, it is changing every moment but we are never aware of that. However, because of the continuity, we experience what is impermanent as permanent. This is the nature of life. From the time of our conception to that of our death is like a snap of the fingers. We always believe that we will wake up tomorrow, and based on that we make plans for breakfast. But one day, due to some karmic condition, death will come and the door to the suffering realms will open.

We are constantly dying, yet we feel like we are permanently alive—until the moment that death stares us in the face and we are shocked. How did that happen? Then there is great suffering in our mind. We grieve for all the things to which we are attached and will never see again; we grieve for all the things we wanted to do but will now never be able to. The greater our attachment, the more we suffer, and as our death approaches we have more and more suffering visions. *Then* we realize just how short life has been.

You see, it's not sure. Every morning we get up with the feeling, "I am going to live for many years—thirty or forty years." Whatever we do we do with this instinctive feeling that we are going to live for a long time, long enough for it to feel permanent. Yet all around us are stories that tell us this is not the slightest bit true. How long we are going to live depends on the breath, which is nothing solid. It depends on how long it will continue to enter and exit our lungs, flowing in, flowing out, flowing in, flowing out. That is what our life is all about. When the time comes that we breathe out and don't breathe in, that will be it. The end of our life. And when that occurs is not up to us.

Everybody has to die. There has never been one being on this planet who has not had to die, who has cheated death. It all depends on the breath. While it functions, we live; when it ceases to function, we die. That's how fragile it is. Like a water bubble that can pop at any moment, this life can cease at any time.

[70] This subject is covered extensively in Rinpoche's book, *Wholesome Fear*.

Death is just there, sitting across from us, looking at us. It is not in another country waiting for us to get our visa and go there. It is not in another city. It is just a breath away. And when that breath stops, what is called hell can start.

Imagine you are lying on an operating table and you know you have very little chance of survival. To your right is a huge pile of diamonds, as high as a mountain. Which would you choose, the mountain of diamonds or your life? Of course, that is a silly question; you're going to choose your life. But that is the choice we face every day, although not on such a dramatic scale. We can choose between worldly concern and life, real life, yet so many of us go for worldly concern, worldly pleasure, unaware that it is costing us our life.

When we die, only our consciousness continues. Our body becomes a corpse; our possessions are useless. Like a hair pulled from butter, our consciousness leaves our body cleanly, without taking an atom of physical matter with it. Whatever material things have been a part of our life are now nonexistent for us. Only the mind with all its imprints remains. If those imprints are negative, we suffer; if they are positive, we're happy. It's as simple as that. Even a mountain of diamonds cannot benefit us at the moment of death, not that it can really benefit us at any time. It can't be the principal cause of happiness in this life, but attachment to it will definitely make us miserable in the next.

Therefore, nothing we do for this life can help us at the time of death. We lose everything we have worked for—body, possessions, relationships, position, reputation—and clinging to such things ensures terrible suffering at death and beyond. All we take with us is our mind, so the one beneficial thing we can do in this life is to make sure our mind is positive. That means practicing Dharma and only practicing Dharma. Every action we do must be Dharma, must be done with a mind of non-attachment, of love and compassion, of wisdom. In other words, we don't need to radically change our life, just our attitude to it.

Even if we just have five minutes left to live, what else is there to do? Go to the beach? Watch TV? Get drunk? Really, there is only one thing to do—practice Dharma. Meditate on renunciation, meditate on bodhicitta, meditate on emptiness. Those five minutes could make all the difference.

Denying death is futile and self-defeating. We will die. We get a phone call from somebody—a mutual friend has died. It is such a shock. We cry and call all our friends. They are shocked too. We never thought that she would die. It is all so unexpected. One day that person is going to be calling all our other friends with the same sad news, but not us, because we'll be the one who's dead. And all our friends will cry and be shocked and say it was so unexpected.

Then this body that we have looked after so well and for so long loses its label "body" and become "corpse" instead. Our friends will come to see our corpse, will cry some more and wonder why it had to happen, and will then go buy some flowers for our funeral. We will never see our body again; we will never see our loved ones again. All our possessions will now mean nothing. All that unfinished work—building a house, writing a book, traveling to other countries, getting promoted at work and so forth—will remain unfinished forever.

This is sure to happen. In the short time we have left we can cling to the mountain of diamonds or do something really worthwhile and die with a happy, contented mind. That shouldn't be such a hard choice to make.

Not preparing for our next life is very dangerous. These days most people have life insurance and go to their doctor for regular checkups. That is simple commonsense. When people trek in Nepal they take cases full of medicine to protect themselves against hepatitis and so forth. Rich people keep in their cabinets all sorts of expensive medicines against high blood pressure, high cholesterol and the like.

What we should all be preparing for, however, is the much more likely event of falling into the lower realms. So isn't it more skillful to practice Dharma ahead of time? Even in this life, practicing Dharma pacifies all our anger and dissatisfied, painful minds, making them weaker, if not destroying them, and consequently we feel more at peace and more in harmony with our surroundings.

Perhaps we see the concept of future lives as some exotic Asian trip, something that is untrue and irrelevant in modern Western society. We deny future lives simply because we can't see them. Yet we can say exactly the same thing about our life in a month's time. Say we're going to Greece on vacation next month. Surely, based on that reasoning—that the future doesn't exist because we can't see it—we shouldn't bother to make arrangements for the trip: buying flights, booking hotels and so forth.

To deny reincarnation is to assert that the Buddha and the great pandits who followed him are wrong. Even though with their clairvoyance they saw the whole process of birth, intermediate state and rebirth, they are mistaken or superstitious and teach such things just to frighten us into being good. If we think like this, and many people do, we are very deluded. Denying another person's experience just because it is not ours is very narrow thinking.

Being reborn or not being reborn does not depend on belief or what culture we come from—as if Tibetans reincarnate but Westerners don't. There may be no ironclad scientific evidence that the mind continues after death but there is also no evidence that it doesn't. Because it is not taught in schools, because people in Western culture don't think about it, does not negate it. Living our life assuming that rebirth doesn't exist is a huge mistake—that's like not booking a holiday or not paying next month's rent because next month doesn't exist.

We can't clearly see what will happen later in this life, yet we still prepare for it with life insurance, retirement plans and things like that. We are trying to avoid suffering in our later years. This is the same thing extended. By assuming that there will be a future life, we can see what we need to do to avoid suffering in that future life. Old age is not definite, the Greek holiday is not definite, but death is definite. As the Buddha said, "It's not sure which will come next, tomorrow or the next life." Instead of spending all our time making arrangements for what's not certain, we should be preparing for what is.

If we know that there is suffering coming, we should prepare for it. Once it arrives it's too late to avoid it; once we have fallen over the precipice and broken our leg we have no choice but to suffer. Before we reach the precipice we can stop and so avoid all that. Dharma is like a dam built before the flood—it helps the present as well as the future.

The decision to practice Dharma from this moment on is by far the most consequential we can make because it affects billions and billions of future lifetimes.

There was an American woman who wrote about the time she died and left her body, but because of some sense of unfinished business she was able to reenter it and resume her life. This made her realize that consciousness doesn't stop at death, that there is a future life. But what was interesting for me is that she also said that the incident showed her clearly that everything she had done from the time of her birth up to her "death" had been completely meaningless because none of it had been done for the happiness of the future life.

Like that woman, we should understand how meaningless the work for this life is and do everything to make this precious human body highly meaningful. Then, at the time of death our mind will be very happy—like going on a picnic, like going back home to visit our family. Perhaps, with such a positive mind, we will be reborn in a pure land where we will be able to attain enlightenment quickly, but even if we can't, we will certainly attain another perfect human rebirth and again have the opportunity to practice Dharma. But we need to prepare now. It is too late to realize at the moment of death that the only thing of benefit is the holy Dharma.

Now that we have this perfect human rebirth we have the chance to make every moment meaningful and because of that we have the chance to have a happy, peaceful mind at death and a good rebirth. Reflecting on death is not intended to scare us into depression but to wake us up to the need to put all our energy into turning our mind from nonvirtue to virtue.

We should meditate on death and impermanence constantly, reinforcing the truths that death is definite and can happen at any time. When we really start to see this, there is no way we will lose even one second of this precious life and there is no way we will ever want to create nonvirtuous actions again. If a delusion arises, we will see the danger and quickly avert it. Instead of short-term selfish ends, we will now be working for long-term goals that will bring us true happiness and enable us to profoundly help countless others.

# 7. Turning Away from Worldly Concern

EARLIER WE LOOKED at the quote from Lama Tsongkhapa's *Hymns of Experience* where he compared this life to a flash of lightning and all worldly activities to a husk.

In Asia, farmers winnow grain by putting it on bamboo mats and tossing it in the air. The grain gets separated from the worthless chaff, which is blown away by the wind. The grain is the thing of value, the food that will sustain them, whereas the chaff is of no value at all. In the same way, what we do with our life can be of great value, but the worldly affairs we get so wrapped up in are utterly meaningless.

## THE MEANINGLESS AFFAIRS OF THIS LIFE

Lama Tsongkhapa's words are the words of a highly realized being and have great power. They are medicine to cure the suffering of the mind, a breeze to cool the fever of the deluded mind. Not a single word is superfluous; each resonates with incredible richness. And so, just as we need to understand that death can happen at any moment in order to seize every moment and make it meaningful, we also need to look beyond the façade of this worldly life and see its meaninglessness. This is the husk we need to discard in order to extract the essence from this perfect human rebirth.

I often use the less poetic analogy of used toilet paper. This is how much meaning our worldly affairs have. And we should treat them exactly as we treat used toilet paper.

That is not the way most people see chasing worldly concern. When we see desire as positive, as something that will give us the happiness we crave, then talking about the perfect human rebirth and its causes and about the consequences of various karmic actions can seem very heavy. We just don't want to know. People who don't understand how the mind works feel that it is oneness with attachment, that somehow the mind and attachment cannot be separated and therefore renunciation is suppression of desire, something burdensome and unpleasant.

Thinking like that is totally misunderstanding both what attachment is and what the Buddhist path entails. It is not like that at all. Generating renunciation is lifting ourselves beyond suffering. People think that enjoying food and being attached to it is the same thing, and that therefore renunciation means that enjoying food is wrong; maybe even *eating* is wrong. When they are cold they crave warmth and therefore think that renunciation means always being cold, that wanting to be warm is wrong. In fact, they draw a pretty bleak picture of what being a Buddhist is all about.

I remember once when Lama Yeshe talked to professors and students at a Melbourne university on how attachment causes problems, there was a lot of surprise at his assertion. During the discussion period there were many questions—how can a person live without attachment, how can there be pleasure without desire, and so forth. The students were incredibly intelligent and had such enquiring minds. It was very interesting to see how they went from their usual perspective—the one that society takes as the norm—to actually starting to see the truth of Lama's argument.

In fact, Buddhism is not trying to make us more unhappy by telling us that whatever we enjoy is evil. Quite the opposite. The goal of Buddhism is to become truly, deeply happy, not this thing that we now call happiness by chasing sense pleasure. The simple fact is that attachment, or desire, or whatever we call it, is suffering. The object isn't suffering; having the object isn't suffering; enjoying the object isn't suffering; but attachment to the object is suffering. We expect an object to bring us happiness and want that happiness, so we become attached to that object. That attachment is a disturbed, agitated mind.

Happiness, by definition, is peace, so happiness and attachment are opposites. One cannot exist with the other. Happiness is the mind resting in contentment; attachment is the mind following disturbing thoughts. Attachment, quite simply, is dissatisfaction. In his *Lam-rim Chen-mo,* Lama Tsongkhapa said,

> Following desire hoping for complete satisfaction is the most painful suffering of samsara. No matter how much you follow desire, the result is always more suffering.[71]

We try something but it fails to satisfy us, so we try something else, but get the same result, dissatisfaction. On and on, chasing a satisfaction that is impossible to get. As Lama Tsongkhapa said, "As long as you follow desire, suffering has no end." The nature of samsaric life is like this. We buy a car but somehow the happiness it seemed to promise does not result, so in a year we think, "Oh, if only I can buy that bigger, newer car, *then* I'll be happy." And so on and so forth, without end. On the other hand, as soon as we stop chasing desire, we find satisfaction. The confused mind stops and so does the suffering.

As we have seen, there is no correlation between wealth and happiness. If there were, then the more money we had, the more possessions we had, the happier we would be. According to that, millionaires should always be a million times happier than poor people. Of course, that's not what we see.

If peace of mind increased and disturbing thoughts decreased as we became wealthier, then millionaires would all have realizations of renunciation, bodhicitta and emptiness and beggars wouldn't have any; if all this depended on education and intelligence rather than wealth, then highly-educated, intelligent people would be the ones with all the realizations whereas poorly educated ones would have none.

Without an understanding of the cause of happiness it is too easy to chase happiness in the wrong way. Not seeing that nonvirtuous actions lead to suffering, we harm ourselves and others. A bank robber is very clear in his thinking: he wants money, there it is, so he takes it. If he gets away with it, it looks as if his nonvirtue made him rich, but in fact his wealth results from previous virtue. Stealing can only ever result in suffering.

Similarly, we see a rich butcher and assume his wealth is due to his profession, killing, or that a businessman's great success is due to exploiting others. For ordinary people who do not understand karma, this seems so, but it is quite the opposite. In *The Thirty-seven Practices of the Bodhisattva*, Thogme Zangpo said,

---

[71] Volume 1, p. 282, the fault of insatiability (one of the six types of suffering).

Sensual pleasures are like salt water:
The more you indulge, the more thirst increases.
Abandon at once those things which breed
Clinging attachment—This is the practice of Bodhisattvas.[72]

Here this great bodhisattva clearly explains the shortcomings of following desire. All the energy we worldly beings expend in our daily life is to obtain pleasure. Our expectation is that everything we do will bring us satisfaction, but in fact that never happens. However hard we work to obtain temporal pleasure, that desire is never fulfilled. Since we can never find satisfaction by following attachment, the work we do looking for it will never cease. That is how we continually cycle in samsara, tied to searching for an unfindable satisfaction. In this, it's exactly like drinking salt water—the more we drink, the thirstier we get. We can never quench our thirst by drinking salt water. We follow attachment trying to quench our desire but all that happens is that our desire gets worse.

Mental peace, which is real happiness, comes from just the opposite. By decreasing attachment we decrease dissatisfaction and thereby increase peace and happiness; by decreasing selfishness, we open our hearts to others and, as a result, true happiness comes to us naturally and effortlessly.

Equating happiness with material possessions is mistaking the contributory conditions for the main cause. If we understand karma we'll see that acquiring things is not the route to happiness, creating virtue is. A new car is a condition, not a cause, for happiness, and if our motivation for acquiring a new car is nonvirtuous—for example, attachment—then we're creating the cause for misery, not happiness. Sooner or later that car will let us down because it never was the cause of happiness. But it will also not be the cause of unhappiness—it is our attachment that betrays us, promising us a happiness that does not exist.

If we examine our material possessions, and even our friends, we will detect a kind of veneer of attractiveness that gives them a false appearance of being good from their own side. Our dear friend appears to be permanently wonderful because of our attachment to her, but in reality she is not. Even to our deluded mind she changes—sometimes she's less wonderful, and sometimes, when she's done something that annoys us, quite unappealing. The special qualities of the objects of our desire are fantasies, creations of

[72] V. 21.

our attachment. As such, they have no power to give us happiness, whereas our attachment to them will certainly lead us to dissatisfaction and disappointment and, ultimately, rebirth in the lower realms.

Until we understand this, we will always chase external objects in the mistaken belief that they will make us happy. And, of course, that does not just mean material possessions. Power, reputation, good experiences, success in our career—all these things are false friends, promising what they can't deliver. None fulfill the meaning of human life. Even incredible concentration, unless it is used as a tool for becoming a better person, is an object of attachment that will let us down. We could have incredible clairvoyance gained from our unshakable concentration, we could see past and future lives and have the psychic power to fly, but this would still not be the meaning of life.

Mundane accomplishments are meaningless. We can have all these psychic powers, but how does that help others? We can go to the moon, we can be the first person on Venus, but it is hollow unless it serves some useful purpose, unless it is used in the service of others. Think of the world's top scientists—how much energy they have spent in training their minds, how much money has gone into their education, how much money is spent on their research. And yet, apart from a very few, most work only to increase the technology of this world or the understanding of chemicals, all of which can enhance the material things we have but none of which can add one tiny bit to the happiness we have.

If we are successful in our career and everybody praises us and wants to be our friend because of the power our success has brought, that is the result of previous good karma. As I mentioned before, the external conditions are contributory factors, not principal causes. Karma is everything. That is why some people with advanced degrees are still unable to get work or a profitable business with unique products can still fail. If the person has not created the karma to succeed it can never happen, no matter how brilliant or inventive he is.

We are so habituated to worrying about short-term self-interest alone that it is almost instinctive. As a result, we ignore our long-term interest, our enlightenment. If we are bitten by a snake, the very real fear of death arises and we are happy to accept the pain of an anti-venom injection in order to live; we are willing to put up with some immediate suffering in order to avoid much greater suffering in the future. Yet we are not prepared to put up with the difficulty of abandoning attachment to worldly pleasure—which is far worse than the most poisonous snake's bite and results in far more suffering—in order to experience real happiness in the future.

Desperate to have a little happiness and avoid a little suffering in the present, we opt for no happiness and incredible suffering in the future. This is completely ignorant, especially when, by practicing Dharma, not only do we assure future happiness, but even in the present we experience a happiness far beyond that which mundane things can give us.

We have seen that the meaning of Dharma is that which saves us from suffering. Conversely, any action done with one of the three poisons of attachment, anger or ignorance or the branch delusions such as jealousy, malice and so forth are deluded, disturbed minds that are themselves suffering and the cause for future suffering. That does not mean we must never eat again because we like eating.

Once we have a clear understanding of how mundane concern wastes our life, it is very good to constantly watch our motivation to see which of our actions done during the day are virtuous and which are nonvirtuous. Which have been done with a mind of ignorance, clinging to the happiness of this life alone, and which have been done with the thought of liberation or enlightenment? Perhaps that should be our last task every day, before getting into bed; we should review all the actions we did from the time we got up in the morning and determine whether they have been virtuous or nonvirtuous. Which were done with a motivation seeking only the happiness of this life? Drinking that first cup of tea, eating breakfast, driving to work, talking to colleagues, going shopping—which was not done out of self-interest?

I suspect, if we honestly appraise our day like that, we will be shocked. Most actions we do are driven by attachment and the wish for mundane happiness, an instinctive need for comfort and looking after our own interests. This subtle but pervasive attachment is what we need to confront and destroy. But it takes time.

## The eight worldly dharmas

It can be disheartening to look back on our life and see how much of this precious opportunity we've wasted. However, we should not be discouraged. Instead, we should take note of the incredible potential we still have and resolve to never, ever, from this moment on, waste another second.

How do we waste our life? By chasing mundane pleasure. This is explained in the teachings on the eight worldly dharmas, the eight objects of our attachment: four that we crave to have and four that we crave to avoid. Within these eight lies the whole of samsara. It is very useful to examine them and see how much they dominate our life.[73] They are:

- craving for material possessions
- craving to be free from lack of material possessions
- craving for happiness and comfort
- craving to be free from unhappiness and discomfort
- craving for a good reputation
- craving to free from a bad reputation
- craving for praise
- craving to be free from criticism

Spending this perfect human rebirth desiring only the eight worldly dharmas and working for the enjoyment of samsaric pleasures is like trading universes full of jewels for kaka. But because it can be used as manure or by insects, even this very dirty thing is much more useful than attachment.

We want to be free from the suffering that is samsara yet we work for samsara, ensuring that we have all the attachment and ignorance we need to keep us in it forever. We can't have samara and be free from it at the same time. Either an action is a virtuous one and leads away from suffering toward true happiness or it is a nonvirtuous one and leads us into more suffering, without one atom of true happiness. And as we have seen, working solely for this life keeps our mind under the control of attachment and is therefore non-virtuous; if we are controlled by attachment there is no way we can renounce samsara. When we look at what we are attached to, we will find it is one or more of these eight worldly dharmas.

The great yogi Padmasambhava[74] said,

No matter how much effort we put into samsaric work, there can never be an end, but there is an end to the effort we need to put into practicing the Dharma. Although there might be some

---

[73] See Rinpoche's *How to Practice Dharma: Teachings on the Eight Worldly Dharmas.*

[74] The eighth-century Indian tantric master mainly responsible for the establishment of Buddhism in Tibet, revered by all Tibetan Buddhists, especially by followers of the Nyingma tradition, which he founded.

benefits from samsaric work at the beginning, they never last.
The benefits of practicing the Dharma never finish.

These words of Padmasambhava are very true. In all our lives since beginningless time we have worked for samsaric pleasure and still the work has
not ended. We have bought an unlimited number of possessions to make
our life happy, yet we still need more. We have worked extremely hard to
make people respect us and to have a good reputation, but we still have to
keep working on it. We have set up our life to be as comfortable as possible,
but we can't sit back and enjoy it. We still have to work to maintain it. Samsaric work is beginningless and endless. If we follow the evil thought of the
worldly dharmas, our work will never finish. How could it when we're trying to feed an insatiable desire?

Instead, we should put effort into changing our attachment to non-
attachment, our self-interest to compassion for others. Although at the
beginning practicing Dharma requires effort, the more we progress the less
effort we need to exert and finally, when we reach enlightenment, the work
ends but the happiness lasts forever. It is completely opposite to worldly
work.

Samsaric work might bring a tiny amount of pleasure for a short period
of time, but that pleasure definitely ends and we then have to work for more
pleasure. That is the nature of samsaric happiness. We have a relationship
but it ends; we have a profitable business but it goes bust; we have a good
reputation but somebody slanders us. Whatever object of attachment we
have, it must end, leaving us dissatisfied. That's its job. The Dharma is not
like that at all. The happiness we get from practicing Dharma increases the
more we practice it and never finishes.

Worldly activities are meaningless. Every action done with the expectation of samsaric happiness is hollow, false, and has the power to cheat us.
We need to check to see how the eight worldly dharmas dominate us. Do
we crave praise? Do we hate criticism? How important are new possessions
to us? Is success at work a big factor in our life? We should check on each
of the eight worldly dharmas in this way to see what in our life needs to be
changed.

All the mood swings to which we're prone are the fault of the eight
worldly dharmas. We wake up happy but the slightest thing on the way to
work triggers a depression. Somebody doesn't smile at us or our car breaks
down. Needing to always have "good" things happen to us, we can't take

even the smallest unpleasant thing happening. That's our life—up and down, up and down, kicked from one extreme to the other by the thought of the eight worldly dharmas. Any work for samsara is like this. Even if it seems good at the beginning, even if we seem to be winning, like backing the fastest horse in a race or being on the winning football team, we always end up losing.

When we view samsaric life from a distance it looks very strange. With a few exceptions, almost everybody is doing the same thing with exactly the same motivation as the creatures that fly and walk and crawl—concern for only the comfort of this life. Look at the people shopping, the people driving their cars, up and down, back and forth, always busy, day and night, day and night. What is everybody doing? Why are they all working so hard? What is in all their hearts? It's all the same thing; they're trying to obtain the pleasures of this life. They are so busy! When His Holiness the Dalai Lama goes to a city most people there are far too busy to see him but never too busy to shop or drink in a bar.

When I'm on a plane I sometimes observe the other passengers. They're trapped there for many hours but still keep so busy. Each is in his or her own world, right there on the plane. They're sitting there eating or reading or doing work, yet their minds seem to be somewhere else, busy trying to secure whatever piece of samsaric happiness they think of as "mine." They all seem so wrapped up in the meaningless affairs of this life. None of them seem to have the slightest idea of the difference between virtue and nonvirtue. No matter how well-dressed they are, no matter what delicious food they eat, to me they seem to be very uncomfortable, like they have some skin disease they need to scratch but can't; they're like a goat on a very steep mountain, unable to take one step forward because of the danger of falling over the cliff.

The very sad thing is that this is exactly right. They are standing on a cliff, very close to slipping off. If samsaric happiness is so good, why aren't they calm and relaxed, why are they so twitchy? I feel quite sad watching them, like watching a friend crossing a dangerous bridge but being unable to help.

We need to see through the surface attraction of samsaric pleasure to the danger below; we need to see how it's like honey on a razorblade. I remember once being inspired by watching a film on space travel—but it didn't inspire me to travel in space; it inspired me to practice Dharma.

It is absolutely incredible how much effort went into getting people on the moon—so many years of endeavor, so much money, so many new scientific discoveries. And when those astronauts walked on the moon, it was as if something amazing had happened. Yet, when you think about it, they went there filled with the three poisons of ignorance, anger and attachment and came back filled with the three poisons, so what worthwhile thing happened while they were on the moon? All that research, all that money, all that effort did not provide a solution to eliminate even an atom of ignorance, anger and attachment. They didn't come back with wisdom, just a few rocks! If they had put even a fraction of that effort into something meaningful, like trying to develop compassion, they would have made fantastic progress, but they didn't. They wasted that precious opportunity.

There is nothing more harmful than the thought of the eight worldly dharmas. This is the thought that keeps us trapped in samsara. When we want to do something worthwhile, this is the thought that creeps in and distracts us, showing us a new sense pleasure that falsely promises us happiness, and somehow that worthwhile thing never gets done. This is the thought that distracts our mind when we try to meditate, that sends it off speculating on what awaits us at work or reminiscing about the nice holiday we just had. This is the thought that tells us we are too tired to read a Dharma book and should watch a little bit of television instead.

The need for comfort, possessions, friends, praise and reputation and freedom from discomfort, poverty, loneliness, blame and a bad reputation traps us. It locks us into endless work and never allows us to turn our mind toward Dharma. It makes us so busy that we never even have time to see how destructive our neediness is. The thought of the eight worldly dharmas is the greatest distraction to the practice of the holy Dharma. It is the thing that most wastes this perfect human rebirth.

The thought of the eight worldly dharmas is even more harmful than the wrong concept of the self-existent I. We can have this basic wrong view, seeing our self as inherently and independently existent, and still renounce nonvirtuous actions. Even with a false sense of I we can practice generosity and other virtuous actions that will ensure a good future rebirth. It's not until we attain enlightenment that we're completely free from the very subtle wrong view of the self-existent I, so that means that even with this wrong view we can attain liberation. However, with the thought of the eight worldly dharmas we can't even renounce samsara, so liberation and enlightenment are totally impossible. Enlightenment depends on having bodhicitta, the selfless aspiration to benefit all beings; the thought of the eight worldly dharmas the exact opposite—it seeks only the happiness of this life for ourselves alone. Bound to samsara with such a mind, even a good future rebirth is impossible.

Just as where there is water there can be no fire, where there is seeking the happiness of this life there can be no seeking liberation. To attain liberation and enlightenment, we need to create their causes, so as long as we are creating the causes to remain in samsara, it is impossible for us to attain those ultimate goals.

The thought of the eight worldly dharmas destroys even the positive things we do in this life. We might try to be generous, giving money to charity, for example, but behind the action lies our actual motivation for other people to think we are a good person—we crave a good reputation—so that potentially good action becomes nonvirtuous because of the sneaky negative motivation.

When we see how this need for *my* happiness now dominates our life and makes us harm others to get what we want, we can easily extend that to everybody else and see where all of society's problems come from. Here is the cause of all conflicts, all wars; here is where the environmental disasters come from—we place our own short-term needs before the long-term needs of others (and ourselves).

## No better than animals

If we squander the promise of our human existence by following the thought of the eight worldly dharmas, we're no better than animals: stupid, self-serving and unable to avoid suffering. Animals cannot rise above their suffering; we can. Therefore, to be too lazy to do anything about it is shocking. There is nothing more ignorant than this.

In fact, there is nothing "higher" in anything we normally do. We work solely to obtain mundane pleasure and to avoid mundane suffering. So do animals, so there is no difference. If we observe nature, we will see that this is so. Everything that every fish, bird, animal or insect does is solely to obtain the happiness of this life and to avoid suffering. Are we any different from the fish swimming in a river or the bird building its nest? We might have more possessions, we might be more sophisticated, we might think ourselves superior, but in reality there is no difference at all between us and the creatures that crawl on the ground or the bugs that get into our clothes.

We see TV programs that glorify the achievements of the human race. We see how man invented flight, but birds are still more skilled at flying than we are, so where is the difference? Just as an animal takes what it wants from something weaker, so do we. Just as an animal fights to keep its home, so do we. Many animals kill, but so do many of us, and not just to eat.

Animals are more skilled at taking what they need to survive and defending themselves than humans. We think we are so good at getting what we want, but a tiger is a much better hunter. She looks very cute when she is not hunting, yet when we see her killing a deer she looks so ferocious. Deer appear to be very defenseless when they are grazing in the long grass in India but they can be very skilled at defending themselves. Watch how they alert each other when there is a tiger about and how skilled they are at running and dodging, suddenly changing direction just as the tiger is about to pounce. And they can also be quite sneaky. I remember some deer that would always steal the food from a bird feeder at a neighbor's place near our retreat center in Washington. The mother deer had taught her young to jump the fence and reach up to the feeder to steal the food.

Beings everywhere are searching for the comfort of this life, doing actions motivated by greed, ignorance and hatred. How many of us can say that we are free from those three poisons? Whether we are in our office, flying in a plane, sunbathing on the beach, what is the difference between the fish in the sea, the bird in the sky or the worm on the ground? The shape is different, but other than that we are essentially the same.

If we are in the army, we might pride ourselves on our discipline, but really ants have far more discipline than the best trained soldier. Ants are incredible. They have a tiny body but ferocious bravery. I once saw a fight between an army of red ants and an army of black ants on TV. It was a real war. If it had been filmed close up I'm sure it would have been more exciting than a football match. Perhaps we pride ourselves on our bravery, but ants will attack even an elephant if it threatens their home. However, bravery is not the meaning of life. There have been many brave people who have also been very cruel. Hitler's soldiers may have been brave but they killed millions of people.

Perhaps we think we have wonderful perseverance and can do the most demanding job well, but that is nothing compared to the perseverance of the insects and squirrels who collect food all summer so they can survive the winter. Perhaps we think we can steal better than animals, but there are plenty of animals who are expert thieves. Animals can even beat us at sexual misconduct. We have an incredible ability to generate ill will, but even the lowest insect is capable of that; there are animals whose miserliness is so great, who are so skilled at collecting and hording food, that even the most miserly person seems generous.

There are many stories about mice in Tibet. For monastic ceremonies the monks would make elaborate, beautifully decorated tormas from tsampa and butter and put them on the altar as an offering. Even though they did everything possible to keep the mice away, the mice were more clever. They would sneak in from behind and nibble away at the back of the torma when nobody was there, so from the front the torma looked perfect but in fact, half the back was eaten away. Humans pride themselves on their cunning but animals are just as smart. They are expert cheats and even have their own politicians.

Kadampa Geshe Langri Tangpa was nicknamed "Gloomy Face" because his main practice was contemplating the suffering of others. It is said that he laughed only three times in his life. One of those times was when he was meditating in his cave and saw a mouse taking grains of rice from his mandala set. When the mouse got to a big piece of turquoise that was in there and could not lift it, he went and got some other mice to help. One mouse lay on his back, the others put the turquoise on his stomach and then they dragged him by his legs to their mouse hole. When they got there they found that the turquoise was too big to go through, so they just had to leave it. This is what made the geshe laugh.

Mice are very clever at working for the happiness of this life. They are experts at stealing even though they never went to school. No matter how many stories a building is, if there is food somewhere, the mice will know how to climb up and steal it. They are also really good at cheating other sentient beings. And if somebody harms them, they know how to take revenge.

I'm not sure if this was revenge or not, but once a mouse ate my zen, the shawl a monk wears over his shoulder. There had been some mouse problems—stolen food and mouse droppings—at Kopan and some of the other monks had tried to get rid of them. After a lot of disturbance the monks thought the mice were gone. At that time I had a special zen made for me by Mummy Max, one of our earliest students. Lama Yeshe and I were going to go to Japan where it was very hot, so Max made me this zen of very lightweight material. She folded it neatly and put it in my cupboard for the trip. However, when I took the zen out a few days later I found that a mouse had been eating it. There seemed to be just one small hole, but when we opened out the folded zen it made a pattern of about four or five holes. We had harmed the mouse, so in return he harmed my object of attachment.

In Tibet, there are mice that know how to collect a tiny sweet plant, like a raisin, which they store in one place. They are very ingenious. Unfortunately, people can tell where these stores are by the softness of the ground and dig them up.

All the honey we love comes from the hard work of the bees. We just wait until they have finished and then we steal it. They collect for the happiness of this life and we steal for the happiness of this life.

When I was a small child I had two teachers who taught me the Tibetan alphabet. I had to spend the whole time from early morning to night learning to read texts. The only real break I got was to make pipi, but sometimes my teacher would give me a free hour as well. Our house was very simple and there were a lot of spiders living inside, so instead of reading the texts I would often watch the spiders. I was amazed at how skillful they were at catching flies. They didn't wait in the middle of the web but at the edge, in a crack in the wall or something, and they'd stay there until the fly was completely trapped. Then they would run out and eat the fly, but always from the bottom up, leaving the head and wings, which they would then throw away, like dropping something from an airplane. Sometimes I would tease them by dropping something onto the web to watch them run out, but as soon as they saw it wasn't food they would run back to safety.

We have become so sophisticated that we don't have to kill to get our food. We get somebody else to do it for us while we work at meaningless jobs to get the money to buy it. But even there animals can claim equality. There are many animals that work for their food rather than kill it directly. Farm and transport animals do this; so do those in circuses and zoos. Just as some humans have to tell jokes to earn a living, elephants and donkeys in a circus do tricks to make people laugh. Tigers, usually so fierce, stand on chairs and jump through hoops. Dolphins carry surfboards and wave goodbye with their tails. So it's not just humans who make fools of themselves.

Unless we can find a higher meaning in life, we are in no way different from animals and in many ways inferior. We have the name "human" and a different shape, but we are no higher than the lowest animal. We have rational thought and with that the ability to understand the distinction between virtue and nonvirtue, but if we then spend our life chasing worldly pleasure alone, we forfeit the right to call ourselves human.

However, there is one way we should emulate the animals. It is not their bravery or cleverness we should copy; not their ability to defend territory or take revenge. It is this. A dog will grab its food and gobble it down right away, afraid of losing it or never finding food again. If the dog were sure that it could always get plenty of food it could relax, but its fear of losing something very precious causes it great worry. In the same way, we should see this perfect human rebirth as something extremely precious, something to be closely guarded. We should grab this unique chance to practice Dharma while we have it, never let it go, and never be satisfied with just a little bite but always want more and more.

## Our past, present and future lives are squandered

Wasting this very precious human rebirth is many millions of times worse than losing universes full of precious jewels in three ways:

- ▸ it wastes the past work we have done
- ▸ it wastes all our future rebirths
- ▸ it wastes our present potential

We have expended so much effort over countless lives practicing morality and generosity in order to get this perfect human rebirth, and unless we utilize the potential we created with such difficulty while we are here in this human form, it will all have been for nothing. Not only that, but wasting this perfect human rebirth also destroys the possibility of better future lives. Like having a winning lottery ticket and not bothering to cash it in, we waste all this amazing potential and ensure untold suffering for ourselves in future lives. Finally, it wastes this present moment. Rather than using every moment to its full potential, we utterly squander it. This perfect human rebirth is like high-yielding soil, and wasting the possibilities it offers is like planting infertile seeds—there's no return on our efforts.

Let's say a father works extremely hard to buy a gold ring for his son, saving every cent he can from his wages over a long, long time, going without for many years. Then, when he gives his son the ring, the ungrateful child just throws it down the toilet. How would that father feel? Of course, this example just shows the waste of the past effort and present potential; in addition, squandering our perfect human rebirth also wastes countless future possibilities.

Seeing how we waste our life in these three ways—past, future and present—is very helpful because it shows what a great mistake it is to do so. Wasting this moment is bad enough, but squandering all the work we did to get here makes it worse, and then, ensuring incredible future suffering by wasting this life makes it incredibly tragic. How could we even think of doing something so stupid?

If we could only realize what a huge effort we must have made to create this perfect human rebirth, we would see clearly how childish it is to take this life for granted. The cause for this perfect human rebirth, with its eight freedoms and ten richnesses, was created in many of our previous lives through dedicated practice of morality and generosity coupled with stainless prayers to bring about the exact result we're experiencing right now. This is not the time to simply relax.

We should check our attitude toward this precious gift. If we see that we have just passively accepted this human rebirth, we will certainly see that we are wasting it. Are we living in morality as perfectly as we had in the past to ensure that this rebirth happened? Are we practicing generosity as well as we must have back then in order to create the causes for the life we now have? Are we still making the pure prayers we need to be making in order to receive such a life again? To answer these questions we need to examine our mind very carefully to see what state it's in.

We *have* received a perfect human rebirth and we should recognize this. It is something that we should constantly feel and always rejoice in. Otherwise we will fail to create the causes of happiness and will create the causes of suffering instead.

We all want happiness. We feel very happy to be offered a cup of coffee or an ice cream or to make a dollar in profit; we think that this is such a fantastic thing. Because we fail to see what is truly important, we can understand the pleasure of a cup of coffee, an ice cream or a dollar's profit but we can't see the importance of creating the causes of a future perfect human rebirth.

Only when we are able to renounce our attachment to sense pleasure will we have the attitude that we find in the wonderful verse of the *Guru Puja* that says,

> Having abandoned the mind that views this unbearable prison
> Of cyclic existence as a pleasure grove, I seek your blessings
> To partake of the treasure of the aryas' jewels by practicing the
>     three higher trainings
> And, thereby, to uphold liberation's banner.[75]

---

[75] *Lama Chöpa*, v. 88. The three higher trainings are morality, concentration and wisdom.

With renunciation, what worldly beings see as pleasure, we see as the center of an intense fire, as a nest of poisonous snakes, as sitting on the tip of a needle or being wrapped in barbed wire. To continue living in the hallucination is to totally waste all the previous hard work we did in getting here. And by wasting the present we set up the only possible result—instead of a good rebirth we get incredible suffering in the lower realms. Of this, the great pandit Chandrakirti said,

> If you have the possibility and freedom to achieve enlightenment
> But do not follow the methods,
> When you fall over the precipice into the lower realms
> And are under the control of others, who will lift you back up?

At present we are not in the lower realms, where we would be unable to help ourselves. We have the perfect guides to show us the path and all the right the conditions to put their guidance into practice. If we don't avail ourselves of this rare and incredible opportunity and do end up in the lower realms, nobody will be able to help us, not even ourselves. Therefore, before that terrible thing happens we need to do everything possible to avert it. We are the beggar who has found the jewel; now we must use it to ensure our future happiness.

### The greatest folly

In his *Guide to the Bodhisattva's Way of Life*, Shantideva said,

> After having found this freedom,
> If I do not train my mind in virtue,
> There is nothing more deceptive,
> There is no greater folly than this.[76]

There is nothing more ignorant than having this perfect human rebirth and wasting it. It is the greatest deception, the greatest folly. Just as an animal is always trapped in its own ignorance, if we squander this chance for happiness we lock ourselves in the very same prison of ignorance and deception. If we continue to act exactly as animals do and create only nonvirtue when we have the choice to forestall all suffering, that is surely the greatest folly of all. In *Friendly Letter*, Nagarjuna said,

[76] Ch. 4, v. 23.

> Even more foolish than someone who uses
> A golden vessel adorned with gems to collect vomit
> Is someone who, having been born human,
> Performs negative deeds.[77]

Here he is saying that the foolishness of using an exquisite golden urn covered in jewels as a receptacle for vomit is nothing compared with using this precious human body, which we receive only once, to create negative karma.

Among the mistakes we make in our daily life, this is the most foolish. The worst mistake we can make, the one that leads us to rebirth in the lower realms, is to create negative karma when we can so easily avoid it. To not make the best use of this perfect human rebirth is to be like a businessman who risks his life traveling to a distant country, finds himself on an island where there are jewels everywhere and then leaves empty-handed. There are jewels everywhere—on the ground, in the trees, in the water—all there for the taking. He can fill his ship with the most precious jewels imaginable, take them all home and become the richest person in the world. But instead, he doesn't pick up a single jewel, turns around and returns home leaving them all there.

If that seems crazy, it is not nearly as crazy as what we are doing. We have this perfect human rebirth and are not taking advantage of it. And we are not just failing to take advantage of this golden opportunity; what we are doing is worse. We are not just going home empty-handed; we are using this incredible opportunity to create negative karma and ensure ourselves eons of unbearable suffering in the lower realms.

Surely we've created many more causes to be born as a crocodile or a turtle than to be born as a human with the eight freedoms and ten richnesses. Looking at the karma we create every day, perhaps we should be learning ant or cockroach language to prepare for our next life. We have something so precious, this amazing body and mind with all their qualities, and are using it as toilet paper.

Having the chance to practice Dharma and not taking it is just like seeing a big hole in the ground that leads straight to the fiery pits of hell and jumping in without hesitation. If we saw a person who, for no apparent reason, fell into a deep hole, we would naturally wonder why. Was she drunk? Was she badly handicapped in some way? Was it spirit harm? We would never

---

[77] V. 60.

think that she did it on purpose. If intentionally jumping into a hole that leads straight to hell is unfathomable, how hard must it be to understand what we are doing: ignoring the opportunities that this perfect human rebirth has given us?

Perhaps people laugh and call us stupid because we have never learned to drive or are hopeless at business. Worldly people see this as foolish and ignorant, but Shantideva says the greatest deception, the greatest folly, is having this incredible opportunity and not using it. He then goes on to say,

> If once I have realized this
> I ignorantly continue to be lazy,
> When death occurs
> I will experience terrible suffering.[78]

One day, and we have no idea when, death will come. If we do not prepare for it now, while we have the freedom to do so, we will die with great anguish and experience unimaginable suffering. At that moment we will have no time to practice Dharma. Then, no matter how repentant we feel, no matter how much we regret having wasted this incredibly precious time, nothing will stop us from falling into the terrible suffering of the lower realms. Only now, only while we have this perfect human rebirth, can we avert rebirth in the lower realms and ensure ourselves of a happy rebirth.

## TAKING THE ESSENCE

### Turning away from worldly concern

As human beings we have a great many advantages that other beings don't, and as human beings with the eight freedoms and ten richnesses we have a great many advantages that the vast majority of other humans don't. We are extremely privileged. That is why we must never waste one second by following the thought of the eight worldly dharmas.

The value of all the material wealth on earth is nothing compared with that of this perfect human rebirth. All the goods that fill all the department stores in the world, all the money in the banks, all the jewels and gold are just so much garbage compared with the perfect human rebirth; completely worthless. Worldly people use their human rebirth to become slaves to their

---

[78] Ch. 4, v. 24.

possessions, to the thought of the eight worldly dharmas, whereas in every second, a person practicing Dharma generates wealth greater than that of diamonds equal in number to the atoms of the earth.

We have to sacrifice many of our samsaric pleasures to follow the spiritual life. Others will see this as turning our back on fun. Even if that is so, even if we do have to endure hardships for the sake of the Dharma, it is incredibly worthwhile. And it is still nothing compared to the hardships that worldly beings endure for the sake of their samsaric pleasures. They work their entire lives—forty, fifty, sixty years—for samsaric pleasures that don't last even a few years. Any hardship a Dharma practitioner undergoes is not for just happiness in this life but for everlasting happiness; for the happiness of the next life, the one after that and so on, forever.

As long as we believe the myth that samsaric pleasure is the only happiness, we will always have problems practicing Dharma. It takes great determination to turn away from samsaric life, and that is where a thorough understanding of the lam-rim is essential.

It all depends on our motivation. I cannot emphasize enough the importance of motivation. The imprints that we accumulate on our mindstream every second come not from the actions we do but from the mind behind them, the motivation that impelled that action. Therefore, at the beginning of each day we should generate the strong motivation that we are going to spend the entire day doing only virtuous actions; in particular, we are going to do everything with bodhicitta, with the determination to attain enlightenment for the sake of all sentient beings. This will set us up and make our day highly meaningful. And then, if possible, we should check before we start each action whether or not we still have the same motivation. This, in fact, is how we make that crucial choice between virtue and nonvirtue. Pabongka Dechen Nyingpo quotes Lama Tsongkhapa as saying,

> If you see the great meaning of this perfect human rebirth and realize how difficult it is to find, there is no way you can live without practicing Dharma. To waste even a moment of it feels to be a great loss. By reflecting on death you prepare for the journey to your next lives; by reflecting on karma you change from being careless to being careful in everything you do.[79]

---

[79] *Liberation* p. 287.

Similarly, Geshe Potowa:

> When we understand the freedoms and richnesses we have with
> this perfect human rebirth and how difficult it is to find this life
> again, there is no way we can feel any comfort unless we are prac-
> ticing Dharma.[80]

There are many stories that exemplify this need to only practice Dharma
and be unconcerned with worldly life. Pabongka Dechen Nyingpo also says
that Kadampa Geshe Gönpawa was so focused on his meditation practice
that once, when he went out of his meditation hut, a sharp thorn from his
incense plant lodged in his flesh. Instead of bothering to pull it out, he simply continued with his practice.[81]

There was one old meditator who had a thorn bush growing next to his
cave. Every time he went outside for pipi it tore his robe. Gradually his robe
got more and more ragged but, thinking that death might come at any
moment, he couldn't see the point of losing meditation time by cutting the
bush. With a mind like that, realizations of impermanence and death and
the perfect human rebirth come very easily.

In *Friendly Letter*, Nagarjuna said,

> Even if your head or clothes suddenly catch fire,
> Don't bother trying to put it out.
> It's far more worthwhile trying to extinguish further uncontrolled
>     rebirths.
> There's nothing more urgent than this.[82]

If our clothes or hair suddenly caught fire, our instinct would be to immediately do whatever was necessary to extinguish the fire. Nothing would be
more urgent. But here Nagarjuna is saying that it is far more important to
extinguish future rebirths taken under the compulsion of karma and delusion. Having our hair and head burnt is nothing compared to the fire of
the hell realms that we are bound to experience if we don't do something
about it.

Therefore we need to distinguish clearly between what is a worldly action

---

[80] Ibid.
[81] Ibid.
[82] V. 104.

and what is a Dharma action and determine to renounce the former and do only the latter. We should see that "practicing Dharma" means much more than reciting prayers or sitting in the meditation posture, that it is our attitude in everything we do. Eating can be a worldly activity or a Dharma activity depending on our motivation. So too can listening to music. And seemingly "good" actions—doing pujas, helping neighbors—can be worldly activities if they're done with a worldly motivation. Actually, any activity done with awareness and a positive motivation is meditation, whether we call it meditation or not. The term for meditation in Tibetan is *gom*, which means to habituate the mind, and, of course, that means habituating the mind to virtue.

In *The Adornment of the Mahayana Sutras*, Maitreya defines meditation as making the mind familiar with the object. This is the training we so desperately need. By acting with love and generosity, for example, we habituate our mind to love and generosity and those traits become stronger and stronger in our mindstream. Whether in formal meditation or in our daily actions, by always motivating with bodhicitta we become familiar with and habituated to bodhicitta. Then, slowly, as this great quality deepens within us, we go from a conceptual, wishing state of mind to a genuine realization, where our mind is one with bodhicitta. But even at the stage we're at right now, where our mind is still quite clouded, if we always act with pure motivation, all our actions will become pure Dharma actions.

This is how we can make every moment of our perfect human rebirth meaningful. Even the simple act of breathing can be meaningful. Every in-breath can be a step toward enlightenment; every out-breath can be a step toward enlightenment. There is no ulterior motive in breathing; we breathe to stay alive. In doing so, we harm nobody, but when we breathe with awareness and a mind imbued with the wish for enlightenment, we create the perfect peace of awakening with each breath.

Establishing a strong motivation in the morning is the crucial factor. This is what lends power and purity to the whole day. His Holiness the Dalai Lama often says that we should take the essence all day and night. This means creating a strong motivation in the morning through meditating on a subject like guru devotion or death and impermanence, followed by generating strong compassion based on that meditation. Then, for the rest of the day and evening, everything we do is suffused with that feeling of compassion and we receive the benefits of the meditation throughout the entire day.

Say our meditation has been on impermanence. Every situation we meet that day has that flavor. We see through the deceptive appearance of permanence and understand that no matter what we encounter—an object, an experience, an emotion—it is not permanent in any way; it is not the permanent cause of permanent happiness or suffering, but transient and constantly changing. It's the same with other lam-rim topics. And when we combine this understanding with bodhicitta motivation, every action becomes so powerful.

If extracting the essence from our perfect human rebirth means practicing Dharma, then striving to attain bodhicitta and enlightenment is the heart of the essence. This is something we should do "all day and night." There is not one second to waste; and with bodhicitta, every second becomes infinitely valuable.

We face situations that require a choice a thousand times a day. Before, we would have had to choose between the better of two samsaric situations or between profit and loss at work, but now the choice is so simple. Do we choose to do something beneficial or something destructive? Do we take the essence of our precious life or waste it? Do we choose between what will benefit ourselves and others and ensure we make the most of this perfect human rebirth and have truly worthwhile rebirths from now on, or do we follow self-interest and ensure suffering for ourselves and others and the certainty of rebirth in the lower realms? We have the freedom to choose between enlightenment or hell every second of the day, in even the smallest, most insignificant actions. The choice between profit and loss—real profit and loss—is completely in our hands.

Perhaps, if we knew we had a long time ahead of us, we could take our time. "I know I need to train in the Dharma but there are a few things I need to sort out first, and then I need to take a nice long holiday before I can start thinking about studying and meditating. I do have this wonderful opportunity now but it's not going anywhere and later—perhaps when I retire—I'll be able devote more time to it."

Of course it is not like that. I don't mind repeating a million times what Lama Tsongkhapa said, that this perfect human rebirth is difficult to find, doesn't last long and can finish at any moment. Thinking we can start our Dharma practice tomorrow is very dangerous, because tomorrow, when we wake up, there will definitely be some other urgent matter to attend to before we can start meditating. And the day after tomorrow there will be another one. And then we are sixty, seventy, eighty, and when people ask us what we regret about our life we will say that we regret that we never quite got around to practicing Dharma.

### Only with a precious human body can we travel the whole path

Only a human being can practice Dharma because only humans can differentiate between virtue and nonvirtue. Beings in other realms might live for eons, but they do not have the capacity to make this distinction. Humans, on the other hand, can understand the definition of virtue within a few seconds of hearing it. This gives them a unique and wonderful freedom to choose happiness over suffering.

This potential is the internal condition needed to attain enlightenment. The external condition is the existence of the entire Buddhadharma and the vows that we as human beings can receive, and that is all due to the kindness of our spiritual friend, our guru.

The ultimate guru is our own inner wisdom, but we can reach our inner guru only through an external guru, a teacher who can introduce us to the Dharma and guide us skillfully in accordance with our own propensities. The guru might appear in different forms in different lives, or even in this life, but the essence of the guru is always the same.

It is only through the guru that we can meet the entire Buddhadharma, especially the advanced Vajrayana teachings and practices. It is only through the guru that we can take the vows necessary to practice perfect morality. We have received the perfect human rebirth we now enjoy through the kindness of the guru. This is why the very first topic in the lam-rim is on developing the correct attitude toward our guru and why proper guru devotion is called the root of the path.

With our guru's guidance the whole path is laid out before us. Whatever we wish to achieve, the unmistaken method is there. This is not something that we might be able to do at some time in the future; this is something that we can definitely do this hour, this minute, this second. Every action we do from now on can be the cause for enlightenment. That is what makes this perfect human rebirth so highly meaningful. The entire path to enlightenment is laid out before us and we have the ability to follow it to its very end. We need refuge, equanimity, compassion and wisdom. All the tools are there ready for us to use and we can acquire not just a small amount of these precious qualities, but a vast amount. They can fill our mind.

Just reciting the refuge and bodhicitta prayer with the motivation to attain enlightenment for the sake of all sentient beings creates infinite merit.

Just saying the prayer of the four immeasurable thoughts rids our mind of any partiality. Four short lines and we have created the cause for complete enlightenment. With such practices, we can easily generate compassion in our mind and from that, great compassion and the precious mind of bodhicitta can grow in a short time. With bodhicitta, enlightenment is easy.

This is the potential that we, as human beings with a perfect human rebirth, have. That is our goal; that is the project we need to undertake. Whether we are at work, at home relaxing, on holiday, with friends—whenever—day and night, that is the main thing.

Just as success in worldly projects requires constant effort and determination, success in our enlightenment project requires continuous meditation on all the lam-rim topics. Wherever we are, whatever we are doing, we are faced with a Dharma teaching if we have the wisdom to use every situation in that way. By always being aware of what is happening, and constantly watching the actions of our body, speech and mind, we can turn our life around so that every moment becomes a Dharma moment, a moment that takes us one step closer to enlightenment.

Otherwise it's like trying to climb an ice mountain without equipment, painfully moving up a few paces on our hands and knees, trying to get hold of the slippery ice with our bare fingers, and then slipping back to start again. Despite the hard effort, there is nothing to cling to and we always end up back at the bottom. Our Dharma practice can be like this too. We try to establish a good motivation for our meditation session, do it properly, but then slide back when we step out into the outside world.

We have the potential to attain full enlightenment. The only thing stopping us is our lack of determination. But if we can truly see how precious this opportunity is, we can use every situation as a step on the path to enlightenment and always offer perfect service to others. When our mind is suffused with bodhicitta, every action has great meaning. Only the Mahayana can take us to this level of mind, and only as a human being in this world system at this time do we have access to the Mahayana.

Therefore, we are incredibly fortunate to have this method freely available, great masters who can explain it to us skillfully and the potential and determination to benefit from this wonderful gift.

# 8. This Precious Life

## The preciousness of this life

I N THE VERSES from Lama Tsongkhapa's *Hymns of Experience* that I mentioned before, he says that our body qualified by the freedoms and richnesses is more precious than a wish-granting jewel. We need to recognize this crucial fact. A beggar rummaging through the garbage looking for something to eat might find a huge diamond and, because it's inedible, throw it away, unaware that if she sold it she could live in luxury for the rest of her life.

Imagine if, when we were a child, our father had given us a bag of diamonds to save us from any difficulties in our life, but, being a child and not understanding what it was, we threw it into a river. Now, as an adult, we realize what we did. How terrible we would feel. That's how we should feel whenever we realize that we have wasted a moment of this perfect human rebirth. If we could really understand how precious our life is we would never think about wasting even a second, and the thought of using it for even a moment's nonvirtue would feel a greater loss than having thrown that bag of diamonds into the river.

We need to see the value of this body; we need to see that there are higher goals than temporary pleasure. We think that a beggar who throws a huge diamond away is incredibly foolish, but we are just as foolish if we don't recognize and seize the chance that we now have.

### More precious than a wish-granting jewel

Life is very, very precious. There is nothing in the world that is as precious as life, especially a life enriched with the eight freedoms and ten richnesses.

We greatly treasure our possessions and our money but scarcely think about the real treasure, taking it for granted and even abusing it.

Imagine winning the lottery, with the hundreds of millions of dollars that is the main prize these days. Of course, we would be insanely happy. It would seem as if the most unbelievable thing that could possibly happen in our life had happened. People dream about this all the time; they buy tickets every week, hoping and praying that they will be the ones to win. Yet one second of this perfect human body is infinitely more valuable than all the lotteries in all the countries in the world.

Think of all your possessions: your house, car, television, computer, clothes, jewels, money and so forth—everything you have now and have ever had. Think how precious all that is to you. Think how upset you would be if you lost all your possessions or all your money was stolen. Yet all of these material possessions are nothing compared to the most precious possession of all, the human body with its potential for real happiness. Wasting that most precious possession is infinitely worse than losing all your worldly possessions.

Think of all the incredibly rich people in your country, the millionaires and billionaires, and all the things they have, the mansions and the yachts and the jewels that you could never even dream about. Think of all the rich people in all the other countries too, each as wealthy as a small country. Imagine all that money and all those possessions piled up, great mountains of riches—every jewel in the world, every piece of gold, every precious thing making huge mountains of wealth. All that is nothing compared to this body.

All the wealth now and that ever has been in this world plus all the wealth of the god realms is nothing. It is impossible to describe the god realms' wealth. As we have seen, one earring of one god is more valuable than all the wealth of the human world put together. Yet that too is nothing compared to this precious human rebirth.

There is one thing that is considered even more valuable than the treasures of the god realms and that is the wish-granting jewel, a jewel that has the power to grant any wish.

In previous times, on auspicious days such as full moon days, bodhisattvas who had created great merit were able to go to the bottom of the ocean to get these most precious jewels. These wish-granting jewels were covered in mud, so they had to be cleaned three times, the final time with very fine cotton, to completely remove the mud. When one of these jewels was placed on a banner on top of a house on a full-moon night, any material wishes the people had—for money, a long, healthy life and so forth—were granted immediately.

But even though a wish-granting jewel can grant wishes in this way, it has no power to save somebody from the lower realms. The material thing itself is the external condition but whether we can benefit from it or not depends entirely on our karma. A match can burn, but whether it burns wood in a fire and makes us warm or burns down our house and brings us misery depends on our karma. An atomic reaction can create electricity and help many people or detonate a bomb and kill hundreds of thousands of people. The material element may be there but the result depends on the mind.

Even if we had a wish-granting jewel, what good would it do? Nagas are animal realm beings who are often incredibly wealthy. It is said that in previous lives many of them practiced great generosity but not morality, so that is why they have ended up with great wealth but in the animal realm. The richest have storehouses filled with such jewels yet they have no opportunity to practice Dharma or escape the suffering of the animal realm.

If one wish-granting jewel is worth far more than all the wealth of all the universes, then one second of this precious human rebirth is worth infinitely more than the whole sky filled with wish-granting jewels. The preciousness of this precious human rebirth is beyond compare.

We get very unhappy when we have something stolen or lose some money, even just ten dollars. It can feel like a huge loss; our mind can be unhappy for days. And if we lose a hundred dollars, it's a tragedy. Yet we feel nothing about wasting a minute, an hour; we don't even feel the slightest loss at having wasted thirty or forty years—however long it is since we were born—squandering this perfect human rebirth.

If we found we had cancer or had inadvertently swallowed poison, we would do everything possible to find a cure, desperate to prolong our life. If we didn't know, however, we would do nothing. We take incredible care of our retirement account or our house, we're so worried about their losing value, but we fail to understand that we are wasting something far more precious. Not knowing the actual value of this life, we do nothing to protect it.

We simply don't understand how unbelievably precious this life is. Pour a little dirt into a horse's ear and it will shake its head to get rid of the irritation; pour in some gold dust and it will do exactly the same thing. It doesn't think one is worthless and one is valuable; dirt and gold are all the same to a horse. Similarly, we have received a perfect human rebirth—a rebirth that gives us the opportunity of achieving all these highly meaningful results, a rebirth that gives us the possibility of gaining any level of happiness we desire—but failing to appreciate this, we totally waste it, like shaking an irritation out of our ear.

Sooner or later, material possessions will let us down and, unless we understand impermanence and karma, when they do, we will be very unhappy. When some rich people lose their business they jump off a high bridge, as if losing their money is worse than losing their life. If they don't go that far, they have a nervous breakdown and end up in a mental hospital. They place so much importance on the value of money. They know to the nearest cent what their profits and losses are, they know every exchange rate, they know what type of possession they must own to be happy, yet they have no idea of the value of their own precious life.

I heard about a Hong Kong businessman who lost a billion dollars in a market crash. He still had four billion left, but that did not stop the poor man being terribly miserable about the billion he had lost. A billion dollars is nothing. Skies filled with wish-granting jewels are nothing. The only truly precious thing is the perfect human rebirth.

People think bargains are great; they feel very happy to have bought something for less money than the next person. They travel miles to a cheaper supermarket to save a few dollars; they wait for the sales and go through much hardship to buy discounted products; their whole day becomes bright and wonderful when they save a few dollars. Yet they think nothing of an act of kindness they might have done.

With the eighteen attributes of the perfect human rebirth we can do anything we want, yet we don't really appreciate them. On the other hand, say we inadvertently pay eighteen dollars instead of seventeen when buying something. Later, when we discover our loss, we are horrified. We have wasted a whole dollar through our carelessness. We feel as if something precious has been torn from our heart. One dollar of that eighteen has been lost, meaning we possibly can't buy a few extra candies. Whether we have $10,000 or nothing in the bank, we still feel the loss of that dollar. Why don't we get the same feeling when we lose one of our freedoms or richnesses? Because we value money much, much more than this perfect human rebirth.

We feel frustrated and annoyed if we miss out on a party because our car has broken down but can waste a whole day and not feel upset about wasting this precious life.

Imagine that you're supposed to go to someplace but are too tired and stay home instead. Then you find out that everybody who went was given a million dollars and you missed out. I'm sure you would be horrified. You'd go crazy thinking that if you hadn't been so lazy you'd have received a million dollars. You wouldn't sleep for days thinking about it. Yet we don't feel any loss sleeping a day away and wasting twenty-four hours of our perfect human rebirth, which is a far greater loss than not getting a *billion* dollars. Again, this is because we don't see clearly how precious this life is.

We are so habituated to believe in the value of money that it might seem impossible to be happy without it, but of course that is not so. Take the great yogis of the past, who owned nothing yet were incredibly happy. The most famous example is Milarepa, the great Tibetan meditator who became enlightened in one brief lifetime of this degenerate age. Other than a place to meditate and a cooking pot, he had nothing—absolutely no money and not even any clothes other than a thin ragged cotton shawl. And what he ate was nettle soup, day after day after day; nettles were all he could pick and they were all he ate. As a result, he was not only very skinny but his skin turned a bluish-green as well.

He lived in a bare cave high in the mountains; just one space you couldn't even call a room. That space was his kitchen; that space was his meditation area; that space was his bedroom. It was totally simple and bare. One night a thief came to steal whatever he could find but found nothing. Milarepa was surprised that the thief even found the cave. "How can you find it in the dark?" he asked. "I can't even find it in daylight." He showed the thief his one cooking pot, which had cracked, but because there was such a thick residue of nettle sludge on the inside, it held together in the shape of the pot. He was making his meal at that time and he offered some to the thief.

The thief asked for some salt and Milarepa sprinkled in some dried nettle, saying, "Here's the salt." Then the thief asked for some chili and again Milarepa added more nettle, saying, "Here's the chili." That was all he had.

Yet he was unbelievably happy because he had the freedom to practice Dharma, and he had this freedom because he had—and valued—his perfect human rebirth. Because of this he was able to attain enlightenment in one brief lifetime.

By our worldly standards, nagas with their great storehouses of wish-granting jewels should be much happier than Milarepa. But even with all that wealth they have no chance to escape the terrible suffering of the lower realms, whereas Milarepa's happiness just increased and increased until he attained complete and perfect enlightenment.

Perhaps we think that Milarepa was somehow special or that it was easier to gain realizations in those days, whereas today things are much more difficult. But we have exactly the same kind of body and mind that Milarepa had. Furthermore, he had killed many people earlier in that very life, so he had to purify all that as well. With the body that we have right now, we can achieve anything we want. We don't need any special circumstances other than the freedoms and richnesses we already have. Right now, at this moment, we have it all. And what we have is worth more than all the wealth of all the universes combined. This perfect human rebirth is that precious. We have the ability to rise above our obstructive delusions as Milarepa did and the ability to help all other sentient beings overcome their suffering and attain peerless happiness as well.

What greater wealth can there be than renouncing the source of suffering, understanding the nature of reality and cherishing others more than ourselves? What can be of more value than acquiring the most precious mind of all, bodhicitta, the mind that seeks enlightenment in order to help all other sentient beings? Those are riches far beyond skies full of wish-granting jewels.

This perfect human rebirth allows us to avoid rebirth in the lower suffering realms relatively easily. No amount of wealth can do this. Nor can it bring us to liberation and enlightenment. In fact, wealth usually has the opposite effect; it activates attachment and weighs our mind down with negativity.

It is important to contemplate these facts again and again because, as I have said, we are habituated to the misconception that money and possessions are the principal path to happiness, whereas they are not. We need to see clearly that money—even skies of jewels—will not bring us one atom of happiness; money will not help us develop along the path to peerless liberation nor will it save us from the lower realms. Money and possessions are false friends in that they promise happiness but bring only misery.

We need to see just how valuable this precious body is. We have been born human before; perhaps we have even had some of the freedoms and richnesses. But we have never had all of them at the same time, so our attempts at real happiness have been flawed and doomed to failure. Now we have all eighteen and, if we apply ourselves, liberation and enlightenment are possible. Only at this time, only with this body can we do that.

We also have to see how morality and generosity are far more important than wealth, otherwise we will continue to misconceive the actual source of happiness and place too much importance on material things. On the one hand, we need to see the poison in the honey of sense pleasure and fear it; on the other, we need to see the true meaning of the human life and feel great joy in utilizing it correctly.

That we have found such a perfect human rebirth is like a dream, as incredible as that beggar finding a diamond in the garbage. Somehow we have that most precious of all jewels in our hand at this moment. It's a miracle, and one we must not waste.

### The preciousness of the human body

What was it about Milarepa? How could he attain complete and perfect enlightenment in one brief lifetime of this degenerate time? It wasn't his cave or his diet. Throughout Asia, Milarepa is revered as a great meditator and a highly realized yogi and even people in the West have heard of him and respect what he did. He had nothing other than his small, almost naked body and the determination to use it to achieve his goal, and so he did. Caring absolutely nothing for comfort, he did what he had to do to attain enlightenment.

We could not even contemplate not wearing clothes, especially in the snows of the Himalayas, but to Milarepa, wearing clothes and going naked were the same, and he went about with his scrap of cloth thrown carelessly over his shoulder, leaving everything exposed. Sometimes his sister would visit him and she was always extremely embarrassed by his appearance. She would constantly scold him, complaining, "Elder brother, I'm so ashamed by your always wandering about naked with everything hanging out." She used to work for various families and once saved up enough money to buy a roll of white cloth. She offered it to him, insisting that he make some clothes out of it: "How can you complete the work of this life with a naked body?"

When she came back later to check on what he had done she found that, instead of making trousers or a jacket, he had made gloves and a finger-like thing that he put on his penis. Naturally, she was very upset that he had wasted the cloth and again criticized his appearance. He said, "Look, everybody has one of these; everybody knows I was born with it. If I should be ashamed of this, you should be ashamed of your breasts," because they were kind of big. I don't know what she replied.

The only difference between Milarepa and us is that we do not have his degree of renunciation. We think that we need comfort and warmth, a good diet and all the external conditions just right, and to get that we need to work and make money. We don't understand what is important. Milarepa did. Other than determination, we have exactly the same potential as Milarepa. Like him, we have this precious body. There is no reason we cannot be just like him.

All beings have the potential to achieve buddhahood; all have buddha nature. But only with this human body can we actualize that potential; it is now that we have the chance to destroy our delusions and develop all our positive qualities. Only with this precious human life can we make every moment meaningful and, by the way, come to enjoy perfect happiness, even in this life; the happiness of practicing Dharma.

The other main advantage of having a human body is that only with a human body, only on this southern continent—the world system we live in—can we achieve the pure morality needed to eliminate all our delusions. And we can achieve that pure morality only by taking the various vows the Buddha formulated. We can't take them in any other form. On that basis we can complete the three principal aspects of the path: renunciation, bodhicitta and the wisdom realizing emptiness. From there, nirvana, the cessation of all suffering, and enlightenment are an easy step.

As there are innumerable universes, there are also many other continents where there human beings exist. Earth is not the only place. But on the other continents, the human beings are different; the human body on this continent is the only one suitable for vows and ordination. Ordination is the foundation for the renunciation of samsara, so a mind unwilling to renounce samsara cannot take ordination. To give up attachment, we need to want to give it up. In the other non-suffering realms[83] it is very difficult to see the nature of suffering, so the beings in those realms remain locked in suffering through following attachment.

Therefore, we are very fortunate that we have neither too much suffering nor too much sense pleasure and are thus able to understand the shortcomings of attachment and realize the nature of suffering. Accordingly, we are suitable receptacles for vows and ordination and are able to keep them. This enables us to develop perfect morality. With pure morality, we can develop perfect concentration. As long as our mind is scattered because of attach-

---

[83] The god realms.

ment and other delusions, it is impossible for us to develop good concentration; with pure morality it is much easier. Then, with strong concentration we can perfect the higher training in wisdom, the realization of emptiness. This, in turn, becomes the basis for our entering the Vajrayana path and achieving enlightenment in the brief lifetime of this degenerate age.

## MAKING LIFE TRULY MEANINGFUL

We have all the eighteen qualities we need to make our life incredibly worthwhile. If just one or two are missing, we have the means of attaining them; we have all the conditions we need to practice Dharma. We know enough about the teachings of the Buddha to understand that it is a philosophy that contains the complete unerring path that leads all the way from here to the ultimate goal of enlightenment. We know how to live the Buddha's middle way, free from extremes. We know the mistakes of both extreme action—self-denial and self-indulgence—and extreme view—denial that anything exists and belief that things exist truly.

Society might try to tell us what we should be, but we can't be pushed. With wisdom, we can see the best way to live, even if everybody is telling us the complete opposite. There are millions of ways of living—the Italian way, the American way, the Nepalese way, the Australian hippie way, the French businessman way—but we have been shown the only way to live that leads to the end of all suffering.

We have the chance to attain full enlightenment, but the road ahead is long and death can come at any moment. Therefore we must at least ensure that we can continue the journey in our next rebirth, and that means creating the causes for another perfect human rebirth. Otherwise it's like, with incredible effort, we almost make it to the top of Mount Everest and, just as the peak comes into view, we slip and slide all the way down to the bottom again.

We still don't have enough wisdom to enjoy worldly pleasure without becoming attached to it, so we suffer. It's really quite logical. If we put our hand in a fire, it gets burned; if we don't want that suffering we should not put our hand in the fire.

If we are not attached to this life, then whatever we do will be Dharma and will lead to happiness. Whatever we are—a soldier, a president; it doesn't matter—if we do what we do without the thought of the eight worldly dharmas, that evil thought can never harm us; if we do what we do with the wisdom realizing emptiness conjoined with bodhicitta, we will attain enlightenment and enlighten all other sentient beings.

Therefore, a major part of our practice at this time should be to recognize the disadvantages of the thought of the eight worldly dharmas and to avoid the attachment clinging to this life that that evil thought fosters. This doesn't mean we should actively seek discomfort and poverty, a bad reputation and blame. That kind of mind training is probably well beyond us at this stage.

However, simply avoiding attachment is not enough. Just as we find ourselves trapped in worldly concern, mistaking desire for happiness, just as we wish to avoid suffering at all costs, so too do all other sentient beings. All beings throughout infinite universes are exactly the same in this regard. But not all beings are the same in their ability to realize their potential for complete happiness. We have all the conditions; they do not. Even if they have a human body, even if they have relative freedom, they probably don't have access to the teachings, the infallible route out of suffering. And they certainly don't have a teacher with the wisdom to give them the flawless guidance they need to achieve freedom from all suffering.

By understanding the nature of suffering, we can see the way out, and by understanding karma and rebirth, we can see that we have had every type of relationship with every one of these sentient beings. More particularly, each sentient being of each universe, of each realm, has been our mother again and again, sacrificing herself in just the same way that our current mother has. Now each kind mother sentient being is experiencing terrible suffering and is unable to help herself, whereas we have the perfect tools to help not only ourselves but each and every one of them as well. But in order to do that, we must first attain full enlightenment ourselves. Then we will be in the best position to help them. But their suffering is so unbearable that we must do this quickly.

How do we do that? There are thousands of actions we can do; there are positive actions that help a little and ones that help a lot. We must choose skillfully. Helping one or two people with their material needs is excellent, but helping a hundred is better. Helping a community out of poverty is wonderful, but best of all is to help all beings—all humans, gods, animals, hungry ghosts and hell beings—attain complete and lasting happiness by leading them to enlightenment. And that is why we must first become enlightened ourselves. To become enlightened we need a completely pure mind. That means never creating any more nonvirtuous actions and destroying all the nonvirtuous seeds left on our mental continuum by our previous negative actions.

## Vows and purification

As we have seen, there are vastly more hell beings than hungry ghosts, vastly more hungry ghosts than animals, and vastly more animals than human beings. And of the humans on this planet, there are very few living in pure morality compared with those who are not. It is extremely difficult to live in pure morality, yet this is what we need to do if we are to attain another perfect human rebirth and continue our spiritual journey.

As above, we first need to avoid creating any more negative actions in the future and at the same time we need to destroy the mental imprints of previous negative actions. Fortunately, Buddhism provides us with the perfect means of doing just that. There are various levels of vow we can take in front of a spiritual teacher that can keep us from engaging in nonvirtue and there are extensive purification practices that can cleanse our mind of the negative habitual tendencies that currently plague it. That does not mean it is easy. Taking vows not to kill, steal and so forth means making every effort not to do these actions, and that means fighting against many lifetimes of habit.

Some of the vows we can take as a lay person are the five lay vows, the eight Mahayana precepts, the bodhisattva vows and the tantric vows. We can also become ordained as a monk or nun and take novice or full ordination vows. Not everybody has the karma to become a monk or nun, so these lay vows are a vital step to happiness. Whatever the number of vows we take—whether those of the lay person or those of the monk or nun— our future happiness and freedom are ensured.

Not only do we protect ourselves from committing negative actions, we also free ourselves from confusion in this life and assure ourselves of good rebirths for tens of thousands of lifetimes, rebirths in which we can again practice morality and establish even more strongly our route to ultimate happiness. Because karma is expandable, all this can come from keeping just one vow for one day, so think of what keeping all the vows every day can do.

When we take vows we accumulate merit all the time. It is very important that we know this. We accumulate great merit every second of our life until we die, even while eating and sleeping. Even in a coma! And while we are doing everything we can to ensure happy future lives, liberation and enlightenment, this life just naturally gets taken care of. By practicing Dharma with the motivation of attaining liberation or enlightenment, we avoid all negativity and create only positive actions, so obstacles to the happiness of this life are automatically eliminated.

By keeping vows made in front of our guru or the Buddha, we create the incredibly strong positive imprints that we need to propel us on the path to enlightenment. But precisely because the vows we take are so powerfully positive, they are very dangerous to break and we create considerable negative karma when we transgress them.

Vows give us responsibility; they add weight to our determination. To live in discipline through having taken various vows, our mind is incredibly strengthened. Taking vows in front of a holy object or a teacher is a big responsibility. Its weight is with us all the time, and if our mind leans toward committing a negative action, we can feel that responsibility.

The various levels of vow taken by monks and nuns and the five lay vows are classified as pratimoksha, or individual liberation, vows. We take the five lay vows for life and they are often given at the same time as a formal refuge ceremony. We can choose to take one or more of the five, which are to refrain from killing, stealing, sexual misconduct, lying and taking intoxicants.

We can also take the eight Mahayana precepts, which are similar to the five lay vows but kept for only twenty-four hours. It is very good to take these vows regularly. They are to refrain from killing, stealing, sexual activity, lying, taking intoxicants, eating more than one meal a day, sitting on a high, expensive bed and wearing jewelry, perfume and makeup, and singing or playing music.

We normally receive the bodhisattva vows in a special ceremony or when we take certain initiations. Tantric vows are given when we take a Highest Yoga Tantra initiation. There are fourteen root vows and eight branch. Of the bodhisattva vows, there are eighteen root vows and forty-six branch. In both cases, breaking a root vow is heavier than breaking one of the secondary ones. While the bodhisattva vows are very subtle and easy to break, the tantric vows are even more profound and much easier to transgress.

One commentary on the *Wheel of Sharp Weapons*[84] says that we need all three levels of vows to receive a perfect human rebirth. We can interpret this to mean that until we can keep the tantric vows—the highest level of vow— purely, we will still have subtle obscurations blocking our complete attain-

---

[84] This text, written by Dharmarakshita, the renowned tenth-century Sumatran teacher who was one of Lama Atisha's teachers, is one of the seminal mind training texts.

ment of the path. On the other hand, if we can keep purely as many vows as we feel comfortable keeping, we should feel very happy. It does not mean that everybody must take tantric vows right away. Aspiring to take and keep the highest vows in the future in order to complete the path as quickly as possible, we should assess our current ability realistically and take just the vows we feel we can, and do our best to keep them purely.

When we look at the vows we have taken and see that we have not broken any, we can truly rejoice. If we see that there are some that we have broken, we should apply one of the methods of purifying broken vows immediately. We should never think that breaking a vow somehow doesn't matter. Transgressing a sacred vow creates a huge disturbance in our mind and generates much negativity. Pabongka Dechen Nyingpo says that it is much more serious to carelessly break a vow than it is to kill a hundred human beings and a hundred horses.

Avoiding negativity through taking vows is one aspect of the Buddhist path; purifying the negative imprints that remain on our mindstream is another. There are many powerful purification practices. They include prostrating to and reciting the holy names of buddhas such as the Thirty-five Confession Buddhas; reciting purifying mantras such as the Vajrasattva mantra; making holy objects such as thangkas, statues and *tsa-tsas*;[85] reciting perfection of wisdom texts such as the *Heart Sutra* or the *Diamond Cutter Sutra*; meditating on emptiness, bodhicitta and similar subjects; and making offerings to the Buddha, Dharma and Sangha.

Any merit we create is a form of purification. Studying the Dharma, meditating, practicing generosity, even cleaning holy places—all the things that constitute our Dharma practice—contribute to freeing our mind from the delusions that currently weigh it down. There are, however, some specific actions associated with purification. Making statues and stupas is considered excellent purification, as is simply painting a small tsa-tsa.

Of the specific meditation practices designed to purify our mindstream quickly, Vajrasattva is considered supreme, but there are others that are also very effective. The nyung-nä retreat is an incredibly powerful practice too. Based on prayers and prostrations to Chenrezig, the Compassion Buddha, this two-day fasting practice focusing on the suffering of others helps cleanse our mind of self-cherishing.

---

[85] A thangka is an image of a deity, usually painted on canvas and set in a brocade border. A tsa-tsa is a small bas relief deity image made by pressing clay or plaster into a mold.

Whatever practice we do, it should be combined with taking refuge, and to be really effective it should be part of the four opponent powers, where we take refuge and generate bodhicitta, remember a specific negativity and regret it, and resolve never to repeat that action again.

The more purification we do with the aim of attaining enlightenment, the closer we get to being able to help sentient beings in the highest possible way. Whatever purification we do builds and builds, freeing more and more of our potential. If we want to accumulate a million dollars for a charity, we start with one dollar; in the same way, if we want to destroy the delusions that obscure our mind, we start with one prostration. Even one prostration done purely has great effect. And just as the thought of collecting a million dollars seems impossible when we don't have even one, it is definitely possible, so even though the thought of completely purifying all the negativity we have collected over countless eons seems an impossible task before we start, we can do it. Many, many beings in the past have done just that.

The Buddha is extremely skillful in the way that he guides sentient beings. With great kindness and compassion he showed us the infallible route away from suffering to full enlightenment. He created the different levels of vow for both lay and Sangha to fit the different propensities of the various sentient beings. The main point is to practice morality as best we can, and taking vows is the most skillful means of doing this.

## MEDITATING ON THE LAM-RIM

We have the intelligence to see what needs to be done. All we need is the determination. When we truly understand the advantages of practicing Dharma—purifying, keeping vows—and the disadvantages of not, we will definitely have the energy and perseverance to make rapid progress on the path.

Perhaps at present it's still an effort to get up that half hour earlier to meditate. Our bed is so comfortable and it's so cold out there. So we stay in bed until the last minute, rush breakfast and hurry off to work. However, feeling that we don't have time to meditate is a misconception. There's time if we make the time. At present, comfort and breakfast seem more important than meditating, but when we understand the shortcomings of the thought of the eight worldly dharmas and the urgency of turning our attitude around, then meditation will always win over sleeping in and even breakfast. But usually we'll find we have time for everything. We can make time.

At the moment we delay and procrastinate because we think that practicing Dharma is too hard or requires too much effort. We want to do a retreat but somehow things are never quite right. We think we need all the right conditions but they never seem to materialize. We can't find a comfortable enough place or are worried about the quality of the food. Our mind throws up all sorts of complications. But really, this is just our reluctance to let go of worldly life. If we could really see the advantages of retreat we wouldn't worry about such superficial conditions.

Overcoming laziness is simply a matter of understanding the importance of doing something. We have no problem working hard to organize a holiday or make a profit at work because these things are important to us. When the Dharma assumes that degree of importance in our life, we will never think of lying in bed when we need to purify the obstacles from our mind or meditate on the lam-rim. The difficulties are only in our mental attitude, which we can change. It is extremely useful to understand this.

Say we're planning to climb Mount Everest. We know to expect many dangers and will make extensive preparations to combat them. We understand that there will be no easy roads or comfortable beds; it will be cold and difficult. Despite all these anticipated difficulties, we still make plans to go because we are determined to conquer the world's highest mountain. We should have the same resolve in our Dharma practice.

If we are discouraged by heat, sore knees or poor food, that is almost certainly our worldly mind making excuses for why we should abandon the Dharma. That is the evil thought of the eight worldly dharmas telling us that life is easier away from the meditation cushion. But with just a little effort now, and possibly a little discomfort, we have the chance to put an end to the need for effort forever and will certainly save ourselves from not just extreme discomfort, but suffering beyond imagination. Pain in the knees, no matter how bad it gets, is nothing compared to being hacked to pieces again and again on red-hot ground in one of the hells. We have endured unimaginable suffering for countless lives; now is the time to endure a little discomfort and inconvenience to never have to experience any of that ever again.

Therefore, this is the time, this very second, to turn our life completely around; to renounce the concern for worldly pleasure that keeps us trapped in suffering and embrace the mind that actively destroys the delusions that are the cause of suffering. Now is the time to study and meditate on the lam-rim, to actualize bodhicitta, to practice the six perfections, to meditate on emptiness and understand the nature of reality. Now is the time to take on a Vajrayana practice, the quick path to enlightenment that enables us to benefit countless sentient beings in a very short time.

If we don't start now, when will we? There will never come a time when the conditions are better for Dharma practice. Everything is waiting for us here, right now.

The foundation upon which all this is based is the lam-rim. Bodhicitta, emptiness, the very special practices of the Vajrayana are impossible without a firm understanding of the lam-rim. Vajrayana especially needs all the other aspects of the path to be in place, otherwise it will not only be useless; it could well be dangerous. There are stories of meditators who have done very powerful tantric practices without the basis of equanimity, compassion and the understanding of emptiness as taught in the lam-rim and have been reborn as hungry ghosts in the aspect of the deity they were practicing. The lam-rim is the main road, the direct highway to enlightenment. Whether we walk, ride a bicycle or drive, we still must take the road from here to there, and if we take any of the side roads, we're just wasting time.

Kadampa Geshe Chengawa[86] asked one of his disciples, "If you had the choice, which would you prefer, all eight common *siddhis*[87] or one lam-rim realization?" Of course, the answer is that one lam-rim realization is infinitely preferable. We have had all these psychic powers numberless times in the past; we have also been a formless realm god numberless times, with the perfect concentration that brings all these powers. None of this has helped us in the slightest. One lam-rim realization, however, is of incredible benefit.

## Bodhicitta is the best motivation

Arhats, those incredible beings who have completely freed themselves from samsara by destroying all their delusions, are still unable to create the infinite merit that we can in such a short time. Isn't that an amazing thought? This is purely because we have this perfect human rebirth, have met the Mahayana teachings and understand the importance of bodhicitta. There is nothing throughout all of space as precious as bodhicitta. With every moment of bodhicitta in our mind, we create infinite merit.

Every action we do with bodhicitta, no matter how great or small, helps other sentient beings because we are doing it to purify our negativity in

---

[86] One of Dromtönpa's main disciples.
[87] See the glossary for details.

order to enlighten them. Enlightenment is impossible with a self-cherishing mind; it cannot be attained for ourselves alone, only with the aim of helping others. That is why we must do everything possible to destroy all our self-cherishing thoughts.

The entire purpose of our life, its whole meaning, is to cherish others and help them as best we can. To free others from the confusion that brings suffering, we must be free from confusion ourselves. If we are still trapped in our own confusion, we have less time to deal with the others' problems and less ability to help them skillfully. That is why we *must* be enlightened. Trying to clean a floor with a dirty mop just moves the dirt around. The mop needs to be clean. Similarly, our mind needs clarity and purity if we are to see how best to help others and have the ability to do it. This is why bodhicitta is vital.

Practicing Dharma is an amazing way of destroying our delusions but that is not the ultimate reason for practicing it. We destroy our delusions in order to become enlightened in order to best help all sentient beings. The real reason for everything we do should be this highest of all motivations—to free each and every living being from suffering and place them in the peerless happiness of enlightenment. Along the way, as a by-product, we attain peerless happiness ourselves and, it goes without saying, will never have to suffer in the lower realms again.

We have the method and now we need to use it, not for our own ends but to free all beings from suffering. Without bodhicitta, there will always be something missing; with bodhicitta, we are on the infallible road to full enlightenment and nothing can divert us or slow us down.

This is a huge mind. We take on the full responsibility of freeing all sentient beings from suffering by ourselves alone. Anything less—most sentient beings but not all; all sentient beings but not completely free from suffering—is not going all the way, is still a mind with limits, so we can never go all the way ourselves. Therefore we need a mind without limits, and that comes from having a motivation without limits. Then, whatever we do, from the most trivial thing to the biggest we can imagine, becomes utterly full of meaning. Drinking a cup of tea, donating a million dollars to charity, anything done with a bodhicitta motivation brings us the greatest possible profit.

We have the full responsibility of freeing all beings. We have met the Dharma, we have understood our own situation and that of all the beings around us, we have seen what has to be done. We have limitless skies of reasons why we need to achieve full enlightenment by completing the path. Aiming at anything short of this ultimate goal is wasting our life.

Bodhicitta makes everything else we need to do on the path so much easier. The mind aspiring to bodhicitta makes the practice of morality most meaningful and therefore much easier to achieve. Because we have love and compassion, of course we have no thought of harming others. Every second we delay means countless sentient beings are suffering, so bodhicitta is the essential spur for us to enter tantric practice, the lightning quick vehicle to enlightenment.

There is actual engaging bodhicitta, the mind that completely, spontaneously and continuously focuses on the benefit of others alone, and there is aspirational bodhicitta, the mind that wishes to have such qualities. We probably haven't achieved the full realization of bodhicitta yet, but even to have wishing bodhicitta is a truly amazing thing. Even with this, we create limitless skies of merit with every action we do. Aspirational bodhicitta takes effort, though, so we should re-energize our motivation as often as we can. Before we begin an action we should start with bodhicitta motivation; while we are doing it we should remind ourselves of bodhicitta; and when we finish, we should dedicate what we have done with a bodhicitta dedication. That way, everything we do becomes extremely pure and powerful.

After meditating on the three great purposes that we can accomplish with this perfect human rebirth, we should think, "Every day, from my birth until now, everything I have done with my body, speech and mind has been done with a selfish attitude, following worldly concern. None of these actions has become the cause of enlightenment, so I have wasted them. I have completely wasted my highly meaningful perfect human rebirth."

Feeling that this is a greater loss than losing diamonds equaling the number of atoms of this earth, we should think, "So far, all the actions of my body, speech and mind have not become even the cause of liberation, because they have been done with attachment and the dissatisfied mind. I have wasted so much of my highly meaningful perfect human rebirth. So far, not one of my everyday actions has even become holy Dharma, the cause of happiness in future lives. My actions haven't even become the cause of mundane happiness. I have wasted so much of my meaningful perfect human rebirth."

We should meditate like this on how much of our life has been wasted, how our actions have not even become Dharma, and then think, "If I had been practicing correctly and continuously all these years, from the time I first met my virtuous friend and received lam-rim teachings up to now, I would have generated bodhicitta or at least renunciation of samsara. Therefore, from this moment on, I shall always watch my mind and never do any action without bodhicitta."

We can wash with bodhicitta, dress with bodhicitta, cook with bodhicitta, for the sake of all sentient beings. We might be eating just one small piece of toast, yet, with the right motivation in our mind, it is helping countless sentient beings. It all depends on our attitude.

We can train our minds to always have bodhicitta and an awareness of emptiness. That does not mean we have to be in a continual state of meditation, but by setting up a strong motivation at the beginning of our day, the whole day can be suffused with bodhicitta and emptiness, thus flavoring any activity we do.

The road is there ahead of us and we have all the things we need for the journey. We have the map and provisions, we have our means of transport, and now is the time to start the journey, but it will be a long one. We need to have a vast view. We will have to purify negativities and collect merit for a long time. But there will come a time when our negativities have been completely purified and our positive qualities have been completely developed. Collecting merit will end; purification will end. Unlike the work of samsara, which never ends, the effort we need to put into our Dharma practice does.

We should therefore not be discouraged if we encounter difficulties on the path. We should not have a small heart but a heart as big as the universe, one able to withstand any physical or mental hardship. We should see that working for worldly concern always comes with hardship, so any hardship that comes with Dharma practice is not unexpected but nothing by comparison and will end.

With this kind of attitude we transform problems into happiness. We see why a particular problem is happening and how it is actually helping us. This makes us happy. We even welcome problems. Just as we are happy to feel pain in our legs when we near the top of a high mountain after a day's climbing, we are happy when we experience problems as part of our mental development; it is simply a stage our mind is going through in its growth toward full enlightenment. And just as it is unrealistic to climb Mount Everest unprepared for serious difficulties, it is foolish not to be ready for obstacles on the lam-rim highway to enlightenment. Therefore we need to keep focused on the ultimate goal and not be discouraged.

We think that the person who climbs Mount Everest is a hero, but the *real* hero is the person who practices Dharma. Western movies are full of superheroes, but when you think about it they are pretty stupid, wasting all that energy in fighting and bending metal.

When I first traveled to the West and saw how materialistic it was, I realized how easy Tibetans have it, constantly surrounded by Dharma and immersed in a culture that treasures the teachings and the great teachers. Devotion comes naturally to most Tibetans, but it takes a brave heart for a Westerner to turn his or her back on such a strong culture. There are distractions in Tibet, but they're nothing compared with the world of distractions created by Western culture. Rejecting the drug of pleasure that most people take to be happiness and deliberately facing and overcoming the demon of the delusions takes a true hero, and I really admire Westerners who are able to practice Dharma.

As I said at the beginning, if you think realistically about how excited so many people get about soccer and other sports heroes, it looks pretty crazy. So much effort for something so meaningless. The real heroes are those trying to practice Dharma.

There is no greater meaning in life than leading all sentient beings to peerless happiness, and the perfect human rebirth that we now have for this brief period gives us the ability to do just that. That is why we need to understand just how precious it is and determine never to waste a second of this rare and amazing opportunity.

# APPENDIX 1
## Meditating on the Perfect Human Rebirth

As we have seen, the purpose of studying teachings on the perfect human rebirth is to realize how incredibly rare and unique this opportunity is. So often, when we have something precious we take it for granted until we have lost it and then feel deep regret that we failed to appreciate what we had. Well, there's nothing more precious than the perfect human rebirth and there's no greater loss than not using it to realize our potential as a human being. Thus, once we understand this subject intellectually we need to meditate on it again and again until we realize it.

If we see a diamond worth millions of dollars, we appreciate its worth; we don't think the ten dollars in our pocket will buy it. Of course, that ten dollars can buy something else, like Coca-Cola, but not that diamond; it is beyond us. However, the perfect human rebirth, which is worth infinitely more than billions of diamonds, is something we already have. It is extremely rare and precious, and we have it. Just as we wouldn't take that diamond for granted, we should check and see that we have each of the eight freedoms and ten richnesses and determine never to take this life for granted, for even one second. The more we understand what an incredible opportunity this is, the less we will carelessly waste even a moment of it.

We'll know that we have realized the perfect human rebirth when we can't bear to think of wasting even a second of this precious life and when just the thought "I have a perfect human rebirth" brings us the sort of surge of joy that winning millions of dollars would.

By meditating deeply on each of the topics within the perfect human rebirth we can make those understandings part of our life. In doing so we become softer and we grow; we become more open to others and less wrapped up in worldly affairs; we become more accepting of problems when they arise. In short, we become a better person.

Crucially, by meditating on the topics of the perfect human rebirth, we come to understand deeply the need for morality, generosity and stainless prayer if we are to take the work we are starting now into the next life. This gives us the determination to take and keep the various levels of vow that Buddhism contains. They are like the key to the door to enlightenment. We are also able to develop our compassion until it becomes bodhicitta, which then allows us to enter the tantric path and achieve enlightenment quickly.

## MEDITATING ON THE EIGHT FREEDOMS AND TEN RICHNESSES

A good way to meditate on the perfect human rebirth is to go over each of the eight freedoms and ten richnesses individually, reflecting on each one in depth, trying to see just why we are so fortunate to have these eighteen qualities.

But don't meditate on each of the freedoms and richnesses as if you're an observer. Really put yourself into the situation as if that were you and feel what it would be like. Then you can really get an appreciation of the actual situation you're in at the moment.

If you are meditating in retreat or as part of a daily practice and focusing on purely lam-rim subjects, then you can do one freedom or richness each day, or each session, or stay with one freedom or richness for a few days until you have a strong feeling for it. Conversely, you can do a glance meditation on a range of freedoms or all of them to give yourself an overview. The purpose is to understand each subject at as deep a level as possible so that it really means something very profound to you.

Meditating on each of the eighteen qualities can be done in conjunction with a deity practice. For example, if you are practicing a Chenrezig sadhana, when you get to the mantra recitation, after a while you can bring in this topic and meditate on it as part of developing compassion. His Holiness the Dalai Lama says that when your mind gets bored or can no longer concentrate on visualizing yourself as the deity, doing a lam-rim meditation stops superstition arising. If you were to continue simply reciting the mantra with a distracted mind, delusions such as anger, attachment, jealousy or pride could arise, and so an hour of reciting the mantra with your mouth could be an hour of creating negative karma with your mind. Incorporating a lam-rim meditation such as that on the perfect human rebirth can prevent this from happening.

By going over each of the freedoms and richnesses while reciting the Chenrezig mantra, you become aware of how other beings lack these vital qualities and naturally develop great compassion for them. You also become aware of how having that quality yourself allows you to practice the holy Dharma so that you can truly help those beings. After contemplating each quality, conclude: "This human body is extremely precious; there is no time to waste. I must attain bodhicitta."

The way to make the experience of your perfect human rebirth deeper is to move from analytical meditation on that freedom or richness to single-pointed fixed meditation on it. Sooner or later there will come a time when you are analyzing the topic and you get a strong feeling for it. When that happens, instead of continuing with the next part of the analysis, do a fixed meditation on this point by thinking over and over, "This is so precious, this is so precious, this is so precious...." You can either recite, "This is so precious" over and over again or recite the mantra while you do fixed meditation on how precious your perfect human rebirth is. With your mind placed on this, recite a mala or half a mala of mantras. This is very effective. If you do analytical meditation followed by a little fixed meditation, your understanding of the preciousness of your perfect human rebirth will become stronger and more stable.

Whether you are in retreat or meditating on the perfect human rebirth as part of your daily practice, it is very good to take what you have done on the cushion into the outside world. If you have meditated on the freedom of not being an animal, whenever you see an animal, think how unfortunate they are, unable to understand even one word of the Dharma. If you have meditated on one of the freedoms or richnesses relating to humans, when you see people in the street, think how few have the circumstances to hear and accept the Dharma.

Most of what you read in newspapers and magazines or see on television is an advertisement for the perfect human rebirth. Reading the news with this attitude is very helpful. Whatever happens in the world, you can see people's lack of freedom and the suffering that comes from it and understand how fortunate you are not to be in that situation. Everything around you becomes a powerful teaching on the perfect human rebirth, a great inspiration for you to make the most of your life.

Seeing the great value of this life, you feel incredible joy that you are protecting and not wasting it. This precious human body is the basis for your entire Dharma practice and without it you have no possibility of following the true path. It was on the basis of the perfect human rebirth that great yogis such as Milarepa attained enlightenment.

You should not rush your meditation on the perfect human rebirth. It is not fast food to be gobbled down mindlessly but a wonderful meal to be cooked slowly and enjoyed. Like cooking, meditation needs time. You need to see each point clearly and note what is missing and what needs to be developed. Savor each point and try to understand it fully.

### Meditation on the specific points of the eight freedoms and ten richnesses

The purpose of meditating on each of the eight freedoms and ten richnesses separately is to completely convince yourself that there is no possibility of practicing Dharma in any realm other than the human one, and that even as a human there is virtually no possibility of practicing Dharma unless you are free from living in an irreligious country, having wrong views and so forth. In this way you conclude that the only chance of practicing Dharma is to have exactly the set of conditions that you have at this very moment.

If you do this meditation effectively you will come to see how there is really only one route to true happiness. Although all beings everywhere are trying to find happiness and avoid suffering, most think that happiness is found in external things. It takes profound and repeated meditation on topics such as the perfect human rebirth to replace that delusion with the conviction that only practicing Dharma brings happiness.

You can make each meditation as elaborate or as simple as you like. It really depends on what is most effective for your mind, and how much time you have.

The meditation on each freedom and richness follows the same format. For instance, with the first meditation, on the freedom of not being born as a hell being, go through the detailed descriptions of each of the hot, cold, surrounding and occasional hells that you find in the lam-rim texts. You can do this in one meditation session or many, but the point is to really feel how unbearable that suffering is and how impossible it is to practice Dharma in the hells. Feel great joy that you do not have to suffer as a hell being suffers: "How fortunate, how lucky I am, not to have been born as a hell being." Then reflect on how being free from rebirth in hell and having this perfect human rebirth allows you to practice Dharma to the full and achieve the three great purposes of attaining a happy future rebirth, liberation or enlightenment. Finally, determine to never waste even a moment of this perfect human rebirth but use it to attain full enlightenment in order to free all the kind mother sentient beings from the unbearable sufferings in which they are trapped.

So each meditation has these four elements:

- reflect on the suffering and lack of freedom of that situation and how it would be impossible to practice Dharma if you were in it
- reflect on how at the moment you are free from that situation and rejoice that as a result you are able to practice Dharma
- reflect on how this freedom allows you to attain the three great purposes
- determine not to waste a moment of this perfect human rebirth from now on

For the richnesses, rather than the feeling the joy of being free from an unfavorable situation, feel fortunate at having received that wonderful quality and think how those who have not received it cannot fully practice Dharma. Relate to each freedom and richness in this way and consider how meaningful it is and how difficult it will be to find it again. Also reflect on the fact that the situation you are now in will not last. This life is very short and can stop at any time, even today. It could even stop during this very meditation session. By considering each freedom and each richness in this way you realize how unbelievably precious each of these eighteen qualities is.

After you have done analytical meditation in this way on each of the freedoms and richnesses, reflect on how extremely difficult it is to gather together all eighteen attributes of the perfect human rebirth. Knowing that you have managed to do so, appreciate how precious this rebirth is and rejoice from the bottom of your heart.

As I explained above, if you get a strong feeling for the point during analysis, stop and do a fixed meditation on that feeling, making it stronger, more profound and more stable. Here, you can repeat the idea over and over, "This is so precious, this is so precious, this is so precious...."

If you train your mind in this way, even in the break times the thought that your perfect human body is extremely precious will arise effortlessly, just as thoughts of hunger or attachment arise effortlessly. As your understanding of the preciousness your perfect human rebirth grows, you will automatically stop creating meaningless actions, even in the break times.

*The freedom of not being born as a hell being*

Think: "Since beginningless time I have been trapped in samsara, circling from one state to another, mostly in the three lower realms, but this time I have found a perfect human rebirth, which gives me every opportunity to practice Dharma. In my previous lives in the lower realms, most times I was born in the hells."

Think about the suffering of the hell realms; go through the various hells in some detail. If you are in retreat, you can concentrate on one hell each session, or all the hot hells in one session, the cold hells in the next and so forth. But don't meditate on the hell beings as if you're watching TV. Put yourself in the place of each type of hell being and try to experience what it's like, what they're actually going through, what it would be like if it were you.

Think how unbearable it is when a spark from a fire or a stick of incense touches your skin for just a second. It is so painful that it fills your mind and all you can think about is getting it off, stopping the pain. At that moment you have no thought of Dharma at all, no compassion for others, no understanding of anything, just a blind desire to be free from pain.

Think that if you were born in any of the hot hells, the suffering would be billions of times worse than a spark on your skin, not only in the intensity of the pain, but in that it is all over your body and lasts for eons. If you were suffering like that, of course you couldn't practice Dharma. Think what it would be like to be trapped in an iron house that is consumed with fire that is hotter than the fire at the end of this world system. Imagine yourself born in a pot of boiling water. Think of the horror. There is no way you could have any rational thought; your mind would be overwhelmed by the suffering.

Go through the cold hells and the surrounding and occasional hells in the same way.

Then realize how, even though the vast majority of sentient beings are in this situation, you are not. Furthermore, you have a perfect human rebirth, that rarest of all rebirths. Rejoice, "How lucky, how fortunate I am." Reflect on the cause of being born in the hell realms—hatred and ignorance—and determine you will never, even for a second, create those causes again.

Think that having the freedom of not being a hell being gives you the freedom to practice Dharma and make your perfect human rebirth highly meaningful in the three ways—creating the cause of a fortunate rebirth; attaining liberation and enlightenment; and making every moment of this life useful.[88] So, this freedom is highly meaningful in general, but especially because you can attain full enlightenment for the sake of all sentient beings. However, this highly meaningful life can come to an end at any moment. Death is certain but when it will happen is completely unknown.

Conclude the meditation by determining to never waste even one second of this perfect human rebirth, but to use every moment to actualize the great potential of this life by developing bodhicitta and attaining enlightenment.

### The freedom of not being born as a hungry ghost

As with each subsequent meditation, start the meditation by thinking, "Since beginningless time I have been trapped in samsara, circling from one state to another, mostly in the three lower realms, but this time I have found a perfect human rebirth, which gives me every opportunity to practice Dharma. In my previous lives in the lower realms, most times I was born in the hells, but when I wasn't, most times I was born as a hungry ghost."

Reflect on the freedom of not being born a hungry ghost by thinking about what you have learned about the conditions of the hungry ghosts. Think about the different types of hungry ghost and how their principal sufferings are terrible hunger and thirst, where they must go for hundreds of years without getting even a scrap of food—not even a tiny piece of dried snot— or a drop of putrid water. Again, don't do this as an observer; visualize yourself as a hungry ghost and try to relive the experience.

Reflect on how you always expect to have enough to eat and drink and, even more than that, you always expect it to taste delicious and be nutritious.

---

[88] Or you can think that it allows you to fulfill the three great purposes of better rebirth, liberation and enlightenment.

You couldn't even go two days without food. Think back to a time when you were really hungry (if there ever was one) and how the thought of food completely filled your mind. You could think of nothing but food; you would have done anything to get some. Would you have had any space to think about Dharma? I'm sure the answer is no; Dharma would have been the last thing on your mind. Think about this and see how such a basic need drives all other thoughts away.

Think how the suffering of the hungry ghost is billions of times worse than the worst hunger you could ever imagine and its chance of finding food is virtually zero. Visualize the hungry ghosts wandering around mad with desperation. Of course they can't practice morality or generosity; they would literally kill for a scrap of food. How terrible that is. Meditate on the various external and internal hindrances they experience in their quest for food and drink.

Then think how, although there are far more hungry ghosts than either animals or humans, in this life you are not a hungry ghost. You have enough to eat and drink and also have the luxury of not having to spend all your time thinking about or trying to obtain food and drink. Even among humans this is a luxury. Furthermore, you have a perfect human rebirth, that rarest rebirth of all. Rejoice, "How lucky, how fortunate I am." Reflect on the causes of being born as a hungry ghost, such as attachment and ignorance, and determine you will never, even for a second, create those causes again.

Think that not being a hungry ghost gives you the freedom to practice the Dharma and achieve the three ways a perfect human rebirth is meaningful and so this freedom is extremely useful. But this highly meaningful life can end at any moment.

Determine to never waste even a second of this perfect human rebirth but to use every moment to actualize the great potential of this life by developing bodhicitta and attaining enlightenment.

### The freedom of not being born as an animal

With this meditation on the freedom of not being born as an animal, as with the others, start by thinking, "Since beginningless time I have been trapped in samsara, circling from one state to another, mostly in the three lower realms, but this time I have found a perfect human rebirth, which gives me every opportunity to practice Dharma. In my previous lives in the lower realms, most times I was born in the hells, but when I wasn't, I was born as a hungry ghost, and when I wasn't born in the hells or as a hungry ghost, I was born as an animal."

Reflect on the situation of the beings of the animal realm that you can see— the mammals, reptiles, birds, fish, insects, worms. Although a few, like pets, are pampered, the vast majority have to face terrible suffering every day. There is never a moment of peace or happiness for them. Take time to put yourself in the place of the different types of animals, fish, birds and so forth and what they face every day, and see how their lives are dominated by suffering and fear. Again, don't judge their lives so much by their bodies as by their minds. Try to experience having the mind of an animal.

Think what it would be like if you were born as an animal, even as your own pet dog. Dominated by stupidity, you would have no ability to understand anything except the most rudimentary commands of your master. Even if your master explained Dharma to you for a hundred years, you would still have no understanding; you couldn't recite even one syllable of a mantra. You would have no chance to accumulate even a tiny shred of good karma. And here we are talking about the most favored of all animals. Imagine yourself as any wild or farm animal and try to live its life, seeing how trapped in suffering it is.

You have not been born in the animal realm but as a human and, furthermore, you have received a perfect human rebirth with its eight freedoms and ten richnesses. Rejoice, "How lucky, how fortunate I am." Reflect on the causes of being born in the animal realm, such as ignorance and stupidity, and determine you will never, even for a second, create those causes again.

Reflect on how incredibly precious this life is, how highly meaningful every moment of your life is, unlike that of the poor animal, and determine never to waste even one second of it.

Determine to do everything possible to attain the realization of bodhicitta and to attain enlightenment.

### The freedom of not being born as a long-life god

Think, "Since beginningless time I have been trapped in samsara, circling from one state to another, mostly in the three lower realms, but this time I have found a perfect human rebirth, which gives me every opportunity to practice Dharma. In nearly all my previous lives I was born in the lower realms, but even when I wasn't and was born in the upper realms, most times I was born as a long-life god."

Reflect on the various types of god in the desire, form and formless realms. Think of the dream-like state that is the life of the form and formless realm gods and the overwhelming indulgence in sense pleasure that is the life of the desire realm gods and how impossible it is for them to practice Dharma.

Think of a time when you were under the control of attachment, and desire occupied your whole mind—for a possession, for a friend, for success in studies or business. Was there space for anything else at that time, such as compassion? Just as the long-life gods have no chance to practice Dharma, neither do human beings when they are controlled by the thought of the eight worldly dharmas.

Think how, although you haven't overcome attachment yet, you can see its great disadvantages and therefore have the choice not to follow it. Rejoice, "How lucky, how fortunate I am." Reflect on the causes of being born as a god and determine that you will never, even for a moment, create those causes again.

Think that this freedom of not being a god gives you the freedom to practice Dharma and make your perfect human rebirth highly meaningful in the three ways.

Determine never to waste even one second of this perfect human rebirth, but to use it to actualize bodhicitta and attain enlightenment.

*The freedom of not being born when no buddha has descended*

Think, "Since beginningless time I have been trapped in samsara, circling from one state to another, mostly in the three lower realms, but this time I have found a perfect human rebirth, which gives me every opportunity to practice Dharma. In nearly all my previous lives I was born in the lower realms, but even when I wasn't and was born in the upper realms, most times I was born as a long-life god; and even when I was born human, most times it was during a dark period when the teachings of the Buddha did not exist."

In this period, however, the teachings of the Buddha do exist. Even though Guru Shakyamuni Buddha himself has passed away, the lineage of his teachings still lives on in the person of highly realized teachers, and the transmission of his holy Dharma is still pure and undiluted.

Imagine if this were not so. There are certain periods when the teachings of the Buddha have completely finished and there is just complete darkness, no existence of the Dharma, no light of Dharma whatsoever. Those are called dark periods. So, even though you may have been born human, due to karma you were born in one of those dark periods where there was no light of Dharma. Imagine a world shrouded in the darkness of ignorance where the light of Dharma does not shine. Born at such a time, you would have no chance to even understand what virtue is, let alone create it.

Rejoice, "How lucky, how fortunate I am to have been born at a time when a buddha has descended." Reflect how we are coming to the end of the period of the Buddha's teachings and will soon be entering another dark period. Therefore, feel the urgency of doing everything possible now to actualize Dharma in your heart as quickly as possible.

Think how you can die at any moment, but have no idea what lies beyond. Will you still have this precious opportunity in your next life? Determine to spend every moment developing bodhicitta in order to attain enlightenment for the sake of all sentient beings.

## *The freedom of not being born as a barbarian*

Think, "Since beginningless time I have been trapped in samsara, circling from one state to another, mostly in the three lower realms, but this time I have found a perfect human rebirth, which gives me every opportunity to practice Dharma. In nearly all my previous lives I was born in the lower realms, but even when I wasn't and was born in the upper realms, most times I was born as a long-life god. Even when I was born human, most times it was during a dark period when the teachings of the Buddha did not exist, and when I was not born during a dark period, most times I was born as a barbarian."

Think of the places where there is no Dharma, where the people who live there have no understanding of Dharma at all, where religion is suppressed or seen as superstition. Think of how people who live like this are always looking for happiness in the wrong places, led by attachment to worldly pleasure. They have no understanding of Dharma and no wish to practice it.

Think how, if you were in that situation, you would be completely unable to create the causes for happiness and would be trapped in suffering forever. How terrible that would be. But you are not like that, you have the freedom that allows you to understand and appreciate the Dharma.

Rejoice, "How lucky, how fortunate I am." Reflect on the causes of being born as a barbarian and determine never to create those causes again. Being free from this state, you are able to practice the Dharma and achieve the three great purposes of a perfect human rebirth. Conclude the meditation by determining to use every second of this life to develop bodhicitta and attain enlightenment.

## *The freedom of not being born as a fool*

Think, "Since beginningless time I have been trapped in samsara, circling from one state to another, mostly in the three lower realms, but this time I have found a perfect human rebirth, which gives me every opportunity to practice Dharma. In nearly all my previous lives I was born in the lower realms, but even when I wasn't and was born in the upper realms, most times I was born as a long-life god. Even when I was born human, most times it was during a dark period when the teachings of the Buddha did not exist, and when I was not born during a dark period most times I was born as a barbarian, and when I was not, most times I was born deaf or foolish."

Many mentally handicapped people have just enough mental capacity to survive but little else, so of course there is no way they can understand or practice Dharma. Even if an explanation is given, they have no way of understanding even the words, let alone the profound meaning. How terrible to be in such a condition.

Rejoice, "How lucky, how fortunate I am to be able to understand and practice Dharma." Reflect on the cause of being born as a fool, ignorance, and determine you will never, even for a second, create that cause again. Think that having this freedom means you can achieve the three great purposes of a perfect human rebirth, making every second you have highly meaningful. Determine never to waste even one moment of this perfect human rebirth, but use it to attain bodhicitta and enlightenment.

## *The freedom of not being born as a heretic*

Think, "Since beginningless time I have been trapped in samsara, circling from one state to another, mostly in the three lower realms, but this time I have found a perfect human rebirth, which gives me every opportunity to practice Dharma. In nearly all my previous lives I was born in the lower realms, but even when I wasn't and was born in the upper realms, most times I was born as a long-life god. Even when I was born human, most times it was during a dark period when the teachings of the Buddha did not exist; and when I was not born during a dark period, most times I was born as a barbarian; and when I was born neither during a dark period nor as a barbarian, I was born deaf or foolish; and when I was not, I was born as a heretic."

Recall that being a heretic means holding wrong views, views contrary to reality, such as the mistaken beliefs that karma, reincarnation and so forth don't exist. Imagine what it would be like to be trapped in such wrong views—believing that there is no cause and effect, no life after this and that the Buddha never existed and his teachings are therefore false. With no idea of absolute nature, what is to stop such a person sliding into nihilism? Not only is there no way of practicing Dharma, there's little chance of doing anything worthwhile at all.

You are not trapped in wrong views. Rejoice, "How lucky, how fortunate I am." Reflect on the main cause of being born as a heretic, ignorance, and determine that you will never create that cause again. Think how highly meaningful this perfect human rebirth is, with its freedom of not holding wrong views, but that it can finish at any moment. There is no telling whether in your next life you will be a heretic or not.

Determine to do everything possible to receive another precious human body in your next life. Make a firm conviction to use every remaining moment of this life to develop bodhicitta and attain enlightenment.

At the end of this meditation or this series of meditations, reflect on all eight of the freedoms that you have and rejoice at how amazing this precious opportunity is. At any moment you could create the causes to be born as a hell being, a hungry ghost, an animal or a long-life god. At any moment you could create the causes to again be born human but in an irreligious country or with wrong views or with such severe mental problems that it would be impossible to understand anything; at any moment you could create the causes to be born at a time when the teachings of the Buddha don't exist.

How amazing it is that, instead of having been born in any of these eight unfree states, you have been born with all these incredible freedoms. Be aware, however, how easy it is to create the causes for these unfortunate states and determine never to do that again but to create instead only the causes for another perfect human rebirth.

## Meditation on ten richnesses

Meditation on the ten richnesses is similar to meditation on the eight freedoms except that here we don't reflect on the undesirable situations from which we are free but on the desirable situations that we have received. There are five personal richnesses and five relating to others.

Think, "Since beginning less time I have been taking rebirth in samsara, nearly always in non-human realms, but this time I have the great richness of having been born as a human being, which gives me every opportunity to practice Dharma." Meditate on the great advantages of being human and, from the bottom of your heart, rejoice at your good fortune.

Think, "For countless lifetimes I was born human but not in a religious country, but this time I have the wonderful richness of having been born human in a religious country, which gives me every opportunity to practice Dharma." Meditate on the great advantages of being human in a religious country and, from the bottom of your heart, rejoice at your good fortune.

Think, "For countless lifetimes I was born human in a religious country but without perfect organs, but this time I have the wonderful richness of having been born human with perfect organs in a religious country, which gives me every opportunity to practice Dharma." Meditate on the great advantages of being human with perfect organs in a religious country and, from the bottom of your heart, rejoice at your good fortune.

Think, "For countless lifetimes I was born human with perfect organs in a religious country but weighed down by having committed one of the five immediate negativities, but this time I have the wonderful richness of having been born human with perfect organs in a religious country without having committed any of the five immediate negativities, which gives me every opportunity to practice Dharma." Meditate on the great advantages of being human with perfect organs in a religious country and not having committed any of these and, from the bottom of your heart, rejoice at your good fortune.

Think, "For countless lifetimes I was born human with perfect organs in a religious country not weighed down by having committed one of the five immediate negativities but lacking devotion in the teachings, but this time I have the wonderful richness of having been born human with perfect organs in a religious country without having committed any of the five immediate negativities and with great devotion to the teachings, which gives me every opportunity to practice Dharma." Meditate on the great advantages of being human with all these richnesses and, from the bottom of your heart, rejoice at your good fortune.

Think, "For countless lifetimes I was born human with perfect organs in a religious country not weighed down by having committed one of the five immediate negativities and having strong devotion to the teachings but not at a time when the buddha had descended, but this time I have the wonderful richness of having been born human with perfect organs in a religious country without having committed any of the five immediate negativities, having strong devotion to the teachings at a time when the buddha has descended, which gives me every opportunity to practice Dharma." Meditate on the great advantages of being human with all these richnesses and, from the bottom of your heart, rejoice at your good fortune.

Think, "For countless lifetimes I was born human with perfect organs in a religious country not weighed down by having committed one of the five immediate negativities, having strong devotion to the teachings at a time when the buddha had descended but before the teachings had been revealed, but this time I have the wonderful richness of having been born human with perfect organs in a religious country without having committed any of the five immediate negativities, with strong devotion to the teachings at a time when the buddha has descended and revealed the teachings, which gives me every opportunity to practice Dharma." Meditate on the great advantages of being human with all these richnesses and, from the bottom of your heart, rejoice at your good fortune.

Think, "For countless lifetimes I was born human with perfect organs in a religious country not weighed down by having committed one of the five immediate negativities, having strong devotion to the teachings at a time when the buddha had descended and revealed the teachings but the complete teachings did not exist, but this time I have the wonderful richness of having been born human with perfect organs in a religious country without having committed any of the five immediate negativities, with great devotion to the teachings at a time when the buddha has descended and revealed the teachings and the complete teachings still exist, which gives me every opportunity to practice Dharma." Meditate on the great advantages of being human with all these richnesses and, from the bottom of your heart, rejoice at your good fortune.

Think, "For countless lifetimes I was born human with perfect organs in a religious country not weighed down by having committed one of the five immediate negativities, having strong devotion to the teachings at a time when the buddha had descended and revealed the teachings and the complete teachings did exist but nobody was following them, but this time I have the wonderful richness of having been born human with perfect organs in a religious country without having committed any of the five immediate negativities, with strong devotion to the teachings at a time when the buddha has descended and revealed the teachings, the complete teachings still exist and are being followed, which gives me every opportunity to practice Dharma." Meditate on the great advantages of being human with all these richnesses and, from the bottom of your heart, rejoice at your good fortune.

Think, "For countless lifetimes I was born human with perfect organs in a religious country not weighed down by having committed one of the five immediate negativities, having strong devotion to the teachings at a time when the buddha had descended and revealed the teachings and the complete teachings did exist and were being followed but I did not receive help from kind benefactors or a compassionate guru, but this time I have the wonderful richness of having been born human with perfect organs in a religious country without having committed any of the five immediate negativities, with great devotion to the teachings at a time when the buddha has descended and revealed the teachings, the complete teachings still exist and are being followed and I am receiving the help of kind benefactors and a compassionate guru, which gives me every opportunity to practice Dharma." Meditate on the great advantages of being human with all these richnesses and, from the bottom of your heart, rejoice at your good fortune.

By taking each richness in turn and building on it, you can see just how unique having a perfect human rebirth is. It's amazing to have a human body at all, but to have one and live in a religious country, is even more amazing. And more amazing still is to be a human being in a religious country and to have perfect organs with which you can practice even Highest Yoga Tantra. Having just one richness is quite rare and having several of them together is far rarer still. To have all of them at once is unbelievably rare.

Really try to feel the preciousness of each freedom and each richness and use that feeling to motivate your Dharma practice. The more precious you feel your rebirth to be, the greater the happiness in your mind. Just as a beggar finding a diamond in the garbage would be overjoyed, that's how you should feel whenever you simply think, "I have received a perfect human rebirth." In this ordinary, mundane life full of work and problems, you have suddenly discovered a priceless jewel. When that happens and your Dharma practice becomes a ceaseless joy, it is a sign that you are making the most of your perfect human rebirth.

## MEDITATING ON THE OTHER ASPECTS OF THE PERFECT HUMAN REBIRTH[89]

You should also do analytical and fixed meditation on the other outlines of the perfect human rebirth according to the teachings in this book. After you have meditated deeply on the freedoms and richnesses and feel how rare and precious this rebirth is, move on to contemplating its great usefulness in helping you achieve both temporal and ultimate goals and make every single moment of this life highly meaningful until you cannot bear even the *thought* of wasting a second of this incredible opportunity.

Then, to deepen your understanding of the rarity and value of the perfect human rebirth and the great difficulty of finding it again, meditate on the relative numbers of sentient beings in the various realms to see how few are human and how far fewer still have the perfect human rebirth. Also try to get a feeling for the unlikelihood of the perfect human rebirth by visualizing the various analogies, such as the blind turtle, dirt under the fingernail, rice grains sticking to glass and so forth.

Then move on to the next lam-rim topic, impermanence and death, to understand that this rare and precious chance will not last, is running out rapidly and could end at any moment, even today.[90]

---

[89] See also Appendix 2, "How to Meditate on the Stages of the Path to Enlightenment."
[90] See Rinpoche's next FPMT Lineage Series book, *Good Life, Better Death.*

# APPENDIX 2
## How to Meditate on the Stages of the Path to Enlightenment[91]

### *by Pabongka Dechen Nyingpo*

[This is part of Pabongka Rinpoche's extensive description on how to meditate on the entire lam-rim.]

INSTRUCTIONS ON DEVELOPING THE SPIRITUAL REALIZA-
TIONS THAT RELATE TO LEISURE AND FORTUNE

Divide each day's meditation periods into three parts.
During one part, meditate only on serving your spiritual teacher;
During one part elicit successively the realizations for the topics
Ranging from leisure and fortune [freedoms and richnesses] to the pre-
    cious enlightenment mind [bodhicitta];
And during one part apply analytical meditation to the profound view.

So when you divide your meditation into these three periods,
The way to contemplate serving a spiritual teacher is as I explained
    before.
And the way to gain the realizations starting with leisure and fortune
Is first to identify what the essence of leisure and fortune is.

---

[91] Excerpted with permission from *Liberation in Our Hands*, Part II, Appendix F. See LamaYeshe.com for the full text.

Reflect on what it would be like if you had been born into any of the
   inopportune conditions[92]
And how fortunate you are not to have been born there in this life.
Don't consider the qualities of leisure and fortune in a shallow or
   detached manner;
Reflect again and again, applying sharp analytic meditation
So that you will imbue yourself with a deep awareness of how you cur-
   rently possess them all.
When you are overcome with joy, like a pauper who has found a
   treasure,
Then you have generated the realization of identifying leisure and
   fortune.

Next switch to the topic of viewing leisure and fortune as having great
   value,
And repeatedly scrutinize it with the subtle analysis of scripture and
   reasoning.
You will have realized the great value of leisure and fortune
When you become distressed if even an instant of time is vainly spent.

Then go on to the next meditation topic, the difficulty of finding
Leisure and fortune, and reflect on it with powerful analytic
   meditation.
When you become as upset about being idle for even an instant
As another person would if he spilled a bag of gold dust into a river,
Then you have realized the difficulty of finding leisure and fortune.

---

[92] The eight inopportune conditions are the opposite of the eight freedoms, hence as a hell
being, a hungry ghost and so forth.

# Glossary[93]

*Abhidharma (Skt; Tib: chö-ngön-pa)*. One of the three baskets (*Tripitaka*) of the Buddhist canon, the others being the Vinaya and the Sutra; the systematized philosophical and psychological analysis of existence that is the basis of the Buddhist systems of tenets and mind training.

*aggregates (Skt: skandha)*. The association of body and mind; a person comprises five aggregates: form, feeling, discrimination, compositional factors and consciousness.

*Amitabha (Skt; Tib: Ö-pag-me)*. One of the five Dhyani Buddhas, red in color, representing the wisdom of analysis and the fully purified aggregate of discrimination.

*anger (Skt: krodha; Tib: khong-dro)*. A disturbing emotion that exaggerates the negative qualities of an object and wishes to harm it; one of the three poisons and six root delusions.

*arhat (Skt; Tib: dra-chom-pa)*. Literally, foe destroyer. A being who, having ceased his or her karma and delusions, is completely free from all suffering and its causes and has achieved liberation from cyclic existence.

*arya (Skt; Tib: phag-pa)*. A being who has directly realized emptiness.

*Ashoka*. Indian emperor of the Maurya Dynasty (about 250 BC) who converted to Buddhism and spread it throughout Asia.

*aspirational bodhicitta*. The mind that wishes to develop actual, engaged bodhicitta.

*asura (Skt)*. Demigod.

*Atisha, Lama* (982–1054). The renowned Indian master who went to Tibet in 1042 to help in the revival of Buddhism and established the Kadam tradition. His text *Light of the Path* was the first lam-rim text.

---

[93] For a more detailed glossary go to LamaYeshe.com.

*attachment (Skt: raga; Tib: dö-chag).* A disturbing thought that exaggerates the positive qualities of an object and wishes to possess it; one of the three poisons and six root delusions.

*Avalokiteshvara (Skt).* See *Chenrezig.*

*bardo (Tib).* The intermediate state; the state between death and rebirth, lasting anywhere from a moment to forty-nine days.

*bhikshu (Skt; Tib: gelong).* A fully-ordained monk.

*bhikshuni (Skt; Tib: gelongma).* A fully-ordained nun.

*bhumi (Skt; Tib: sa).* Literally, stage or ground. Bodhisattvas must traverse ten bhumis on their journey to enlightenment, the first being reached with the direct perception of emptiness.

*bodhicitta (Skt; Tib: jang-sem).* The altruistic determination to achieve full enlightenment in order to free all sentient beings from suffering and bring them to enlightenment.

*bodhisattva (Skt; Tib: jang-chub-sem-pa).* One who possesses bodhicitta.

*bodhisattva vows.* The vows taken when one enters the bodhisattva path and required for the development of actual, engaged bodhicitta.

*Boudhanath.* A village just outside Kathmandu that is built around the Boudhanath Stupa, a famous Buddhist pilgrimage site.

*buddha, a (Skt; Tib: sang-gye).* A fully enlightened being. One who has purified all obscurations of the mind and perfected all good qualities.

*Buddha, the (Skt).* The historical Buddha, Shakyamuni. See also *enlightenment, Shakyamuni Buddha.*

*Buddhadharma (Skt).* See *Dharma.*

*buddhahood.* The state of being a buddha; enlightenment.

*Buxa Duar.* The refugee camp in West Bengal, India, where Lama Zopa Rinpoche and many other incarnate lamas and monks lived after fleeing Tibet in 1959; where Rinpoche met Lama Yeshe.

*capable being (lower, middle or higher).* See *three levels of practice.*

*chakras (Skt; Tib: khor-lo).* Energy wheels; the focal points of wind energy within the central channel. The main ones are at the brow, crown, throat, heart, navel and sex organ.

*Chandrakirti (Skt; Tib: Dawa Dragpa).* The seventh century CE Indian Buddhist philosopher who wrote commentaries on Nagarjuna's philosophy. His best-known work is *A Guide to the Middle Way (Madhyamakavatara).*

*Chandragomin.* A famous seventh-century CE Indian lay practitioner.

*chang (Tib).* Beer made from fermented grain, often barley.

*channel (Skt: nadi; Tib: tsa).* A constituent of the vajra body through which energy winds and drops flow. The major channels are the central, right and left.

*Chengawa Tsültrim Bar, Geshe* (1033–1103). One of Dromtönpa's three main disciples.

*Chenrezig (Tib; Skt: Avalokiteshvara).* The Buddha of Compassion. A male meditational deity embodying the compassion of all the buddhas. The Dalai Lamas are said to be emanations of this deity.

*chöd (Tib).* A tantric practice aimed at destroying self-grasping, where practitioners visualize dismembering their ordinary body and distributing its parts to spirits and other beings as a feast offering.

*compassion (Skt: karuna; Tib: nying-je).* The sincere wish that others be free from suffering and its causes.

*conventional bodhicitta.* The altruistic mind that wishes to attain enlightenment for the sake of all sentient beings. The word "conventional" is used to distinguish it from "ultimate" bodhicitta, the realization of emptiness with bodhicitta motivation.

*daka (Skt; Tib: kha-dro).* Literally, "sky-goer"; a male being with tantric realizations of the generation or completion stages.

*dakini (Skt; Tib: kha-dro-ma).* Literally, "female sky-goer."

*Dalai Lama, His Holiness* (b. 1935). Gyalwa Tenzin Gyatso. Revered spiritual leader of the Tibetan people and tireless worker for world peace; winner of the 1989 Nobel Peace Prize; a guru of Lama Zopa Rinpoche.

*deity (Tib: yidam).* An emanation of the enlightened mind used as the object of meditation in tantric practices.

*delusions (Skt: klesha; Tib: nyön-mong).* The disturbing negative thoughts, or minds, that are the cause of suffering and negative karma. The three main delusions, the three poisons, are ignorance, attachment and anger. The six principal delusions add pride, doubt and deluded views.

*Denma Lochö Rinpoche* (b. 1928). A learned Gelug lama and former abbot of Namgyäl Monastery who is one of Lama Zopa Rinpoche's gurus.

*desire realm (Skt: kamadhatu).* One of the three realms of samsara, comprising the hell beings, hungry ghosts, animals, humans, demigods and the six lower classes of gods; beings in this realm are preoccupied with desire for objects of the six senses. The other two are the form and formless realms.

*deva (Skt; Tib: lha).* A god dwelling in a state with much comfort and pleasure in the desire, form or formless realms.

*Dharamsala.* A village in Himachal Pradesh, northwest India. The residence of His Holiness the Dalai Lama and seat of the Tibetan Government-in-Exile.

*Dharma (Skt; Tib: chö).* In general, spiritual practice; specifically, the teachings of Buddha, which protect from suffering and lead to liberation and full enlightenment.

*Dromtönpa* (1005–64). Dromtön Gyalwai Jungne. Lama Atisha's heart disciple and chief interpreter in Tibet; founder of the Kadam tradition and Reting Monastery.

*eight common siddhis* (Skt: *astasadharanasiddhi*; Tib: *thün-mong gi ngö-drub gyä).* As opposed to the supreme siddhi (enlightenment), these mundane, or common, attainments are often listed as: the sword of invincibility (*rel-dri ngö-drub*); the eye potion enabling one to see the gods (*mik-mem gyi ngö-drub*); swift footedness—the ability of being able to cover great distance extremely quickly (*kang-gyok kyi ngö-drub*); invisibility (*mi-nang-ba'i ngö-drub*); the art of extracting the essence (rejuvenation) (*chü-len gyi ngö-drub*); becoming a sky-traveler—the ability to fly (*kha-chö kyi ngö-drub*); the ability to make medicinal [invisibility] pills (*ril-bü ngö-drub*); and the power of perceiving treasures under the earth (*sa-ok ngö-drub*). Slight differences may be found in other lists.

*eight freedoms.* Along with the *ten richnesses*, the defining feature of the perfect human rebirth: freedom from birth as a hell being, hungry ghost, animal or long-life god, when no buddha has descended, as a barbarian, with defective mental or physical faculties or as a heretic, holding wrong views.

*eight Mahayana precepts.* One-day vows to abandon killing, stealing, lying, sexual activity, taking intoxicants, eating at the wrong time, sitting on high seats or beds, and singing, dancing and wearing perfumes and jewelry.

*eight ripening qualities.* Eight qualities that are said to be most conducive to spiritual development: long life, handsome or beautiful body, noble caste, wealth, power and fame, trustworthy speech, male body and powerful body and mind.

*eight worldly dharmas.* The worldly concerns that generally motivate the actions of ordinary beings. Craving to have material possessions and to be free from a lack of possessions; craving to have happiness and comfort and to be free from unhappiness and discomfort; craving to have a good reputation and to be free from a bad one; craving to be praised and to be free from criticism and blame.

*emptiness (Skt: shunyata; Tib: tong-pa-nyid).* The absence, or lack, of true existence. Ultimately, every phenomenon is empty of existing truly, or from its own side, or independently.

*empowerment.* See *initiation.*

*engaging bodhicitta.* Conventional bodhicitta, when the mind has moved beyond the wish to develop bodhicitta and is actively engaged in developing it through taking bodhisattva vows and practicing the six perfections.

*enlightenment (Skt: bodhi; Tib: jang-chub).* Full awakening; buddhahood; omniscience. The ultimate goal of Mahayana Buddhist practice, attained when all faults have been removed from the mind and all realizations completed; a state characterized by the perfection of compassion, wisdom and power.

*Ensapa, Gyalwa* (1505–66). A disciple of Chökyi Dorje; achieved enlightenment within a few years without bearing much hardship.

*eon (Skt: kalpa).* A world period, an inconceivably long period of time. The life span of the universe is divided into four great eons, which in turn are divided into twenty lesser eons.

*eternalism.* The belief in the inherent existence of things, as opposed to nihilism; one of the two extremes.

*faith (Skt: shraddha; Tib: dä-pa).* Three kinds: believing, or pure-hearted, faith; lucid, or understanding, faith—faith based on logical conviction; and yearning, or aspirational, faith.

*five degenerations.* The degenerations that occur as human beings evolve over the eon of existence; they are: the degeneration of disturbing thoughts, lifespan, time, view and sentient beings.

*five immediate negativities (or, five uninterrupted karmas).* Killing one's mother, one's father or an arhat, maliciously drawing blood from a buddha and creating a schism in the Sangha community.

*five lay vows.* The vows against killing, stealing, lying, sexual misconduct and taking intoxicants observed by lay Buddhist practitioners.

*five near immediate negativities.* Sexually violating one's mother who is an *arhati*, killing a bodhisattva who is destined to become a buddha, killing an arya who has not yet reached the arhat stage, stealing the property of the Sangha and destroying a stupa.

*five paths.* The paths along which beings progress to liberation and enlightenment: the paths of merit, preparation, right-seeing, meditation and no more learning.

*form realm (Skt: rupadhatu).* The second of samsara's three realms, with seventeen classes of gods.

*formless realm (Skt: arupadhatu).* The highest of samsara's three realms, with four classes of gods involved in formless meditations.

*four great eons.* The four periods of a world system, the great eons of evolution, existence, destruction and emptiness.

*four Mahayana Dharma wheels.* The four external conditions conducive to spiritual development: relying on holy beings, abiding in a harmonious environment, having supportive family and friends, and collecting merit and making prayers.

*four means of drawing disciples to the Dharma.* The second of two sets of practices of the bodhisattva (the other being the six perfections): giving, speaking kind words, teaching to the level of the student and practicing what you teach.

*four noble truths.* The subject of Shakyamuni Buddha's first teaching, or first turning of the wheel of Dharma; the truths of suffering, the cause of suffering, the cessation of suffering and the path leading to the cessation of suffering.

*four opponent powers.* The four-part purification practice, the powers of the object (taking refuge and generating bodhicitta); regret (at having done a specific negative action); resolve (determination not to do the specific negative action again); and remedy (doing a practice such as Vajrasattva recitation-meditation, prostrations to the Thirty-five Buddhas and so forth).

*gelong (Tib; Skt: bhikshu).* A fully-ordained monk.

*gelongma (Tib; Skt: bhikshuni).* A fully-ordained nun.

*Gelug (Tib).* One of the four main traditions of Tibetan Buddhism, it was founded by Lama Tsongkhapa in the early fifteenth century and has been propagated by such illustrious masters as the successive Dalai Lamas and Panchen Lamas.

*Gelugpa (Tib).* A follower of the Gelug tradition.

*geshe (Tib).* Literally, spiritual friend. The title conferred on those who have completed extensive studies and examinations at Gelug monastic universities.

*Geshe Chengawa.* See *Chengawa.*

*Geshe Rabten.* See *Rabten Rinpoche, Geshe.*

*Geshe Potowa.* See *Potowa, Geshe.*

*god.* See *deva.*

*gompa (Tib).* Usually refers to the main meditation hall, or temple, within a monastery.

*graduated path to enlightenment.* See *lam-rim.*

*Great Treatise on the Stages of the Path to Enlightenment.* See *Lam-rim Chen-mo.*

*guru (Skt; Tib: lama).* Literally, heavy, as in heavy with Dharma knowledge. A spiritual teacher, master.

*guru devotion.* The practice of seeing the guru as a buddha then devoting to him or her through thought and action.

*Guru Puja (Skt; Tib: Lama Chöpa).* A special Highest Yoga Tantra guru yoga practice composed by Panchen Losang Chökyi Gyältsen.

*hearer (Skt: shravaka).* Follower of the Hinayana who strives for nirvana on the basis of listening to teachings from a teacher.

*Heart Sutra (or, Heart of Wisdom Sutra, Skt: prajnaparamita-hrdaya).* The best known of a series of sutras on emptiness classified as *Prajnaparamita (Perfection of Wisdom) Sutras.*

*hell (Skt: narak; Tib: nyäl-wa).* The samsaric realm with the greatest suffering; one of the three lower realms. There are eight hot hells, eight cold hells, four surrounding hells and various occasional hells.

*heresy (Tib: log-ta).* A general term for the wrong, or perverse, view of denying karma, past and future lives, liberation and so forth; negative thoughts toward the guru, the opposite of devotion.

*Highest Yoga Tantra (Skt: Anuttara yoga tantra).* The fourth and supreme of the four classes of tantra, it mainly emphasizes internal activities.

*Hinayana (Skt).* Literally, the Lesser Vehicle. The path of the arhats, the goal of which is nirvana, or personal liberation from samsara. Although not synonymous, the term *Theravada* is often preferred.

*hungry ghost (Skt: preta; Tib: yi-dag).* One of the six classes of samsaric beings, one of the three lower realms, hungry ghosts experience the greatest sufferings of hunger and thirst.

*ignorance (Skt: avidya; Tib: ma-rig-pa).* A mental factor that obscures the mind and prevents it from seeing the way in which things exist in reality. There are basically two types of ignorance: ignorance of karma and ignorance of ultimate truth. The fundamental delusion from which all others arise; one of the three poisons and six root delusions.

*impermanence (Tib: mi-tag-pa).* The gross and subtle levels of the transience of phenomena.

*imprints.* The seeds, or potentials, left on the mind by positive or negative actions of body, speech and mind.

*individual liberation.* The liberation achieved by the Theravada (Hinayana) hearer or solitary realizer as opposed to the enlightenment achieved by the Mahayana practitioner.

*individual liberation vows.* See *pratimoksha vows.*

*inherent existence.* See *true existence.*

*initiation (or, empowerment; Skt: abhisheka; Tib: wang).* The transmission of the practice of a particular deity from a tantric master to a disciple, which permits the disciple to engage in that practice.

*Kadampa geshe.* A practitioner of the Buddhist tradition that originated in Tibet in the eleventh century with the teachings of Lama Atisha. Kadampa geshes were renowned for their practice of thought transformation.

*Kagyü (Tib).* One of the four traditions of Tibetan Buddhism, having its source in such illustrious lamas as Marpa, Milarepa, Gampopa and the Karmapas.

*Kanakamuni (Skt; Tib: Ser-thub).* The second buddha of this eon.

*karma (Skt; Tib: lä).* Literally, action. The workings of cause and effect, whereby positive actions produce happiness and negative actions produce suffering.

*Kashyapa (Skt; Tib: Ö-sung).* The third buddha of this eon.

*Khunu Lama Tenzin Gyaltsen* (1894–1977). A renowned bodhisattva born in northern India, he wrote *Vast as the Heavens, Deep as the Sea: Verses in Praise of Bodhicitta*; a guru of Lama Zopa Rinpoche.

*Kirti Tsenshab Rinpoche* (1926–2006). A highly attained and learned ascetic yogi who lived in Dharamsala, India, and was a guru of Lama Zopa Rinpoche.

*Kopan Monastery.* The monastery near Boudhanath in the Kathmandu Valley, Nepal, founded by Lama Yeshe and Lama Zopa Rinpoche.

*lama (Tib).* See *guru.*

*Lama Atisha.* See *Atisha, Lama.*

*Lama Chöpa.* See *Guru Puja.*

*Lama Tsongkhapa.* See *Tsongkhapa, Lama.*

*Lama Yeshe.* See *Yeshe, Lama.*

*lam-rim (Tib).* The graduated path to enlightenment. A presentation of Shakyamuni Buddha's teachings as step-by-step training for a disciple to achieve enlightenment.

*Lam-rim Chen-mo (Tib.) The Great Treatise on the Stages of the Path to Enlightenment.* Lama Tsongkhapa's most important work, a commentary on Atisha's *Lamp for the Path*, the fundamental lam-rim text.

*Langri Tangpa Dorje Senge, Geshe* (1054–1123). A Kadampa geshe student of Geshe Potowa, nicknamed "Gloomy Face" because he was always meditating on the suffering of sentient beings. Author of the *Eight Verses of Thought Transformation*.

*Lawudo.* A small area in the Solu Khumbu region of Nepal about three hours' walk west of Namche Bazaar just above Mende. Site of the cave where the Lawudo Lama meditated for more than twenty years and now the Lawudo Retreat Centre. Lama Zopa Rinpoche is the reincarnation of the Lawudo Lama.

*liberation (Skt: nirvana, or moksha; Tib: nyang-dä, or thar-pa).* The state of complete freedom from samsara; the goal of a practitioner seeking his or her own escape from suffering (see also *Hinayana*). "Lower nirvana" is used to refer to this state of self-liberation, while "higher or great nirvana" refers to the supreme attainment of the full enlightenment of buddhahood. Natural nirvana (Tib: *rang-zhin nyang-dä)* is the fundamentally pure nature of reality, where all things and events are devoid of any inherent, intrinsic or independent reality.

*Library of Tibetan Works and Archives.* The publishing house and research institute in Dharamsala foremost in preserving and publishing Tibetan Dharma texts.

*lineage lama.* A spiritual teacher who is in the direct line of guru-disciple transmission of teachings, from the Buddha to the teachers of the present day.

*lo-jong.* See *thought transformation.*

*loving kindness.* The wish for others to have happiness and its causes.

*lower realms.* The three realms of cyclic existence with the most suffering: the hell, hungry ghost and animals realms.

*Madhyamaka (Skt; Tib: u-ma-pa).* The Middle Way School of Buddhist philosophy; a system of analysis founded by Nagarjuna, based on the *prajnaparamita* sutras of Shakyamuni Buddha, and considered to be the supreme presentation of the wisdom of emptiness. This view holds that all phenomena are dependent originations and thereby avoids the mistaken extremes of self-existence and non-existence, or eternalism and nihilism. It has two divisions, Svatantrika and Prasangika. With Cittamatra, one of the two Mahayana schools of philosophy.

*Mahayana (Skt).* Literally, Great Vehicle. The path of the bodhisattvas, those seeking enlightenment in order to enlighten all other beings. Its two divisions are *Paramitayana* and *Vajrayana*.

*Maitreya Buddha (Skt; Tib: Jampa).* The Loving One. The next buddha after Shakyamuni and the fifth of the thousand buddhas of this present world age.

*mala (Skt; Tib: threng-wa).* A rosary of beads for counting mantras.

*mandala (Skt; Tib: kyil-khor).* The purified environment of a tantric deity; the diagram or painting representing this.

204 THE PERFECT HUMAN REBIRTH

*mandala offering.* The symbolic offering of the entire purified universe.

*mantra (Skt; Tib: ngag).* Literally, mind protection. Sanskrit syllables usually recited in conjunction with the practice of a particular meditational deity and embodying the qualities of that deity.

*meditation.* Familiarization of the mind with a virtuous object. There are two main types of meditation: analytical and fixed.

*merit (Skt: punya; Tib: sö-nam).* The positive energy accumulated in the mind as a result of virtuous actions of body, speech and mind. The principal cause of happiness.

*merit field, or field of accumulation.* The visualized or actual holy beings in relation to whom one accumulates merit by going for refuge, making offerings and so forth and to whom one prays or makes requests for special purposes.

*method.* All aspects of the path to enlightenment other than those related to emptiness; principally associated with the development of loving kindness, compassion and bodhicitta.

*Middle Way.* See *Madhyamaka.*

*Milarepa* (1040–1123). A great Tibetan yogi and poet famed for his impeccable relationship with his guru, Marpa, his asceticism and his songs of realization. A founding figure of the Kagyü tradition.

*mind (Skt: citta; Tib: sem).* Synonymous with consciousness. Defined as "that which is clear and knowing"; a formless entity that has the ability to perceive objects.

*mind training.* See *thought transformation.*

*Mount Meru.* The mythical center of the universe in Buddhist cosmology.

*mudra (Skt).* Literally, seal. Symbolic hand gestures used in images of buddhas and deities or in tantric rituals.

*nadis (Skt).* The energy channels that run through the body carrying the wind, or *prana*, on which the consciousness rides.

*Nagarjuna.* The great second-century Indian philosopher and tantric adept who propounded the Madhyamaka philosophy of emptiness.

*nagas (Skt).* Snake-like beings of the animal realm living in or near bodies of water, they are commonly associated with the fertility of the land but can also function as protectors of religion. Some are said to be incredibly wealthy.

*Nalanda.* A Mahayana Buddhist monastic university founded in the fifth century near Rajgir, Bihar, not far from Bodhgaya, it served as a major source of the Buddhist teachings that spread to Tibet. HH the Dalai Lama often says that Tibetan Buddhism is in the "Nalanda Tradition."

*negative karma.* See *nonvirtue.*

*nirvana (Skt; nya-ngän-lä).* See *liberation.*

*nihilism.* The doctrine that nothing exists; denying, for example, cause and effect of actions or past and future lives. See also *heresy.*

*nonvirtue.* Negative karma; an action motivated by delusion that results in suffering.

*Nyingma (Tib).* The oldest of the four traditions of Tibetan Buddhism, it traces its origins back to *Padmasambhava,* or Guru Rinpoche.

*nyung-nä (Tib).* A two-day Thousand-Arm Chenrezig retreat that involves fasting, prostrations and silence.

*obscurations (Skt: avarana; Tib: drib).* Also known as obstructions, they hinder the attainment of liberation and enlightenment. The gross are called *disturbing-thought obscurations* or *obscurations to liberation (Tib: nyön-drib);* the subtle ones, the imprints left when the gross obscurations are purified, are called *obscurations to knowledge* or *obscurations to enlightenment (Tib: she-drib).*

*om mani padme hum.* The *mani;* the mantra of Chenrezig, the Buddha of Compassion.

*omniscient mind.* See *enlightenment.*

*Pabongka Dechen Nyingpo (1871–1941).* The author of *Liberation in the Palm of Your Hand,* a very influential Gelug teacher and root guru of HH the Dalai Lama's Senior and Junior Tutors, HH Ling Rinpoche and HH Trijang Rinpoche.

*Padmasambhava, or Guru Rinpoche.* The eighth-century Indian tantric master who played a key role in establishing Buddhism in Tibet; he is revered by all Tibetans but especially followers of the Nyingma Tradition, which he founded.

*Palden Yeshe (1738–80).* Also known as Lobsang Palden Yeshe, the sixth Panchen Lama.

*Panchen Lama.* A Gelug lineage of incarnations of Amitabha Buddha originally based in Tashilhunpo Monastery, Shigatse, Tibet; the Dalai Lama and the Panchen Lama are the two highest spiritual leaders of Tibet.

*pandit (Skt).* A great scholar and philosopher.

*paramitas (Skt; Tib: pha-röl-tu jin-pa).* See *perfections.*

*Paramitayana (Skt).* Literally, Perfection Vehicle. The bodhisattva vehicle; a section of the Mahayana sutra teachings; one of the two forms of Mahayana, the other being Vajrayana. Also called Bodhisattvayana or Sutrayana.

*parinirvana (Skt).* The final nirvana the Buddha attained when he passed away in Kushinagar, Uttar Pradesh.

*Penpo.* A county in Tibet, near Lhasa.

*perfect human rebirth.* The rare human state qualified by eight freedoms and ten richnesses that is ideal for practicing Dharma and attaining enlightenment.

*perfections (Skt: paramitas).* The main practices of a bodhisattva. On the basis of bodhicitta, a bodhisattva practices the six perfections of generosity, morality, patience, joyous perseverance, concentration and wisdom.

*pervasive compounding suffering.* The most subtle of the three types of suffering, it refers to the nature of the five aggregates, which are contaminated by karma and delusions.

*Potowa, Geshe* (1031–1105). Also known as Potowa Rinchen Sel, he entered Reting Monastery in 1058 and became its abbot for a short time; one of the three great disciples of Dromtönpa, patriarch of the Kadampa Treatise lineage.

*Prajnaparamita (Skt; Eng: Perfection of Wisdom).* Shakyamuni Buddha's second teaching, or turning of the wheel of Dharma, in which the wisdom of emptiness and the path of the bodhisattva were explained.

*pratimoksha (Skt).* The vows of individual liberation taken by monks, nuns and lay people.

*preliminaries (Tib: ngön-dro).* The practices that prepare the mind for successful tantric meditation by removing hindrances and accumulating merit.

*preta (Skt).* See *hungry ghost.*

*prostrations.* Paying respect to the guru-deity with body, speech and mind; one of the tantric preliminaries.

*puja (Skt; Tib: chö-pa).* Literally, offering; a religious ceremony.

*pure realm.* A pure land of a buddha where there is no suffering; after birth in a pure land, the practitioner may receive teachings directly from the buddha of that pure land, actualize the rest of the path and soon become enlightened.

*purification.* The removal, or cleansing, of negative karma and its imprints from the mind.

*Rabten Rinpoche, Geshe* (1920–86). The learned Gelug lama who was a religious assistant to His Holiness the Dalai Lama before moving to Switzerland in 1975; a guru of Lama Yeshe and Lama Zopa Rinpoche.

*Rajgir.* A town in Bihar, northern India; ancient capital of the Magadha kingdom. Vulture's Peak, where the *Heart Sutra* was taught, and Nalanda Monastery are nearby.

*refuge.* Heartfelt reliance upon Buddha, Dharma and Sangha for guidance on the path to enlightenment.

*renunciation.* The state of mind imbued by the strong wish for liberation and having not the slightest attraction to samsaric pleasures for even a second.

*rinpoche (Tib).* Literally, precious one. Generally, a title given to a lama who has intentionally taken rebirth in a human body to continue helping others. A respectful title used for one's own lama.

*Sakya (Tib).* One of the four main traditions of Tibetan Buddhism, it was founded in the province of Tsang in 1073 by Khön Könchog Gyälpo, the main disciple of Drogmi Lotsawa.

*samsara (Skt; Tib: khor-wa).* Cyclic existence; the six realms of suffering: the lower realms of the hell beings, hungry ghosts and animals and the upper realms of the humans, demi-gods and gods. It also refers to a sentient being's contaminated aggregates that cycle from life to life.

*Sangha (Skt; Tib: ge-dün).* Absolute Sangha are those who have directly realized emptiness; relative Sangha are ordained monks and nuns. Also used loosely to refer to a lay Dharma community or members of a Dharma center.

*Sarnath.* A small town near Varanasi, Uttar Pradesh; the site of Deer Park, where the Buddha first turned the wheel of Dharma, giving his famous discourse on the four noble truths.

*secret mantra.* See *tantra.*

*self-cherishing.* The self-centered attitude of considering one's own happiness to be more important than that of others; the main obstacle to the realization of bodhicitta and, consequently, enlightenment.

*sentient being (Tib: sem-chän).* Any unenlightened being; any being whose mind is not completely free of ignorance.

*Sera Monastery.* One of the three great Gelug monasteries near Lhasa; founded in the early fifteenth century by Jamchen Chöje (1354–1435), a disciple of Lama Tsongkhapa; now re-established in exile in south India. It has two colleges, Sera Je, with which Lama Zopa Rinpoche is connected, and Sera Me.

*Shakyamuni Buddha* (563–483 BCE). The founder of the present Buddhadharma. Fourth of the one thousand founding buddhas of this present world age, he was born a prince of the Shakya clan in north India and taught the sutra and tantra paths to liberation and full enlightenment.

*Shantideva* (685–763). The great Indian bodhisattva who wrote *A Guide to the Bodhisattva's Way of Life,* one of the essential Mahayana texts.

*Sherpa.* A native of the Solu Khumbu region of Nepal. Two famous Sherpas are Sherpa Tenzin, the first person to climb Mt. Everest, and Lama Zopa Rinpoche.

*siddhi* (Skt; Tib: *ngö-drub*). A realization or attainment, either common or supreme. Common siddhis refer to psychic powers acquired as a by-product of the spiritual path; supreme siddhi refers to great liberation or enlightenment. See also *eight common siddhis.*

*single-pointed concentration.* The ability to focus effortlessly and for as long as one wishes on an object of meditation.

*six perfections* See *perfections.*

*six realms.* See *samsara.*

*spirits.* Beings not usually visible to ordinary people; they can belong to the hungry ghost or god realms and be helpful or harmful.

*stupa (Skt; Tib: chör-ten).* A reliquary symbolic of the Buddha's mind.

*subtle obscurations.* See *obscurations.*

*sura (Skt; Tib: lha).* Another term for deva, or god.

*sutra (Skt; Tib: do).* The open discourses of Shakyamuni Buddha; a scriptural text and the teachings and practices it contains.

*Sutrayana (Skt).* The pre-tantric division of Mahayana teachings stressing the cultivation of bodhicitta and the practice of the six perfections. Also called Paramitayana or Bodhisattvayana.

*tantra (Skt).* Also called Vajrayana, Mantrayana or Tantrayana; the secret teachings of the Buddha; a scriptural text and the teachings and practices it contains. Tantric practices generally involve identifying oneself as a fully enlightened deity in order to transform one's own impure states of body, speech and mind into the pure states of that enlightened being.

*tantric vows.* Vows taken by tantric practitioners.

*Tara (Skt; Tib: Drölma).* A female meditational deity who embodies the enlightened activities of all the buddhas; often referred to as the mother of the buddhas of the past, present and future.

*ten nonvirtues.* The three nonvirtues of body are killing, stealing and sexual misconduct; the four of speech are lying, slander, harsh speech and gossip; the three of mind are covetousness, ill will and wrong views.

*ten richnesses.* Along with the *eight freedoms*, the defining features of the perfect human rebirth: being born as a human being, in a Dharma country and with perfect mental and physical faculties; not having committed any of the five immediate negativities; having faith in the Buddha's teachings; being born when a buddha has descended, the teachings have been revealed, the complete teachings still exist and there are still followers of the teachings; and having the necessary conditions to practice Dharma, such as the kindness of others.

*Theravada (Skt).* A tradition of Buddhism that upholds the Pali Canon and the noble eightfold path, which leads practitioners to liberation (nirvana), a state free from the suffering of conditioned existence; one of the eighteen schools into which the Hinayana split not long after Shakyamuni Buddha's death; the dominant Hinayana school today, widely practiced in Sri Lanka and most of continental South-east Asia.

*Thirty-three Realm.* A god realm in the desire realm; the abode of Indra.

*Thogme Zangpo* (1297–1371). Also known as Gyalsä Ngulchu Thogme. A great master of the Nyingma and Sakya traditions and author of the *Thirty-seven Practices of a Bodhisattva* and a famous commentary on Shantideva's *Guide.*

*thought transformation (Tib: lo-jong).* Also called *mind training*; a powerful approach to the development of bodhicitta in which the mind is trained to use all situations, both happy and unhappy, as a means of destroying self-cherishing and self-grasping.

*Three Baskets.* See *Tripitaka.*

*three doors.* Body, speech and mind.

*three great meanings, or purposes.* The happiness of future lives, liberation and enlightenment. See also *three ways a perfect human rebirth is highly meaningful.*

*three higher trainings.* The higher trainings in morality, concentration and wisdom.

*Three Jewels (Skt: triratna; Tib: kon-chog sum).* Also called Triple Gem; the objects of Buddhist refuge: Buddha, Dharma and Sangha.

*three levels of practice.* Also known as the three scopes, the three levels of lower, medium and higher capable being, based on the motivations of trying to attain a better future rebirth, liberation or enlightenment.

*three poisons.* Ignorance, attachment and anger.

*three principal aspects of the path.* The essential points of the lam-rim: renunciation of samsara, bodhicitta and right view of emptiness.

*three ways a perfect human rebirth is highly meaningful.* It allows us to seek the happiness of future lives, to seek liberation and enlightenment, and to make this life useful in every moment. See also *three great meanings.*

*torma (Tib).* An offering cake used in tantric rituals. In Tibet, tormas were usually made of tsampa, but other edibles such as biscuits and so forth suffice.

*transmigratory beings (Tib: dro-wa)*. Sentient beings, those who transmigrate from one realm to another, trapped in cyclic existence.

*Tripitaka (Skt)*. Literally, "three baskets," the way the Buddha's teachings are traditionally divided: the Vinaya (monastic discipline and ethics), Sutra (the Buddha's discourses) and Abhidharma (logic and philosophy).

*Triple Gem*. See *Three Jewels*.

*true existence*. The concrete, real existence from its own side that everything appears to possess; in fact, everything is empty of true, or inherent, existence.

*tsampa (Tib)*. Roasted barley flour, a Tibetan staple food.

*Tsenshab Serkong Rinpoche* (1914–1983). Born in Lhoka, southern Tibet; one of the lineage masters of the FPMT.

*Tsongkhapa, Lama* (1357–1419). The revered teacher and accomplished practitioner who founded the Gelug order of Tibetan Buddhism. An emanation of Manjushri, the Buddha of Wisdom.

*twelve deeds*. The twelve deeds that Guru Shakyamuni Buddha and all buddhas perform: descending from Tushita Heaven, entering his mother's womb, birth, studying arts and handicrafts, enjoying life in the palace, renunciation, undertaking ascetic practices, going to Bodhgaya, defeating the negative forces (the maras), attaining enlightenment, turning the wheel of Dharma and passing into *parinirvana*.

*ultimate bodhicitta*. The realization of emptiness with a bodhicitta motivation. The word "ultimate" is used to distinguish it from "conventional" bodhicitta.

*vajra (Skt; Tib: dorje)*. Literally, "adamantine," often translated as "thunderbolt" but usually left untranslated, the vajra is the four- or five-spoked implement used in tantric practice.

*Vajrasattva (Skt; Tib: Dorje Sempa)*. A male tantric deity practiced for purification.

*Vajrayana*. See *tantra*.

*Vinaya (Skt; Tib: dül-wa)*. The Buddha's teachings on ethical discipline (morality), monastic conduct and so forth; one of the three baskets.

*virtue*. Positive karma; an action motivated by a positive mind that results in happiness.

*virtuous friend (Tib: ge-wä she-nyen)*. See *guru*.

*Vulture's Peak*. The mountain near Rajgir where the Buddha taught the *Heart Sutra*.

*wisdom.* All aspects of the path to enlightenment associated with the development of insight into the nature of reality, often specifically referring to the realization of emptiness.

*wish-granting jewel.* A jewel that brings its possessor everything that he or she desires.

*Yeshe, Lama Thubten* (1935–1984). Born and educated in Tibet, he fled to India in 1959, where he met his chief disciple, Lama Zopa Rinpoche, at Buxa Duar. They began teaching Westerners at Kopan Monastery in 1969 and founded the Foundation for the Preservation of the Mahayana Tradition (FPMT) in 1975.

*yoga (Skt; Tib: näl-jor).* Literally, to yoke. The spiritual discipline to which one yokes oneself in order to achieve enlightenment.

*yogi (Skt).* A highly realized meditator.

*zen (Tib).* The upper, shawl-like robe of a Tibetan monk or nun.

*Zina Rachevsky* (1931–73). Lama Yeshe's and Lama Zopa Rinpoche's first Western student, she helped them establish Kopan Monastery and died in retreat in Solu Khumbu.

*Rinpoche at Chenrezig Institute, 1975.*

# Bibliography[94]

## SUTRAS

*Diamond Cutter Sutra (Aryavajracchedikanamaprajnaparamitamahayanasutra; phag pa she rab pa röl tu chin pa dor je chö pa she ja theg pa chen pö do).* Available in several languages at fpmt.org as *Vajra Cutter Sutra.*

*Four Noble Truths Sutra (Setting the Wheel of Dharma in Motion) (Pali: Dhammacakkappavattana Sutta).* Pp. 1843–1847 in *The Connected Discourses of the Buddha: A Translation of the Samyutta Nikaya.* Translated by Bhikkhu Bodhi. Boston: Wisdom Publications, 2000.

*The Heart Sutra (Prajnahridaya/Bhagavatiprajnaparamitahridayasutra; she rab nying po/Chom dän de ma she rab kyi pha röl tu jin pä do).* Available at fpmt.org.

*The King of Concentration (Samadhirajasutra; ting nge dzin gyi gyäl pö do).* Commentary by Thrangu Rinpoche, translated by Erik Schmidt. Hong Kong: Rangjung Yeshe Publications, 1994.

*The Perfection of Wisdom in Eight Thousand Lines & Its Verse Summary (Astasahasrikaprajnaparamitasutra; she rab kyi pha röl tu jin pa tri gyä tong pä do).* Translated by Edward Conze. San Francisco: Four Seasons Foundation, 1973, 1995.

## INDIAN AND TIBETAN TEXTS

Chandragomin. *Letter to a Disciple.* In *Invitation to Enlightenment*, translated by Michael Hahn. Berkeley: Dharma Publishing, 1999.

Dharmarakshita. *The Wheel of Sharp Weapons Effectively Striking the Heart of the Foe* (Tib: *lo jong tshön cha khor lo*). Pp. 133–153 in *Mind Training*, translated by Thupten Jinpa. Boston: Wisdom Publications, 2006.

Gyältsen, Panchen Losang Chökyi. *Lama Chöpa* (Skt: *Guru Puja*). In *Lama Chöpa Jorchö*. Portland: FPMT, 2011.

---

[94] Since this is not an academic work, in the interests of simplicity we have decided not to use diacritical marks and to use pronounceable Tibetan phonetics rather than transliteration.

Khunu Lama Rinpoche (Tenzin Gyaltsen). *Vast as the Heavens, Deep as the Sea: Verses in Praise of Bodhicitta.* Translated by Gareth Sparham. Boston: Wisdom Publications, 1999.

Maitreya. *Adornment of the Mahayana Sutras (Mahayanasutralamkara; do de gyan).* Published as *Universal Vehicle Discourse Literature.* Edited by Robert A. F. Thurman. New York: American Institute of Buddhist Studies, 2004.

Padmasambhava. *The Tibetan Book of the Dead (bar do thö dröl).* Revealed by Tertön Karma Lingpa, translated by Gyurme Dorje, edited by Graham Coleman and Thupten Jinpa, introduced by HH the Dalai Lama. London: Viking, 2006.

———. *The Tibetan Book of the Dead.* Translated by W. Y. Evans-Wentz. Oxford: Oxford University Press, 1960, 2000.

Nagarjuna. *Precious Garland of Advice for the King (Rajaparikatharatnavali; gyal po la tam cha bar rin po che threng wa).* Published as *Nagarjuna's Precious Garland: Buddhist Advice for Living and Liberation.* Translated by Jeffrey Hopkins. Ithaca: Snow Lion Publications, 1998, 2007.

———. *Friendly Letter (Suhrllekha; she pä tring yig).* Published as *Nagarjuna's Letter.* Geshe Lobsang Tharchin and Artemus B. Engle. Dharamsala: Library of Tibetan Works and Archives, 1979, 1995. Also as *Nagarjuna's Letter to a Friend.* With a commentary by Kangyur Rinpoche. Translated by Padmakara Translation Group. Ithaca: Snow Lion Publications, 2005.

Pabongka Rinpoche (Pabongka Dechen Nyingpo). *Liberation in the Palm of Your Hand (nam dröl lag chang).* Edited by Trijang Rinpoche, translated by Michael Richards. Boston: Wisdom Publications, 2006.

———. *Liberation in Our Hands, Part Two: The Fundamentals.* Translated by Lobsang Tharchin and Artemus B. Engle. Howell: Mahayana Sutra and Tantra Press, 1994.

Rinchen, Geshe Sonam. *The Thirty-seven Practices of Bodhisattvas.* Translated and edited by Ruth Sonam. Ithaca: Snow Lion Publications, 1997.

Shantideva. *A Guide to the Bodhisattva's Way of Life (Bodhisattvacaryavatara; jang chub sem pä chö pa la jug pa).* Translated by Stephen Batchelor. Dharamsala: India, Library of Tibetan Works and Archive, 1987.

Tsongkhapa. *The Foundation of All Good Qualities (yön ten shir gyur ma).* Pp. 139–141 in *Essential Buddhist Prayers: An FPMT Prayer Book, Volume 1.* Portland: FPMT, 2009.

———. *The Great Treatise on the Path to Enlightenment, Volume 1 (lam rim chen mo).* Translated by the Lamrim Chenmo Translation Committee. Ithaca: Snow Lion Publications, 2000.

———. *Songs of Spiritual Experience: Condensed Points of the Stages of the Path (lam rim nyam gur).* Translated by Thupten Jinpa. Montreal: Institute of Tibetan Classics, 2007. See TibetanClassics.org under Media/Resources/Text/Other Texts.

————. *The Three Principal Aspects of the Path (lam gyi tso wa nam sum)*. Pp. 143–145 in *Essential Buddhist Prayers: An FPMT Prayer Book, Volume 1*. Portland: FPMT, 2009.

## ENGLISH LANGUAGE TEXTS

FPMT. *Essential Buddhist Prayers, Volume 1*. Portland: FPMT, 2009.

————. *FPMT Retreat Prayer Book: Prayers and Practices for Retreat*. Portland: FPMT, 2009.

Mackenzie, Vicki. *Cave in the Snow: A Western Woman's Quest for Enlightenment*. New York: Bloomsbury, 1999. There's also this nice video: http://vimeo.com/45500914.

Rampa, T. Lobsang. *The Third Eye: The Autobiography of a Tibetan Lama*. New York: Ballantine Books, 1956, 1964.

Sopa, Geshe Lhundub. *Steps on the Path to Enlightenment Volume 1*. Boston: Wisdom Publications, 2004.

Willis, Janice D. *Enlightened Beings*. Boston: Wisdom Publications, 1995.

Zopa Rinpoche, Lama. *Aroma Charity for Spirits (Sur Offering)*. Portland: FPMT, 2006.

————. *How to Practice Dharma: Teachings on the Eight Worldly Dharmas*. Boston: Lama Yeshe Wisdom Archive, 2012.

———— and Kathleen McDonald. *Wholesome Fear*. Boston: Wisdom Publications, 2010.

———— and Lobsang Chökyi Gyältsen and Pabongka Rinpoche. *Practices to Benefit Nagas, Pretas, and Spirits*. Portland: FPMT Publications, 2006.

# Index

# Lama Yeshe Wisdom Archive

The Lama Yeshe Wisdom Archive (LYWA) is the collected works of Lama Thubten Yeshe and Lama Thubten Zopa Rinpoche. Lama Zopa Rinpoche, its spiritual director, founded the Archive in 1996.

Lama Yeshe and Lama Zopa Rinpoche began teaching at Kopan Monastery, Nepal, in 1970. Since then, their teachings have been recorded and transcribed. At present we have well over 12,000 hours of digital audio and some 90,000 pages of raw transcript. Many recordings, mostly teachings by Lama Zopa Rinpoche, remain to be transcribed, and as Rinpoche continues to teach, the number of recordings in the Archive increases accordingly. Most of our transcripts have been neither checked nor edited.

Here at the LYWA we are making every effort to organize the transcription of that which has not yet been transcribed, edit that which has not yet been edited, and generally do the many other tasks detailed below.

The work of the Lama Yeshe Wisdom Archive falls into two categories: archiving and dissemination.

*Archiving* requires managing the recordings of teachings by Lama Yeshe and Lama Zopa Rinpoche that have already been collected, collecting recordings of teachings given but not yet sent to the Archive, and collecting recordings of Lama Zopa's on-going teachings, talks, advice and so forth as he travels the world for the benefit of all. Incoming media are then catalogued and stored safely while being kept accessible for further work.

We organize the transcription of audio, add the transcripts to the already existent database of teachings, manage this database, have transcripts checked, and make transcripts available to editors or others doing research on or practicing these teachings.

Other archiving activities include working with video and photographs of the Lamas and digitizing Archive materials.

*Dissemination* involves keeping up with evolving technology and making the Lamas' teachings available through various avenues including books for free distribution and sale, ebooks on a wide range of readers, lightly edited transcripts, a monthly e-letter (see below), social media, DVDs and online video, articles in *Mandala* and other magazines and on our website. Irrespective of the medium we choose, the teachings require a significant amount of work to prepare them for distribution.

This is just a summary of what we do. The Archive was established with virtually no seed funding and has developed solely through the kindness of many people, some of whom we have mentioned at the front of this book and most of the others on our website. We sincerely thank them all.

Our further development similarly depends upon the generosity of those who see the benefit and necessity of this work, and we would be extremely grateful for your help. Thus we hereby appeal to you for your kind support. If you would like to make a contribution to help us with any of the above tasks or to sponsor books for free distribution, please contact us:

LAMA YESHE WISDOM ARCHIVE
PO Box 636, Lincoln, MA 01773, USA
Telephone (781) 259-4466
info@LamaYeshe.com
www.LamaYeshe.com

The LAMA YESHE WISDOM ARCHIVE is a 501(c)(3) tax-deductible, non-profit corporation dedicated to the welfare of all sentient beings and totally dependent upon your donations for its continued existence. Thank you so much for your support. You may contribute by mailing a check, bank draft or money order to our Lincoln address; by making a donation on our secure website; by mailing us your credit card number or phoning it in; or by transferring funds directly to our bank—ask us for details.

## LAMA YESHE WISDOM ARCHIVE MEMBERSHIP

In order to raise the money we need to employ editors to make available the thousands of hours of teachings mentioned above, we have established a membership plan. Membership costs US$1,000 and its main benefit is that you will be helping make the Lamas' incredible teachings available to a worldwide audience. More direct and tangible benefits to you personally include free Lama Yeshe and Lama Zopa Rinpoche books from the ARCHIVE and Wisdom Publications, a year's subscription to *Mandala* and a year of monthly pujas by the monks and nuns at Kopan Monastery with your personal dedication. Please see www.LamaYeshe.com for more information.

## MONTHLY E-LETTER

Each month we send out a free e-letter containing our latest news and a previously unpublished teaching by Lama Yeshe or Lama Zopa Rinpoche. To see more than one hundred back-issues or to subscribe with your email address, please go to our website.

# The Foundation for the Preservation of the Mahayana Tradition

The Foundation for the Preservation of the Mahayana Tradition (FPMT) is an international organization of Buddhist meditation study and retreat centers—both urban and rural—monasteries, publishing houses, healing centers and other related activities founded in 1975 by Lama Thubten Yeshe and Lama Thubten Zopa Rinpoche. At present, there are more than 160 FPMT centers, projects and services in over forty countries worldwide.

The FPMT has been established to facilitate the study and practice of Mahayana Buddhism in general and the Tibetan Gelug tradition, founded in the fifteenth century by the great scholar, yogi and saint, Lama Je Tsongkhapa, in particular.

Every quarter, the Foundation publishes a wonderful news journal, *Mandala*, from its International Office in the United States of America. To subscribe or view back-issues, please go to the *Mandala* website, www.mandalamagazine.org, or contact:

FPMT
1632 SE 11th Avenue, Portland, OR 97214
Telephone (503) 808-1588; Fax (503) 808-1589
info@fpmt.org
www.fpmt.org

The FPMT website also offers teachings by His Holiness the Dalai Lama, Lama Yeshe, Lama Zopa Rinpoche and many other highly respected teachers in the tradition, details about the FPMT's educational programs, an online learning center, a complete listing of FPMT centers all over the world and, especially, those in your area, a link to the excellent FPMT Store, and links to FPMT centers—where you will find details of their programs—and other interesting Buddhist and Tibetan pages.

# FPMT Online Learning Center

In 2009, FPMT Education Services launched the FPMT Online Learning Center to make FPMT education programs and materials more accessible to students worldwide. While continuing to expand, the Online Learning Center currently offers the following courses:

- Meditation 101
- Buddhism in a Nutshell
- Heart Advice for Death and Dying
- Discovering Buddhism
- Basic Program
- Living in the Path

Living in the Path is particularly unique in that it takes teachings by Lama Zopa Rinpoche and presents them in theme-related modules that include teaching transcripts, video extracts, meditations, mindfulness practices, karma yoga, and questions to assist students in integrating the material. Current modules include: *Motivation for Life, Taking the Essence, What Buddhists Believe, Guru is Buddha, Introduction to Atisha's text, The Happiness of Dharma, Bringing Emptiness to Life, The Secret of the Mind, Diamond Cutter Meditation,* and *Refuge & Bodhicitta.*

All of our online programs provide audio and/or video teachings of the subjects, guided meditations, readings, and other support materials. Online forums for each program provide students the opportunity to discuss the subject matter and to ask questions of forum elders. Additionally, many retreats led by Lama Zopa Rinpoche are available in full via audio and/or video format.

Education Services is committed to creating a dynamic virtual learning environment and adding more FPMT programming and materials for you to enjoy via the Online Learning Center.

Visit us at: onlinelearning.fpmt.org

# What to do with Dharma teachings

The Buddhadharma is the true source of happiness for all sentient beings. Books like this show you how to put the teachings into practice and integrate them into your life, whereby you get the happiness you seek. Therefore, anything containing Dharma teachings, the names of your teachers or holy images is more precious than other material objects and should be treated with respect. To avoid creating the karma of not meeting the Dharma again in future lives, please do not put books (or other holy objects) on the floor or underneath other stuff, step over or sit upon them, or use them for mundane purposes such as propping up wobbly chairs or tables. They should be kept in a clean, high place, separate from worldly writings, and wrapped in cloth when being carried around. These are but a few considerations.

Should you need to get rid of Dharma materials, they should not be thrown in the rubbish but burned in a special way. Briefly: do not incinerate such materials with other trash, but alone, and as they burn, recite the mantra OM AH HUM. As the smoke rises, visualize that it pervades all of space, carrying the essence of the Dharma to all sentient beings in the six samsaric realms, purifying their minds, alleviating their suffering, and bringing them all happiness, up to and including enlightenment. Some people might find this practice a bit unusual, but it is given according to tradition. Thank you very much.

## Dedication

Through the merit created by preparing, reading, thinking about and sharing this book with others, may all teachers of the Dharma live long and healthy lives, may the Dharma spread throughout the infinite reaches of space, and may all sentient beings quickly attain enlightenment.

In whichever realm, country, area or place this book may be, may there be no war, drought, famine, disease, injury, disharmony or unhappiness, may there be only great prosperity, may everything needed be easily obtained, and may all be guided by only perfectly qualified Dharma teachers, enjoy the happiness of Dharma, have love and compassion for all sentient beings, and only benefit and never harm each other.

LAMA THUBTEN ZOPA RINPOCHE was born in Thangme, Nepal, in 1945. At the age of three he was recognized as the reincarnation of the Lawudo Lama, who had lived nearby at Lawudo, within sight of Rinpoche's Thangme home. Rinpoche's own description of his early years may be found in his book, *The Door to Satisfaction*. At the age of ten, Rinpoche went to Tibet and studied and meditated at Domo Geshe Rinpoche's monastery near Pagri, until the Chinese occupation of Tibet in 1959 forced him to forsake Tibet for the safety of Bhutan. Rinpoche then went to the Tibetan refugee camp at Buxa Duar, West Bengal, India, where he met Lama Yeshe, who became his closest teacher. The Lamas went to Nepal in 1967, and over the next few years built Kopan and Lawudo Monasteries. In 1971 Lama Zopa Rinpoche gave the first of his famous annual lam-rim retreat courses, which continue at Kopan to this day. In 1974, with Lama Yeshe, Rinpoche began traveling the world to teach and establish centers of Dharma. When Lama Yeshe passed away in 1984, Rinpoche took over as spiritual head of the FPMT, which has continued to flourish under his peerless leadership. More details of Rinpoche's life and work may be found in *The Lawudo Lama* and on the LYWA and FPMT websites. In addition to many LYWA and FPMT books, Rinpoche's other published teachings include *Wisdom Energy* (with Lama Yeshe), *Transforming Problems, The Door to Satisfaction, Ultimate Healing, Dear Lama Zopa, How to Be Happy, Wholesome Fear* and many transcripts and practice booklets.

GORDON MCDOUGALL first met Tibetan Buddhism in Hong Kong in 1986 and was the director of Cham-Tse Ling, the FPMT center there, for two years. Since then he has been involved with various FPMT centers and projects. In 2001 he became the spiritual program coordinator of Jamyang Buddhist Centre, London, where he worked with the resident teacher, Geshe Tashi Tsering, to develop the Foundation of Buddhist Thought, the two-year campus and correspondence course that is part of the FPMT core education program. He administered the course and worked at Jamyang for seven years, editing the six FBT books, first as study books for the course and then as "stand-alone" books for Wisdom Publications. He has also led lam-rim courses in Europe and India and was involved with the creation of the Discovering Buddhist program. After moving to Bath, England, he became a full time editor with the LAMA YESHE WISDOM ARCHIVE in 2008, managing the Publishing the FPMT Lineage project and editing the books published in the series.